LAW OF VALUE AND THEORIES OF VALUE

Studies in Critical Social Sciences Book Series

Haymarket Books is proud to be working with Brill Academic Publishers (www.brill.nl) to republish the *Studies in Critical Social Sciences* book series in paperback editions. This peer-reviewed book series offers insights into our current reality by exploring the content and consequences of power relationships under capitalism, and by considering the spaces of opposition and resistance to these changes that have been defining our new age. Our full catalog of *SCSS* volumes can be viewed at https://www.haymarketbooks.org/series_collections/4-studies-in-critical-social-sciences.

LAW OF VALUE AND THEORIES OF VALUE

Symmetrical Critique of Classical and Neoclassical Political Economy

TIAGO CAMARINHA LOPES

Haymarket Books
Chicago, IL

First published in 2022 by Brill Academic Publishers, The Netherlands
© 2022 Koninklijke Brill NV, Leiden, The Netherlands

Published in paperback in 2023 by
Haymarket Books
P.O. Box 180165
Chicago, IL 60618
773-583-7884
www.haymarketbooks.org

ISBN: 978-1-64259-814-8

Distributed to the trade in the US through Consortium Book Sales and
Distribution (www.cbsd.com) and internationally through Ingram Publisher
Services International (www.ingramcontent.com).

This book was published with the generous support of Lannan Foundation and
Wallace Action Fund.

Special discounts are available for bulk purchases by organizations and
institutions. Please call 773-583-7884 or email info@haymarketbooks.org for more
information.

Cover design by Jamie Kerry and Ragina Johnson.

Printed in the United States.

10 9 8 7 6 5 4 3 2 1

Library of Congress Cataloging-in-Publication data is available.

Contents

Acknowledgement

My parents offered me with enthusiasm the material and spiritual support that enabled me to initiate a career as a humanist scholar. I dedicate this book to my father, who first showed me more than 20 years ago Adam Smith's *Wealth of Nations* from his multidisciplinary bookshelf.

Figures

Introduction

The law of value is a central concept for political economy. Adam Smith's *Wealth of Nations*, published in 1776, is considered the first work to deal systematically with the law of value. During the 18th and 19th centuries, the law of value was thought of as the gravitational force that organizes production and distribution in an economy that is regulated by markets. After that, the notion of a 'law of value' disappeared from the treatises of political economy, but the reality of social relations of production based on private property, market and capital is stronger than ever.

Before Marx's presentation of his *Critique of Political Economy*—a broad study about economic thought and the rise of capitalism, which led him to the masterpiece *Capital* in the 1860s—the law of value could not be studied properly. This was so not simply because the economists treated market and capitalism as if they were almost the same thing, but mainly because they conceived of the standard metrics of exchange ruled by private property as universal. The idea that markets are natural, non-historical institutions, shows the systemic limitations of bourgeois economics, both classical and neoclassical. The result of this profound error is the naturalization of all theories of value, regardless of how a theory of value is positioned in class struggle. This error also leads to the grotesque idea that the law of value should be understood as a heavenly power able to lead humanity to paradise, as if the intensification of alienation were the solution to all social problems.

The difference between the law of value and the theory of value is profound. The goal of this work is to problematize this difference. The main argument is that all conceivable theories of value describe and study a real phenomenon, called the law of value. A theory is an explanation of something real and there can be various explanations for the same real phenomenon. This is why there are many various theories of value, but only one law of value.

In this book, I focus on the historical development of theories of value between the 18th and 21st centuries and so I analyze all existing theories of value within this period by dividing them into two great strands before dissecting Marx's own approach to the law of value. Marx's theory of value surpasses both strands and stands out as the unique approach that deals with the error of naturalizing a value theory of any kind.

It is especially important to focus on this unique feature of Marx's work when communicating with economists. Marx pointed out that despite making important contributions, the economic thought of the capitalist era is doomed to continue naturalizing social relations of production that are conditioned by very narrow historical and cultural institutions. This book investigates a double effect of this error regarding the theoretical core of political economy. On one side, this error generated the labor theory of value, and on the other side, it generated the utility theory of value. Both theories of value (labor and utility) are rooted in the same fundamental mistake of classical political economy and are both equally valid and limited, despite their differences.

This equal treatment of the naturalized theories of value that oppose each other is essential for introducing economists to Marxian political economy. Radical and critical literature in political economy usually praises the labor theory of value as progressive and depicts the utility theory of value as reactionary. Politically speaking, this division is correct, but it also indicates a serious theoretical deficiency that should be corrected by a symmetrical critique of both naturalized theories of value. Marx's work is not limited to attacking the reactionary development of classical political economy; it is also a critique of the progressive development of classical political economy into general (utopian) socialist economics.

By giving equal attention to both classical and neoclassical economic thought, it is possible to prepare the reader to problematize the differences between utopian and scientific socialism. This differentiation is critical, and it is often overlooked by economists. The clash between the labor theory of value and the utility theory of value represents the fight of labor versus capital, but the problem is not as simple as it might seem. From the standpoint of a value theoretician, it does not matter which side is chosen because both sides err regarding Marx's main scientific contribution to value theory.[1]

The division between a labor theory of value and a utility theory of value that we witness today is a result of changes in economic thought since the end of the 19th century. But this split originated much earlier, if we think of the distinction between objective and subjective approaches to value theory. Since its earliest stages, even when markets were not at the center of the economy, economic thought dealt with quantitative relations between items of different quality. Thinkers from various backgrounds and epochs were creative in

---

1   My problematizing approach to the law of value employs a flexible strategy of fighting against capital-allied economic thinking, as will become clear. I do not make a direct defense of the 'labor theory of value' against the 'utility theory of value'. Instead of confronting mainstream economics directly, as Smith ([1994] 2018) and others do, I investigate non-Marxian economics to try to separate what is scientific analysis from what is only apologetics capitalism (and socialism). Moreover, my analysis of the law of value is very limited in scope in the sense that it does not intend to deal with historical and concrete geopolitical questions, as is the case, for example, in Amin ([1977] 1981) and ([1978] 2010).

determining what might be the cause for these specific relations. It was known that exchange is a process that involved both nature and society. The standard division is that of cost or outcome (supply) versus receipt or income (demand). On one side, we have all aspects of production, while on the other side we tend to see the elements of distribution. Likewise, the first side focuses on an objective approach, while the second side focuses on a subjective approach. Dialectical unity shows that one path is complementary to the other path. Accordingly, there cannot be a decision about which one leads to the correct theory of value.

The economic process is the transformation of matter through human activity and the use of that transformed matter to fulfill different societal needs. As an example, let us take an item from this mass of transformed matter, a single unity of the whole product of the economy, such as a knife. Note that we do not need to specify the details of this knife (it can be an ancient tool made of stone or an industrialized utensil forged in the flow of capitalist production). In the absence of private property, this item (which is called a use value because it serves a specific function) does not have what economists call 'price', but it does have 'value'. From the objectivist perspective, value indicates how much effort must be put into the production of an item if this item is to be brought into existence through the transformation of raw material. Thus, items have value in all types of economy. Price is an indicator of how much the proprietor of the item demands in order to transfer its ownership. It is the amount of abstract wealth that the proprietor is willing to sell it for. In other words, it is the sum of wealth for which the proprietor will not employ direct violence to defend his possession of the item. In economies where private property emerges and commodity exchange takes place even at the margins, traded items not only have value, but also price. The violence behind possession is exerted by the bourgeois state to guarantee private ownership.

However significant the difference in category between value and price is, it is not the focus of this book. The important thing is to know that there are two kinds of nomenclature to designate two different things that are strongly connected to each other. One is the quantitative relations of matter combination that transform inputs into outputs. These relations are determined by the laws of nature. The other is the quantitative relations that suit the preferences of individuals who have appropriated certain outputs privately. These relations are given by social institutions or traditions that describe power relations between individuals who recognize themselves reciprocally as private owners. We may refer to these second setting of relations as social laws that emerge from the commodity relationship or, more precisely, the social relations of production of commodities, the founding stone of the capitalist mode of production.[2]

The labor theory of value and the utility theory of value are derived from each one of these two sides. They are opposing theories because they depart from opposite (though complementary) starting points (supply and demand). But they are also united by their common mistake of naturalizing the quantitative relations that inform how valuable useful outputs are. They treat value and price as purely quantitative dimensions and never question why they chose a certain quality to be the measure of quantity (on one side labor, on the other, utility).

Marx's theory of value, despite often being classified as a labor theory of value, is the only theory of value that overcomes this mistake and powerfully shows that the choice of the qualitative variable to measure quantities expressed in value or price depends on the position of the theoretician in class struggle. Indeed, I argue that it is not precise to call Marx's view a theory of value. Strictly speaking, Marx does not build a theory of value; he builds a theory of the commodity. His perspective on value, use value, value-form, money, capital, and everything other concept in capitalism, derives from his theory of the commodity. If we want to understand Marx's view on the law of value and what kind of theory of value he proposes, we need to look at his theory of the commodity.

Before exploring this insight, we need first to analyze some fundamentals. We will take Adam Smith's hegemony as our starting point and explain how classical political economy came to an end. At this point in the history of economic thought, value theoreticians thought they had to choose whether labor or utility was the true source of value. I present both the major strands of value theory and explain the differences and commonalities between the labor strand and the utility strand. I analyze the nature of this dichotomy and then present Marx's perspective on the theory of value and the law of value,

---

2 In my opinion, the relationship between value and price is that market prices are the empirical information about the conditions of production, that is, about values. I adopt this perspective from Farjoun and Machover (1983) and Rojas (1989). The value system and the price system must be somehow connected by the analyst. I believe each reader must work out his/her own understanding of these two entities, not only to find his/her own solution to the transformation problem of values into production prices, but also to be able to navigate through different worlds of economic thought. In this sense, I am sympathetic to Beggs (2012) teachings on 'how to stop worrying and forget the transformation problem'. Marxist political economy considers that the conceptual difference between value and price is extremely important, while non-Marxist economics does not consider it at all.

which depends on a solid understanding of his theory of the commodity. The structure of the book is as follows:

Chapter 1 presents how economics became an independent field of research when the quantitative relations of exchange began to be studied in a new way. Economic interests were no longer judged by fixed ethical standards but were recognized for what they are. Political economy deals with concrete power relations between individuals and nation-states in history, but it has a clear theoretical core that is quite abstract. Since this book focus on this core, the presentation of political economy will not enter into the details of the political struggle behind historical events and developments. We assume that the reader will complement this presentation with a careful study of the history of the formation, development, and decay of capitalism. In focusing on theoretical issues, I refer to political economy in chapter 1 as the 'science of value'.[3]

---

3   This name is inspired by the title of Michael Heinrich's book *Die Wissenschaft vom Wert* (Heinrich ([1990] 2014)). I agree with Heinrich's approach to differentiating Marx from classical political economists. However, I do not think that Marx's limitations are because he repeats some mistakes of previous economists, as if he could not leave entirely the old system. In my view, the limitations are related to concrete issues that exist in both classical and Marx's political economy. Both Adam Smith and Karl Marx warn their readers about the difficult topic of value. Adam Smith writes in the last paragraph of chapter 4 of *Wealth of Nations*: "I shall endeavour to explain, as fully and distinctly as I can, those three subjects [(i) what is the real measure of this exchangeable value; or wherein consists the real price of all commodities, (ii) what are the different parts of which this real price is composed or made up and (iii) what are the different circumstances which sometimes raise some or all of these different parts of price above, and sometimes sink them below, their natural or ordinary rate; or, what are the causes which sometimes hinder the market price, that is, the actual price of commodities, from coinciding exactly with what may be called their natural price] in the three following chapters, for which I must very earnestly entreat both the patience and attention of the reader: his patience, in order to examine a detail which may, perhaps, in some places, appear unnecessarily tedious; and his attention, in order to understand what may perhaps, after the fullest explication which I am capable of giving it, appear still in some degree obscure. I am always willing to run some hazard of being tedious, in order to be sure that I am perspicuous; and, after taking the utmost pains that I can to be perspicuous, some obscurity may still appear to remain upon a subject, in its own nature extremely abstracted. Smith ([1776] 1981), p. 46."

    Likewise, Marx warns in the preface to the first German edition of *Capital*: "Every beginning is difficult, holds in all sciences. To understand the first chapter, especially the section that contains the analysis of commodities, will, therefore, present the greatest difficulty. That which concerns more especially the analysis of the substance of value and the magnitude of value, I have, as much as it was possible, popularised. The value-form, whose fully developed shape is the money-form, is very elementary and simple. Nevertheless, the human mind has for more than 2,000 years sought in vain to get to the bottom of it all (...). Why? Because the body, as an organic whole, is more easy of study than are the cells of that body. In the analysis of economic forms, moreover, neither microscopes nor chemical reagents are of use. The

Chapter 2 shows how the concept of law of value was conceived of in classical political economy, especially how it derives from Adam Smith's *Wealth of Nations*. Here, the law of value could not be adequately studied due to the limitations of the emerging modern society. Smith's time is one full of hope in the future of humankind. Despite these limitations, it is important to recognize the great advances made in this period. I propose an interpretation that conceives of the law of value in classical political economy in three ways: as the invisible hand, as the exchange of equivalents and as the contradiction between value and price.

Chapter 3 explains that the end of classical political economy opened up two alternative paths. These paths lead to two complementary and naturalizing theories of value. The error of naturalizing commodity relations of production generates on one side the labor theory of value, and on the other the utility theory of value. Both theories of value are rooted in the same mistake made by classical political economy and are both equally valid and limited, despite their differences. I recover Isaak Rubin's pioneering study about the end of classical political economy to assert that the division of value theory into two irreconcilable theories of value should be critically revised.

Chapters 4 and 5 are twin chapters and should be read as parallel. Their relation symbolizes the symmetry in the critique of Classical and Neoclassical political economy I propose. Each one deals with one of the two paths of value theory after the dissolution of classical political economy: the labor theory of value and the utility theory of value. The form in which these chapters are presented reinforces my argument that these two theories of value lack the same fundamental idea that capitalism is a historically determined economic system emerging from the social institution called commodity. Thus, even though they represent on one side a progressive political position, and on the other a reactionary political position, both suffer from the same problem of naturalizing commodity relations of production. This shared deficiency leads both currents to the same dead end: an idealized model of equality based on bourgeois institutions called simple commodity production.

Chapter 4 argues that the labor theory of value is a naturalized form of value theory. This means that its justifications for choosing the input of labor as the responsible element for creating value are rooted in the use-value

---

force of abstraction must replace both. But in bourgeois society, the commodity-form of the product of labour—or value-form of the commodity—is the economic cell-form. (...) With the exception of the section on value-form, therefore, this volume cannot stand accused on the score of difficulty. I presuppose, of course, a reader who is willing to learn something new and therefore to think for himself. Marx ([1867] 2015), p. 6."

analysis (natural sciences). Despite being correct as a value theory for describing exchange value (quantity) it is unable to unveil the mysteries of value (quality). Why is it that labor creates value? 'Because God told us so and he is good to the working poor'—so would progressive non-Marxian economists answer. Utopian socialism is the economics form of this strand of the naturalization of value theory and its result is simple commodity production.

Chapter 5 mirrors chapter 4 and argues that the Marginalist Revolution also develops a naturalized form of value theory. It chooses utility as the main determinant for the quantitative relations of exchange between commodities based on use-value analysis (natural sciences). Thus, it too is incomplete, since it can indeed describe why commodities have the prices they do (quantity) but cannot explain concretely why they measure utility and nothing else (quality). Neoclassical economics is the form of this strand of the naturalization of value theory and its result is also simple commodity production.

After presenting this context, we will have a new look into the core of political economy, which undergoes critique by Marx. Marx's political economy is not simply another contribution to economic science made in the second half of the 19th century, it maps out the frontier of economic science. Marx's political economy is the paradigm of economic science today. It is the most advanced system in this field because it absorbs and signifies anew every novelty that is produced in the intellectual area called economics. Thus, his critique is not only directed at the past—Smith, Ricardo, Stuart Mill, and all the defenders of a naturalized version of the labor theory of value, such as Hodgskin and Ricardian socialists—Marx's missile also targets future authors who would still build upon the basis of utilitarianism. Menger, Jevons, Walras and all subsequent neoclassical author are also subject to Marx's *Critique of Political Economy*. In this perspective, every economic theory and thought of the present must be integrated and domesticated by Marx's system. There is not a *Marxian* political economy or even worse, a *Marxian* economics. What we have is a methodology proposed by Marx to master the science of wealth by separating what is in the interests of one class and what is in the interests of the other.

Chapter 6 presents how Marx began the journey to dominate the field of political economy. The purpose here is to explain how economic science relates to Marx's thought and action in general. I describe Marx's path from law and philosophy towards history, society, and economics in order to contextualize the writing of *Capital*, since Marx planned to present his research on the law of value in this work. In my view, the oeuvre remained open, but not unfinished. This means that the essentials are well established by Marx and that the task of economic scientists who struggle on the side of the working class is to push his system forward. My approach suggests a unifying movement in the development of science, i.e. that various currents dealing with the same object of investigation must be incorporated into one single system that encompasses everything. In that sense I argue that every aspect categorized as economics must be subservient to Marx's system.

Chapter 7 presents in more detail how the law of value may be interpreted according to Marx's theory. First, I present a summary of the relationship between the two great strands of theories of value. Next, I explain how Marx's theory of value and his understanding of the law of value derives from his theory of the commodity. The law of value in Marx has three dimensions: 'unity of value and price', 'lack of control over economic reproduction' and 'objective phenomenon'. This three-dimensional interpretation is not intended to close the debate on the significance of the law of value in Marx's work. It is also not the aim of this work to map the literature about the law of value within Marxism.[4] Rather, I intend to show how Marx's concept of the law of value fits into the totality of his work, specifically how it derives from his critique of bourgeois economic thinking. Chapter 7 also explains the difference between the law of value and theories of value. While the law of value is an objective phenomenon

---

4 There is a longstanding debate about the law of value among Marx's followers. In chapter 8, I present a simple idea that tries to synthesize the current paradigm of this debate, but which does not tell the whole story. This literature is vast, and it spread throughout the socialist world during the 20th century. I advise the reader to begin with Engels' ([1895–1896] 2003) commentary on *Capital*, entitled *Law of value and rate of profit*. The first systematic presentation of the law of value in the context of the formation of socialist economies after the Russian Revolution was made by Preobrazhensky ([1926] 1965). Stalin's ([1952] 1972) pamphlet *Economic Problems of Socialism in the USSR* should also be considered in a survey to map the various points of view. The Soviet Union textbook on political economy (Economics Institute of the Academy of Sciences of the U.S.S.R ([1954] 1957)) was assembled in the 1950s and it was the mainstream reference for the debate in the East. It has been criticized from numerous perspectives by progressive economists worldwide, including the most eminent Brazilian critical economist, Celso Furtado (1956). The topic of the law of value and the transition from capitalism to socialism and communism is controversial. This kind of approach to the law of value focuses on concrete historical developments. It also requires a connection between the law of value and the materialist conception of history which is very important. The main questions in this historical approach are about if and how deeply the law of value operates in real existing economic systems. To explore this area is beyond the scope of this book. In the 20th century, besides the soviet economy, other nations have produced studies on how economic policy relates to the law of value. In Latin America, Cuba produced original ideas on economic planning based on Guevara's ethics regarding labor in the transition to socialism. See Guevara (1982). Today, this line of investigation is studying how economic planning in China can be thought of as the contemporary form of controlling the law of value in the 21st century.

of economic reality given certain historical and social institutions, theories of value are the different ways in which economists try to conceptualize this phenomenon. There are as many theories of value as theoretical economists: every analyst constructs his own abstract apparatus for both describing and researching the law of value.

Chapter 8 deals with the peculiar case of capitalist economic planning. It intends to show that controlling the law of value is not enough to overcome capitalism. Capitalism can function in a fully planned mode where everything is organized to achieve the expansion of capital. The law of value is then no longer a phenomenon of spontaneous character, but one in which all rationality is directed at serving the irrational movement of value expansion. I argue that there is no such thing as free movement of the law of value: it is always under pressure to serve specific material interests. This is the reason why we cannot study economic planning without understanding how the aim of the plan is disputed in class struggle. Economic planning is a necessary stage in the education of the economist, even in the capitalist system. The overall message is the following: since economists are not fully aware of the political forces of class struggle influencing their activities, the most important task of educators in the field of economics is to highlight how professional economists are managed by these forces. Chapter 8 argues that the contradiction between the law of value and economic planning, as it was envisaged in the 20th century, is false. The real struggle is between the economic planning of the capitalist class and the economic planning of the working class.

The final remarks close the book by revisiting the main ideas. In the end, I indicate that to create new insights and lead theoretical political economy into the future, we need to leave the safe waters of our own school of economic thought. Marxian political economists who think it is possible to disdain or ignore the development of non-Marxist thinking in economics must revise their position. We need to have a better grasp of the relationship between Marxist and non-Marxist economics as a necessary condition for gaining control over the mainstream and changing the reality of education in economics. The study of value theory as proposed here is a fundamental step for this task.

CHAPTER 1

The Independence of the Science of Value

In classical political economy the law of value appears in three forms: as the invisible hand, as the exchange of equivalents and as the contradiction between the labor theory of value and the empirical prices observed in the market. The law of value points to the fundamentals of economic liberalism, but it also evokes its opposite, economic planning. The economic thought of the bourgeois era is restricted to only one side of this dichotomy, economic liberalism. Consequently, it abandons consideration of the reality of political struggle around the law of value. Nevertheless, it is true that this limitation enabled economic thinking to develop as an autonomous field of investigation.

Historians of economic thought agree that the founding moment of economic science as an independent field of study was the publication of Adam Smith's book, *The Wealth of Nations*, in 1776. Adam Smith's oeuvre is an important phase in the long history of the science of value. Although Smith does not employ the expression 'law of value' in his works, it is acceptable to argue that the concept is clearly present.[1]

---

1 The expression 'law of value' also does not appear in Ricardo's *Principles of Political Economy*. It seems that the term 'law of value' entered the vocabulary of political economy through the polemic between Marx and Proudhon (Oishi (2001)). Proudhon writes 'law of value' for the first time in chapter 2, section II, of his *Philosophy of Poverty* (Proudhon ([1846] 2007), p. 92). According to my research, it is reasonable to argue that Proudhon has coined the term 'law of value', which will be extensively explored by Marx and Engels. Proudhon is talking about the principle behind the magnitude of values and how this fixed principle contradicts the dynamics of real, empirical prices according to the different conditions of production among industries. In short, Proudhon observes that a static perspective on the law of value will lead to a grave contradiction between real empirical prices and values measured in labor time in each sector. Marx's first mention of the 'law of value' appears in his critique of Proudhon, where he recognizes that the term was put into usage by the French philosopher. Both Proudhon and Marx are building up the concept of the law of value from Ricardo's theory of value. The difference is that while Proudhon thinks it is possible to modify the awful reality of exploitation to match the principle of justice behind the law of value, Marx argues in his work *Poverty of Philosophy*, Chapter One: A Scientific Discovery, Part 2, Constituted Value of Synthetic Value, that it is precisely the existence of this so-called 'law of value' that sustains the exploitation of wage labor: "To sum up: Labor, being itself a commodity, is measured as such by the labor time needed to produce the labor-commodity. And what is needed to produce this labor-commodity? Just enough labor time to produce the objects indispensable to the constant maintenance of labor, that is, to keep the worker alive and in a condition to propagate his race. The natural price of labor is no other than the wage minimum. If the

Until the last quarter of the 18th century, all explanations for value were based on moral judgements. Because prices always reflect a power relationship, it was not possible to analyze it scientifically in the context of the restrained markets of the Middle Ages and pre-capitalist modes of production. Price becomes close to value only when there are no strong impediments to free market bargaining and competition exists to some degree. Thus, the connection between value and price can only be properly studied when many individuals are free from any rule of tradition and can relate to others as private owners of commodities. The greater the equality between private proprietors, the clearer the law of value becomes. It becomes visible when the number of transactions and participants increase in such a way that we have a system in which no single agent is capable of manipulating prices to differentiate them from values.

Philosophers directed all their attention to the qualitative aspects of the relationships between the members of a society before the ascension of the market. Instead of investigating how value appeared as a quantitative relation in the exchange of commodities, they discussed how people behave when entering in social relations with others. Usually, this analysis was also a moral judgement of what was right and wrong. After the market came to dominate the core of the mechanism ruling society, the moral treatment of value gave way to an impartial study of exchange relations expressed in prices. We can observe this change by recovering the origins of Adam Smith's thought and the concept of the invisible hand.

It seems strange for the standard understanding of economics today that the foundation of economic science as an independent field of knowledge is closely related to the theory of the state. In western civilization, we could cite as one major reference the Greek philosopher Plato and his work *The Republic*. In eastern civilization, we could refer to the Chinese thinker Confucius, whose thoughts on various topics, including power, was registered in the book *Analects*.

Political science has a pre-modern founding moment in *The Prince* from 1513 by Machiavelli. Political economy (or economics, as we call it today) has a

---

current rate of wages rises above this natural price, it is precisely because the *law of value put as a principle by M. Proudhon* happens to be counterbalanced by the consequences of the varying relations of supply and demand. But the minimum wage is nonetheless the centre towards which the current rates of wages gravitate."

Thus relative value, measured by labor time, is inevitably the formula of the present enslavement of the worker, instead of being, as M. Proudhon would have it, the 'revolutionary theory' of the emancipation of the proletariat. ((Marx [1847] 1955), p. 21, Emphasis mine.)

founding moment in *The Wealth of Nations* from 1776 by Adam Smith. The science of politics involves identifying the aims of the agents and the means that they utilize to reach those aims. The power and the state are no longer analyzed ethically but asks new questions: How are aims and means articulated so that agents achieve what they seek? How does this free environment for seeking whatever one believes to be one's goal affect the relations of dominance between humans? Based on these new questions, Machiavelli ([1513] 2016) gave valuable instructions on how to overcome the challenges of an ancient Greco-roman model that had returned with the Renaissance.

Political Economy is an episode in the history of the theory of the state. It is an area of investigation where thinkers reduce all relations of power to relations of material or economic interests. With ascension of modernity, they focus on a single modality of economic relations: the commodity relationship. This focus is based on the protection of private property and the rules for moving it from one owner to another. Because of this, economists increasingly pay attention to individuals rather than the totality of society as an organism. Individualism gradually dominates the methodology of inquiry in political economy until its name becomes 'economics' at the turn of the 20th century.

It is important to note that this development is not entirely negative. According to the dialectical principle, we must identify both sides of contradictory movements. The abandonment of the global vision of society as one entity is positive in the sense that it helps to show that social relations do not arise from the wishes of individual humans but are conditioned by the level of the development of the productive forces. This discovery was only possible because all social relations are reduced to commodity relations in capitalism. When the agents are trapped in a social network where the strongest directive is given by the commodity relationship, we can study precisely what the rules of this society are. Pre-capitalist modes of production contain various kinds of social connections that do not let us see what the bourgeois agent is and how an economy entirely dominated by commodity and capital functions. So, methodological individualism is at the same time both limited and progressive in the context of the birth of modern economic science.

The negative side of the transformation of political economy into economics is easier to see. Critical economists do a good job denouncing the limitations of a methodology that leaves aside the broader aspects of history, politics and society. By observing the bourgeois agent without remembering how this agent came into being, economists will think that the social relations of a specific mode of organizing the economy (capitalism) derive from natural patterns of human behavior. This is the greatest mistake to which Marx calls attention in his *Critique of Political Economy*.

Before capitalism, there were various forms of economic organization based on tradition. The cycle of production and distribution followed these cultural determinants, and it was not possible to study social relations without appealing to the wishes of Heaven. When the market ascends and becomes the ruling entity of the economy, thinkers must find a way to explain how production and distribution are organized based on the direct material interests of the members of society. This is the great question of political philosophy in the epoch of Adam Smith and his *Theory of Moral Sentiments* (Smith [1759] 1869).

It is only after this point, from the last quarter of the 18th century, that value will be scientifically studied. Until then, the analysis of value and price was biased towards the dominant moral and cultural standards. Nonetheless, it is accurate to note that Adam Smith is not the first to launch the solid scientific base upon which value will finally be deciphered. Marx indicates, in the preface of the first German edition of *Capital* in 1867, that the human mind has for more than 2000 years tried to understand the value-form (Marx [1867] 2015). Many thinkers had already dedicated time to trying to comprehend the phenomenon of quantitatively equalizing objects that are qualitatively different. In the case of Western civilization, Aristotle may be mentioned as a pioneer. The mysteries of value are an old feature throughout intellectual history preceding political economy. Value was an appendix to every thought on society, and so it was almost impossible to unveil what it really is.

What is the difference between how philosophers approached this riddle before the field of political economy and now, in capitalism? There is a significant difference. Before capitalism, there did not exist the objective conditions for the study of value to establish itself as a proper scientific field of study. Because of this, humanity could not advance in the search for the discovery of natural laws and the social patterns of organization that are limited by those laws. It was not possible to understand capitalism as another mode of production among various others in the history of human civilization. Marx explained that, to arrive at this conclusion (that is, that there are different modes of production and capitalism is one of them), required a development in the social relations of commodity to the degree that allowed the rise of the idea of legal equality between all humans.

Adam Smith's oeuvre and the foundation of classical political economy are historical landmarks of this moment. They are part of the long trajectory of attempts to construct a theoretical system that describes the phenomenon of commodity exchange and its substrate: value. The categories of what we may call 'the theoretical core of political economy', such as value, price, value-form, exchange value, use value, commodity and capital, must be organized in a coherent framework. This is exactly what was initiated by all those who worked to explore further the ambiguities of the word value.

When Adam Smith first mentions value in *The Wealth of Nations*, he employs capital letters to write 'VALUE' (Smith ([1776] 1981), p. 44). This is the climax of the initial pages of *The Wealth of Nations*. He explains that the word value sometimes refers to the power of the stuff to be exchanged by other stuff, and sometimes it refers to the power of the stuff to satisfy human needs. Although the more concrete categories of nation, labor, productivity, wealth are also very important in the realm of political economy, the abstract level is where our attention must be directed if we want to discover the fundamental elements of capitalism and the logic behind its birth, development and decline. These fundamental elements, in turn, will help us better understand the dynamics of different modes of production throughout human history. In this sense, value theory is a strong pillar of historical materialism and its roots lie in Adam Smith's work.[2]

The law of value is one of these fundamental elements and although it does not appear explicitly in every page of the literature in political economy, the concept underpins all explanations of the market mechanism that mediates the wants of the individual and the needs of the collective in which the individual lives. How are these opposing entities (individual and society) harmonized when the only driving force for action is the pursuit of self-interest? Adam Smith's solution to this problem is the first step for describing the real social phenomenon called the law of value. If we want to understand how different theories of value capture and describe the law of value, we need to begin the investigation by recovering the foundations of classical political economy.

Classical political economy is a synthesis of physiocratic and mercantilist doctrines. It merges the notion of natural systems with the desire for constant wealth augmentation. The economy is a self-reproducing system that is composed of two complementary parts: production and distribution. Useful objects, or goods, are produced when human labor transforms nature. The results of these changes become objects, or products that are used by society to meet its needs. Thus, production and distribution are two moments in the full reproduction cycle of the flow of goods that are necessary to sustain society from a purely material point of view. But the relationship between these two parts is complex. It is not possible to interfere in each of them separately,

---

2   Cockshott (2019) presents a novel introduction to historical materialism based on drawing a rigorous connection between Marx and Adam Smith. My approach is similar in the way that I emphasize aspects of continuity without forgetting to stress the singularity of the *Critique of Political Economy* regarding the theory of value.

as if they were independent components. First, economists followed the phys- iocrats, the French physicians of the early 18th century who believed that this complexity was so great that it was useless to try to interfere in the economy. Later, in the 19th century, Marx showed that the social rules for organizing both production and distribution emerge from a historical process related to how well society masters the transformation of nature. The stronger and more sophisticated the tools, the more easily humans can alter their environment to guarantee the material reproduction of their society through time. Both the material aspects of this circular process and the social arrangements employed to guarantee its repetition constitute what we call the economy.

Every economy is a system organizing the use of resources to sustain its own material existence. However, this organization is not a given; it does not fall fully formed from Heaven. It stems from the decisions and actions of each one of its members, whose behavior is shaped both by the traditions of the past and innovation for the future that creates new social relationships.

Before capitalism, tradition played an overwhelming role in the decision making of all societies. The economic decisions of the ancestors were repeated by the younger generations, creating a variety of cults and norms justifying why the world is like it is. Questioning the status quo was an endeavor restricted to the brilliant minds of individual members of the elite itself, and so social cri- tique was not necessarily tied to social revolution. Capitalism, however, has a unique pattern upon which it develops, and it systematically replaces religious tradition by illuminist reasoning and critique. It must rationalize production and distribution to serve a purpose that works as the sole master of the eco- nomic system. It encourages innovation in such a way that everything changes rapidly enough to make traditions disappear. Paradoxically, while science becomes accessible to ordinary people, it also becomes a tool to further the exploitation of the working class. Capitalist society must expand indefinitely the frontiers of capital accumulation. In a certain way, we can also call it a tra- dition, or even religion. It is the most contradictory framework for organizing the economy. All the rationality involved, aided by all scientific achievements hitherto, is compromised by the goal to expand capital. Human needs are met only as a side effect of this logic. Science is put to work to achieve dogmatism, dominance, and exploitation.

This logic could only develop freely when production and distribution became fully dominated by capital. When markets and commodity exchange were only an addendum of the economy, the law of value could not show itself in its true form. There was a limitation to the price system, inhibit- ing it from moving freely, because of the ethical boundaries supported by tradition.

Isaak Rubin ([1928] 1987) indicates the Renaissance as the turning point that initiates the science of value. Feudalism declines and the law of value becomes an object of investigation free from normative evaluations about what the prices of goods should be. Prices must be investigated as they are, not as they ought to be. Before capitalism opened the way to markets and liberated them from any moral and ethical boundaries, price was viewed in a normative sense. All exchange relations had to be judged based on what was called the 'fair price'. The struggle around price was heavily dependent on clear political forces, such as the medieval guilds, which blocked the development of market competition.

Markets have existed since long before the formation of the capitalist mode of production. But it was only when the social relationship of the commodity became central that it became possible to see that economic organization did not have to repeatedly follow traditional practices. The tension between the individual and the collective had a new solution in the emerging capitalist mode of production.

Everything was commodified and the rules for determining resource use became homogenized. A general behavior emerged among individual agents that could be objectively described. Every single agent in this new world tries to perform the movement of value expansion, and the greater the expansion, the better. In this system, this is the unique criterion by which to judge economic decisions. Ideally, there is no choice that is not under the influence of the impetus of value expansion. Capital controls every agent but, according to liberal classical political economy, each one is free to choose. Of course, this contradiction between the strict control of all society by this entity called capital and the idea that the human individual enjoys freedom like that in no other epoch in the history of civilization was and still is one of the great problems of the naive bourgeois economists from the past and today.

Humans make their own history, but this process is not solely dependent on their needs. By analyzing how the bourgeoisie began to block the further development of the revolution in France after it reached a certain stage, Marx showed that each generation is conditioned to act within concrete limitations that impede the immediate application of the communist ideals. The objective conditions needed to fully realize the pledge 'from each according to his ability, to each according to his needs' (Marx [1875] 1970) depend on the development of the productive forces. Moreover, there is also a constant subjective element that, even in the presence of the objective conditions given by a high level of development of the productive forces, restrains the flow of revolutionary change. Old ideas and ideologies are maintained out of plain fear of novelty.

In the case of economic thought, classical economists[3] insist on the illusions of the principles of liberty, equality, and freedom because they do not see what could come after the heyday of modern society. Free functioning markets and the structure of exchange deriving from it is seen as the pinnacle of human history. On this beautiful and peaceful peak, the law of value would govern all in the name of good, and everyone would be sure that he/she is free.

Thus, we have two contradictory aspects during the birth of the science of value. On one side, there is a positive movement that replaces the ethical and moral justifications for the organization of the economy by the rational search driven by self-interest. On the other side, there is a negative movement because this search appears as if it would necessarily lead to social wellbeing, while in fact it only guarantees the dominance of capital over all human action. Considering the transformations of Illuminism, we must recognize the advances for economic science in classical political economy. Value can be now studied as something that stems from the standard behavior of trying to get privately rich. What was once a privilege for the powerful is now democratically done by everyone, since everybody is a bourgeois citizen (at least on paper).

Does this mean that there was no economic thought before the 18th century? Not at all. It means only that, in the modern sense of the word 'science', economics could only be considered an independent field of research from this date on. The general protocol for enhancing the quantity of value, which is

---

3   Who are the classical economists for Marx? Marx himself provides an answer: "Once for all I may here state, that by classical Political Economy, I understand that economy which, since the time of W. Petty, has investigated the real relations of production in bourgeois society in contradistinction to vulgar economy, which deals with appearances only, ruminates without ceasing on the materials long since provided by scientific economy, and there seeks plausible explanations of the most obtrusive phenomena, for bourgeois daily use, but for the rest, confines itself to systematising in a pedantic way, and proclaiming for everlasting truths, the trite ideas held by the self-complacent bourgeoisie with regard to their own world, to them the best of all possible worlds. Marx [1867] 2015, p. 58."

The 'last' classical economists for Marx are David Ricardo (in England) and Sismondi (in France) (Marx [1859a] 1971). It is not clear who would be the 'first' vulgar economist, but maybe John Stuart Mill is the most appropriate name. The traditional division proposed by Marx is between a scientific political economy and a vulgar political economy. Marxist scholarship usually associates scientific political economy with working-class political economy and vulgar political economy with capital-class political economy. I argue in some passages in this book that this association is not precise, because there can also be a politically 'progressive' vulgar economy as well as a 'reactionary' vulgar economy. For a presentation of the entry 'vulgar economy', see Bharadwaj (1990) who correctly indicates that the distinction traced by Marx between scientific and vulgar economics is not only political, but also analytical.

the code written in the (bourgeois) Homo economicus' DNA, is a prerequisite
for seeing the law of value in full action. Before the spread of this protocol,
economic organization was not homogeneous and every society around the
globe had its own logic for arranging production and distribution, based on its
own local beliefs and traditions.

Some historians of economic thought make an overly simplified division
between pre-classical and classical economic thinking. They argue that there
was no rationality whatsoever in previous economic systems, as if only market
capitalism had a coherent frame for organizing the use of resources. The truth
is that every system has its own rules for this organization, and market capitalism presents itself as having 'the best' method as reinforcing propaganda.
We must remember that, since the dawn of the scientific revolution, the term
'rational' is typically applied to everything that is considered good. In this context, rationality means that the economic system most suited to promoting
value expansion is the one based on the liberty of labor power to be freely used
as a commodity in the production process.

But the real dividing line between previous modes of production and market
capitalism is not the absence or presence of defined patterns of organization,
be they rational or irrational. The difference is that the pattern of organization in market capitalism is homogeneous and imperialist: every single human
society on Earth is about to merge into one giant world economy, which also
promotes the homogenization of economic thinking around the globe. Profit,
interest and the cultural ideology surrounding private property have become
the foundations of every thought on economics. From ancient Greek and eastern philosophy up to mercantilism and the physiocrats, the focus of interest
was the description of the complex functioning of society. There was no way
to establish a unified mode for acting economically for all members of society.
Each social group or individual was condemned to follow the traditions and
commandments of the sacred past. Development in understanding the law of
value was impeded because of these ties. Theories of value prior to the ascension of capitalism are consequently not considered scientific.

Let us look deeper into the idea of the scientific birth of value theory. Why
is it that economic thought before Adam Smith is not considered economic
science? The reason is that the criterion for understanding value is based on
the illuminist paradigm that everything must have an explanation that is self-
contained in the system. Value must be explained from within the system itself
and it is not possible to employ external elements to support a theory of value.
The Wealth of the Nations from 1776 was chosen as the founding moment of
the independence of economic science because it represents the first coherent closed system. It gathers scattered ideas together into one single set of

explanations identifying the great causes of the enhancement of productivity. More specifically, it indicates that the social relations governing production and distribution no longer depend exclusively on tradition, but on an individual's evaluations of whether such relations are beneficial or not for him/herself. Pursuit of self-interest is the new standard for judging the rightness of material relations of exchange. This opened the way to studying the law of value from a dispassionate point of view.

The science of value develops fully only after the standard behavior of all members of the society becomes that of maximizing capital accumulation. It is important to note that the mercantile system is not only an evil entity acting against progress. It also opens the way towards an association of free human beings when we consider the past confines of traditionalist societies. Individual goals can be chosen by each of the members and religious control of influence over economic matters may get weaker. Of course, this liberation is just an initial stage, and we will witness more complex and transparent forms of exploitation of the economically dominated working people. As the commodity relation becomes more and more important, all exploitation becomes more homogenized in the circuit of capital expansion. On one side, the dimensions of this exploitation increase; on the other side, its global spread allow the organization and union of working people on a planetary scale.

We must thus receive the pioneers of political economy enthusiastically. Later they will be critically reviewed. The negative consequences of the social relationship of production based on the commodity become evident only when the living conditions of the working class are compared with that of the proprietors of the means of production. It is necessary to recognize the advances that allow the scientific inquiry of the phenomenon of value. This is the starting point for a new kind of relation among members of society, one that is totally free from the prejudices of ancient moral and ethical instructions.

Although we welcome this new view of the phenomenon of value, we also must remember the limits of the bourgeois Homo economicus. The great problem here is that the logic of capital expansion promotes one specific objective function for all agents of this new society. By making decisions based only on the quantitative increase of something as abstract as money, the Homo economicus represents the personification of capital itself. There are no other standards for analyzing one's actions. Everyone is driven by the impetus of maximization, as if the only goal were to increase quantitatively what constitutes value. Of course, it is important to talk about the quality of value, but quantity is a permanent characteristic that we cannot abandon when we consider Marx's *Critique of Political Economy*. Quality and quantity are the two opposing sides of the dialectical unity and any attempt to create a theory of value based on only one of these two sides will result in failure.

Classical political economy brought novelties and prejudices. It would have to be corrected later. Value and all economic relations based on private property are not natural, universal, and just. *The Wealth of Nations* brings both an advance and a limitation in the long journey for the ultimate theory of value. It represents one of the most influential works to systematically describe a real phenomenon called the law of value. For this reason, it is considered the inauguration of the scientific endeavor to unveil the law of value.

CHAPTER 2

The Law of Value in Classical Political Economy

1   The Law of Value as the Invisible Hand

How does a society in which everyone is entirely free to pursue his/her own interests manage to function as a coherent collective of humans? That has been the great question of modern political philosophy. After the decay of feudalism, it was no longer possible to explain the cohesion of the social system with external arguments. The ascension of modernity means that there is no moral, ethical, religious or traditional pressure from outside that keeps the social body together. An explanation must be found within the system itself. Heaven can no longer provide the authority to sustain social relations of economic exploitation. Law must arise from beneath. It must reflect the fundamental condition of the individual free from constraints unrelated to material interests.

But if every individual acts in self-interest, is it possible to have a social system that does not fall apart? Indeed, bourgeois thinkers will develop enthusiastic answers to praise this new kind of social system as something both solid and positive. There were two main visions of how the members of society relate to each other and how they relate to legal authority. The first one is represented by Thomas Hobbes (1588–1679) and the second one is represented by John Locke (1632–1704).

In his work *De Cive* (*On the Citizen*), Hobbes drew on a phrase from the Roman poet Plautus to argue that, if man is a God to another man, then it is also true that a man is a wolf to another man (*Homo homini lupus*) (Hobbes ([1646] 1918), p. 63). So, in the state of nature, without civil society, there would be a war of all men against all men (Hobbes ([1651] 2003), p. 98). According to Hobbes, the only way to overcome this situation is to institutionalize a force that is recognized and respected by all. This is what constitutes the State. It is the result of an agreement between all citizens in which everyone transfers the right of exerting violence onto a third entity. This entity becomes responsible for applying the same rules to everyone. The State absorbs the task of guaranteeing to all members of society enough security so that they can live by means of their own labor and on the fruits of the earth. It means that the State must actively defend the institution of private property as an objective necessity in order to save humanity from a primitive world.

In this philosophical system, the institution of private property is already relatively safe. However, the assurance of private property rests on a power from the outside. Legitimate violence to protect private property is something intrusive as an external force. The power that guarantees private property is based on a myth. It is an invention. It depends on an explanation that makes it explicit that a third party exists to regulate the relations between two citizens. Hobbes' theory of the State is a theory of social contract midway towards a political ideology that is perfectly suitable for market society. It abandons the sovereign-God bond but keeps an ideal element to generate social order. Cohesion is assured by an active subject: the State. It recognizes that each member of society is aware of his/her own 'selfish nature' and sufficiently rational to obey the power surveilling from above, from outside the civil world. Still, for a perfect answer to the question posed by modern political philosophy, it is not enough to argue that this power's origin lies in the civil world itself. This is so, because in Hobbes, the State and society are clearly separated, and so the idea that private property is a natural phenomenon cannot develop properly. The institution of private property must be created, instead of simply being acknowledged. Consequently, in this system, economics is still subordinate to politics. Besides economic matters, there are other aspects of human relations that influence the dynamics of society, so it is not suitable for envisaging a theoretical system that sees only material interests and ignores every other dimension of human relations of power. The kind of State that emerges here is not entirely lined up with the ideology of the market as the natural order regulating human life. The class of proprietors needs a theory of the State that fits better into their own world view. For this class, the entity of private property and the corresponding State that guarantees it should not appear as human creations, as if they came into being after society was already functioning. They must be conceptualized as if they were born together with society itself.

John Locke's explanation for the relationship between the individuum and modern society goes in this direction. For Locke, the natural state includes the existence of private property. There is no need for it to be created by a social contract that constitutes the State. The agreement in this case is consent, humans interact directly and freely without having to count on a third party to watch over them. This reciprocal recognition of the other as a private proprietor is the basis of modern society. In Locke's thought, the naturality of private property is so strong that bourgeois society appears as the only possible arrangement of social relations of production. The commodity producing society appears not only as a natural entity, but also as the only possible way of organizing the economy. It is interesting to notice that for Locke humans have the natural right to the products of their labor. So, there is a strong connection between private property, i.e. wealth, and the process of production in which labor is responsible for transforming nature into goods. If someone works on inputs found in nature, it is right to assert that the resulting outputs are the private property of this person (Locke ([1690] 1999)). This naturalisation of private property gives us a clue about how the labor theory of value becomes gradually integrated into the ideological world of bourgeois society. Later we will see that this theory of value will be violently expelled from official economic thinking, thus helping us understand that there is no 'true' theory of value. All theories of value are expressions of a political force fighting for its share of society's entire wealth.

There is a subtle difference between Hobbes and Locke regarding the concept of the State. While Hobbes assigns an active role for the State, Locke gives the State a passive role. For Hobbes, the State is responsible for institutionalizing private property. However, for Locke, it is as if private property was already present in the state of nature. If the State for Locke is a result of the consensual negotiation between free individuals who recognize each other reciprocally as private proprietors, then the ultimate basis for the political instance is the individual itself and not something that 'comes from above'. This picture is in accordance with commodity relations of production. Commodity is the basic unity that constitutes the whole body of capitalism. In this system, people interact with each other only through the economic nexus of the exchange of properties. It appears as if there is no need of a State to guarantee that everybody is respecting the rules that are created directly by individual negotiation. Metaphorically, we could say that the rules become 'invisible'. The participating agents do not recognize that they are playing a game created by themselves. Exchange relations based on private property shine forth as if they were free from human handling, as if these rules were identical to the rules that govern the universe and the natural world. Accordingly, it is no longer necessary to have a political, ethical, or religious base to explain the social system under observation. Private property becomes such an automatic thing that it gains the status of 'natural' and 'eternal'. Locke's system is perfectly adequate for the bourgeois *Weltanschauung*, because it protects the institution of private property from the inquiring eyes of science.

There is another way to understand why Locke has a more suitable theory of the State for modern society than Hobbes. Locke's thought puts the individual above the collective, as if the Leviathan's purpose was to meet the desires of a single citizen. If the individual experiences oppression from the State, the State must change, and not the individual. So, the State must always be in alignment with what this (bourgeois) individual wants. This individual is free not to obey the ruler if there is disagreement. The liberal model of this current presents various arguments in favor of insurgency, given specific circumstances. For example, social revolution and uprisings against the government are defendable if the legal authority fails to perform the wishes of the individuals. Here we have a clear seed of a future current deriving from (Lockean) liberalism that will openly act against any form of the State: anarchism.[1]

Locke's theory provides a sense of natural order behind the fundamentals of modern society that will reappear in Adam Smith's work. The individual and the collective are linked by an explanation of harmonious naturality. The resulting picture is one in which the specificities of a certain society are presented as universal characteristics. It is an idea of modern society as the pinnacle of a linear and progressive evolution. The formation of modern society had to take place just as gravity pulls everything towards the floor.

Usually, theoretical works in the Marxist tradition that compare Marx with the classical economists emphasize the negative features of bourgeois economic thinking. However, it is important to notice that there are also positive features in Adam Smith's milestone achievement in political economy. Any professional economist educated in the 20th century was introduced to Adam Smith as a champion of liberalism with little profound reflection about the features of his thinking on the complexities surrounding the very concept of liberty. This has led to the idea that Adam Smith's invisible hand is very close to the satirical perspective of Bernard Mandeville (1670–1733), who presented the most provocative answer to the paradox of the relationship between individual and -society in his *Fable of the Bees* from 1714, to which we shall turn in detail later in brief. This superficial reading of Adam Smith does not pay the necessary attention to *The Theory of Moral Sentiments*, which he published in 1759, 17 years before *The Wealth of Nations*.[2]

---

1   For a detailed view of Locke as a precursor of 'philosophical anarchism', see Simmons (1993). Anarchism is one important result of negation of the State deriving from the logical development of liberal philosophy. Instead of justifying the State, the rigorous continuation of liberalism must lead to the full rejection of the State. Libertarianism is a late, reactionary, and completely contradictory form of liberalism where anarchy and the bourgeois State must coexist.

2   There have been numerous efforts to reconsider Adam Smith's thought in its entirety in the last decades. My approach is influenced by Amartya Sen (1999), who aimed at connecting philosophy and ethics to economics. Bertram Schefold (2017) in Germany and Ana Maria Bianchi (1988) in Brazil have similar approaches and I follow their instructions on the recovery of Adam Smith's thought as a whole. For a presentation of the 'Adam Smith problem', that is, of supposed incongruencies between *The Theory of Moral Sentiments* and *The Wealth of Nations*, see Boff (2018). Tribe (2008) explains that modern Smith scholarship originated

In this book, Adam Smith reacts against Mandeville's approach and indicates that self-interest is not something that is detached from the judgement of others. One is free to seek one's own benefits, but this search must happen within the boundaries of what is socially accepted. Achieving individual goals through means that society considers despicable is not the way to sustain the nexus between the private and the public. This is why Smith considers that every individual must understand that his/her particular action not only affects the collective, but also that, besides the result of any particular action, the civil peers will judge the means employed to generate the result.

The most important thing to have in mind here is that, despite what was once thought, *The Theory of Moral Sentiments* and *The Wealth of Nations* do not present conflicting philosophical systems (Tribe 2008). In the history of economic thought, the so-called 'Adam Smith problem or paradox' points to the perceived impossibility of harmonizing his two books. Why? In the first one, Adam Smith deals with the traditional questions of moral philosophy. He tries to build an ethical system in which private interests must be harmonized with public needs. In the second book, Smith addresses more concrete issues related to material wealth and its connections to labor division, commerce, and money. Of course, each work has its own purpose and focus. This has led to the erroneous idea that Adam Smith dispensed with the principles in his previous book in favor of the ideas set out in his more recent and popular *Wealth of the Nations*.

It is a fact that both works show distinct moments in the intellectual development of Adam Smith. He moves from a well-established and vast area, i.e., moral and political philosophy, towards a more specific new terrain, i.e., political economy. The philosophical system proposed in his classes on moral philosophy in Glasgow in the 1750s is totally incorporated into the observations he made during his tutoring tour of continental Europe in the 1760s. This trip provided empirical material and intellectual inspiration for the writing of *The Wealth of Nations*. In Europe, Adam Smith had discussions with economists such as Turgot (1727–1781), François Quesnay (1694–1774) and other intellectuals (Stewart [1811] 2002). Therefore, if we want to understand how the law of value appears in Smith's thought, we need to correctly relate *The Theory of Moral Sentiments* with *The Wealth of Nations*. There is a continuation in Smith's intellectual development that cannot be disregarded.

---

with German writers from the 1850s to the 1890s and that this debate remained long ignored by English speaking scholars.

The main idea in *The Theory of Moral Sentiments* concerns what he calls sympathy. According to Smith, sympathy is a feeling that every human is capable of experiencing. For Smith, sympathy refers to how humans living in society can recognize and respect everyone else as co-existing entities. It is the capacity we all have, with distinct intensity, to imagine how we would feel if we were the other person. The idea of human equality and reciprocal respect is key, since it is not possible to imagine living the life of another person if there is not a common element between you and the other.

In the structure of Adam Smith's course on moral philosophy, the discussion of sympathy was placed in the second part, where he talked about ethics (Stewart [1811] 2002). The general structure of the course indicates that material interests were not the central concern. Typical topics of what would become the field of political economy appear only in later stages of Smith's course on moral philosophy. The first part dealt with natural theology, where he discussed proofs and attributes of God. The third part was dedicated to morality and justice. It analyzed how social rules are evaluated in terms of fairness. The fourth and last part of the course concerned justice and utility and how these principles relate to wealth.

According to Stewart ([1811] 2002) two things are investigated in *The Theory of Moral Sentiments*. First, Adam Smith explains how we learn to judge the behavior of others. Second, he indicates that when we use the same criteria to judge our own behavior, we develop a sense of duty.

But what are the criteria of this judgement? The judgement depends first on an accurate perception of the difference between right and wrong, and second on an understanding of the agent's accountability. Smith offers examples to show that there is an intrinsic ability to put oneself in another's shoes. By doing this, everyone becomes closer to someone else's experience. We become more capable of judging everyone's actions and reactions, including our own, based on what is socially acceptable. For Smith, the capacity to achieve this standard of judgement derives from what he calls sympathy.

Although Smith says this ability is natural, he observes that it is not homogeneous in the population (using statistical terminology we could say that he noted that this ability is normally distributed among the population). He is aware that each person has a different capacity for feeling sympathy. At one extreme, there may be a person who feels the emotions of a stranger with the same intensity as if he/she were the person directly affected by the phenomenon. At the other extreme, there may be someone who is totally incapable of sympathy. In this case, could the individual be labelled an antisocial person?

This is one intriguing way to relate Adam Smith's thought to the field of social psychology, which would develop many decades later.[3]

In chapter 1 of *The Theory of Moral Sentiments*, Smith imagines a situation in which we observe a person about to receive a stroke with a stick on his/her leg or arm. How would we react? Smith suggests "(...) we naturally shrink and draw back our own leg or our own arm (...)" (Smith [1759] 1869). Similarly, when we watch a tightrope walker in a circus, we automatically react as if we were high above the floor in a precarious situation. The crowd would "writhe and twist and balance their own bodies, as they see him do, and as they feel that they themselves must do if in his situation." (Smith [1759] 1859).

Smith is telling us that there is a natural mechanism making us feel the same sensations as someone else just by being aware of what this person is going through. Now, many situations and variations can be imagined, including all other kinds of sentiments: pain, sorrow, joy, etc. All these hypothetical situations serve Smith's purpose of demonstrating that we all have, as a natural principle, the capacity to put ourselves in the place of our fellow citizens. By doing this, we can judge ourselves as we judge others. This ability is called sympathy: "Sympathy, (...) may now, however, without much impropriety, be made use of to denote our fellow-feeling with any passion whatever." (Smith [1759] 1859).

Certainly, Adam Smith knows that there are various situations and there is not always a convergence of feelings. There can emerge what he calls dissonance. For example, imagine you are standing in line for your turn and someone behind you starts shouting in public, disturbing everyone around. It is reasonable to think that such behavior will not necessarily generate a positive connection with others who might be seeing the scene or even be the target of such aggression. Why? Because we do not know what is causing this person's fury. Perhaps the line was the last straw after a series of bad episodes in the person's recent past. Smith's argument here is that, when we trace the causes of someone's feelings, then we all are able to put ourselves in the other's shoes and to judge the other just as we judge ourselves. The consideration of others as real individual entities that exist just like ourselves is something Adam

---

3 For an introduction to Adam Smith as a precursor of social psychology, see Truzi (1966) and Ashraf, Camerer and Loewenstein (2005). In the *Theory of Moral Sentiments*, Smith explains that the sense of duty can be thought of as our awareness that someone is always watching and judging our actions. This is the impartial spectator, a kind of judge created in the mind. This would be the result of a socialization process which every member of society goes through during the transition from infancy to adulthood. So, to Adam Smith, there are natural origins for constructive social behaviors, but they are also a product of human culture.

Smith regards as a concrete phenomenon that allows everyone to be more than self-interested robots. The idea of strict individualism that was spreading at the time, and which is still repeated by the most superficial economic analyses in the 21st century, is counterposed by the following words that open *The Theory of Moral Sentiments*:

> How selfish soever man may be supposed, there are evidently some principles in his nature, which interest him in the fortune of others, and render their happiness necessary to him, though he derives nothing from it except the pleasure of seeing it.
>
> ADAM SMITH [1759] 1869, p. 2

The transition from feudal institutions to a full market society demanded an answer to the mysteries of social cohesion based on self-interest. The great paradox of moral philosophy was to explain how individual interests could generate a social state of peace and abundance. Selfishness and altruism are two opposing tendencies that philosophers knew belonged together in the reality of the human condition. How could these contradictory things be united in a theoretical system capable of explaining social order based on the pursuit of self-interest? Adam Smith knew that a solution had to be found in which both sides must play their role in order to neutralize the dichotomy and tension between them.

We still do not have any real conception of the law of value in *The Theory of Moral Sentiments*. However, we must remember that Adam Smith's initial reflections for merging private interests with public needs in an ideal system begin here. The specialist literature today indicates that the system presented in *The Wealth of Nations* contains all the fundamental insights presented in *The Theory of Moral Sentiments*. So, self-interest is not to be pursued by any means, but only through means that meet societal approval. Economic agents do follow their own goals, but in Smith's eyes, they are conscious of the effects their actions can have on others and must accordingly play by the rules. Individual achievements are not the only source of social recognition and praise: the means through which the individual reached his/her goals also play an important role. This is quite different from what Mandeville's *Fable of the Bees* tries to teach.

The superficial idea of an 'unethical Adam Smith' spread with the help of memorable scenarios in *The Wealth of the Nations*. One of the most famous concerns the famous passage where Smith speaks of the redundancy of the benevolence of the butcher, the brewer, or the baker with regard to providing our dinner.⁴ The butcher, the brewer, and the baker are not primarily thinking about serving others for the sake of humanity but about their own material interests. They contribute to the wellbeing of others as a by-product of their self interest. Such remarks do not involve a denial of the previous social system he conceived in *The Theory of Moral Sentiments*. All features he presented in the past must find their place in the theoretical system of *The Wealth of Nations*. There is no evidence that Smith ever rejected his previous work in favor of his later book. Therefore, our task is to insert the more specific and concrete analysis of *The Wealth of Nations* into the broader and more philosophical framework of *The Theory of Moral Sentiments*. There is a continuity between the two books that shows Smith integrating more specific questions into his overarching system of political philosophy. Political economy is focused on matters of material interests, and it is a part of what constitutes the whole social system. Addition is the keyword to understand the intellectual development here, and not substitution.

At this point, we may have one difficulty. Assuming that there is a linear progression of cumulative knowledge, as if each next theoretical system surpassed the previous system in every sense, one could argue the following: if ethical philosophy is a permanent feature in Smith's thought, then the philosophical system behind Mandeville's *Fable of the Bees* is superior, because it does not have any moral constraints on individual behavior. So, who has a superior system: Mandeville or Smith?

The answer to this problem reveals how dialectical development is present in the progressive movement of philosophy. Real progression is not simply linear overcoming but overcoming through achieving higher levels of dialectical contradiction. The next system surpasses the previous one in the sense of Hegel's *Aufhebung*. With respect to the standard behavior of individuals in

---

4   The example of the butcher, brewer and baker is in chapter 2 of *Wealth of Nations*: "In almost every other race of animals, each individual, when it is grown up to maturity, is entirely independent, and in its natural state has occasion for the assistance of no other living creature. But man has almost constant occasion for the help of his brethren, and it is in vain for him to expect it from their benevolence only. He will be more likely to prevail if he can interest their self-love in his favour, and shew them that it is for their own advantage to do for him what he requires of them. Whoever offers to another a bargain of any kind, proposes to do this. Give me that which I want, and you shall have this which you want, is the meaning of every such offer; and it is in this manner that we obtain from one another the far greater part of those good offices which we stand in need of. It is not from the benevolence of the butcher, the brewer, or the baker that we expect our dinner, but from their regard to their own interest. We address ourselves, not to their humanity, but to their self-love, and never talk to them of our own necessities, but of their advantages. Smith ([1776] 1981), p. 26."

modern society, Mandeville both is *and* is not superior to Smith at the same time. He is superior when he disdains the force of morality to explain the cohesion of this new society. But he is inferior because he also intends to teach a moral lesson in the form of a fable. The vulgarization of Smith's thought through an excessive approximation to Mandeville's is, in a certain way, correct and progressive, because it eliminates the complexities of real contradictions that are present in Smith's thought and impedes a clear view of the idealized invisible hand.[5]

Despite some minor differences, Smith and Mandeville are pointing to a similar solution to the problem of harmonizing private interests with public needs. The important thing here is that both Smith and Mandeville create a perpetual self-reproducing system that does not require any external factor to function. Individuals seek their own aims and generate positive social outcomes (even though the exact way in which this happens may differ).

Indeed, one of the most significant episodes in the birth of political economy was the tremendous impact of Bernard Mandeville's poem *The Grumbling Hive or Knaves turn'd honest* (Mandeville ([1705] 2017)), also known as *The Fable of the Bees: or, Private Vices, Public Benefits*. It tells the story of a hive that undergoes a drastic transformation. The community of bees living in this hive represents human society in the age of modernity. Each member has its function and division of labor is what keeps the colony alive. When they perform their individual tasks, there emerges a collective cohesion that maintains the hive together and makes it grow stronger. Each bee is dedicated to fulfilling its tasks not because it knows that it will contribute to the community, but because this fulfillment is in accordance with its own individual aims.

According to Adam Smith, this striving to perform energetically the various tasks necessary to sustain the entire society derives from the quest for social distinction. In *The Theory of Moral Sentiments,* Chapter II, Session III, called On the origin of Ambition, and of distinction of Ranks, Smith accurately explains that what all members seek is to be admired by their fellow citizens (Smith [1759] 1869, pp. 47–56). It is not a quest to gain material wealth. Material wealth certainly is a means to achieve high rank in society, but it is not the only one. The word 'ambition' captures this phenomenon and it is used in the *Fable of the Bees* as the force corresponding to Smith's 'invisible hand': every member of society, by striving to reach his/her own goals, contributes to a collective process from which all benefit. We can understand that Smith has a broader

---

5   This would be a Hayekian reading of Adam Smith, for example. We should view this kind of reading as limited but in the right direction. See Montes (2010).

interpretation of self-realization. Each one has specific goals that may take different forms, such as greater material wealth, greater knowledge, superior abilities in arts or sports, etc. People struggle to gain social distinction, honor, and reputation.

How does this fit Mandeville's fable? Mandeville is a little more realistic in terms of each person's individual wishes. For him, individual members of a collective do not think about how they are seen by others. Reputation is absent from the parable. So it is not a matter of social recognition, but of pure self-interest, regardless of what others might think. The history the poem tells has three parts. First, there is an initial situation of both abundance and competition. Second, there is a phase in which all the bees complain about how miserable they are because everyone cares only for him/herself and thus asks for a change, which comes magically. Third, there is a final stage where this magical solution, which appeared to be a good thing at first, turns out to be the worst outcome possible.

The pursuit of self-interest is the standard behavior for all bees. During the day, they all give their best to fulfill their own goals. They trick each other, exploit the weaker, and take advantage of every possible occasion. At night, they all complain at home that everyone else is selfish and that society is sick. So, the god Jupiter comes to teach a lesson to all bees. He casts a spell over the hive, turning everyone from knaves, scoundrels, and scamps into honest citizens.

What happens next? Immediately all the bees celebrate the new situation together. It is a great collective festival, as if a war had been won. Many problems simply disappear. Trickery, vengeance, and egoism are gone. All costs necessary to pay for law enforcement, contract protection and agreements vanish in this ethical collectivization. However, in an unexpected turn, other problems appear and direct the fable to a dystopian ending. The complete absence of ambition and individual accountability, which lay behind the self-interested behavior, leads to a lack of responsibility. Everyone leaves to another the tasks necessary to guarantee the economic reproduction of the hive. Since ambition is gone, no one tries to be the best butcher, brewer, baker, cook, barber, shoemaker, etc. Consequently, all labor is performed poorly. The result is economic and social decay, and the remaining bees flee from the hive to other places. Mandeville gives a lesson which will become one of the most popular rules of thumb used against any idea of collectivization. The bees should not complain about the fact that everyone is selfish and thinks only of his/her own success. Why? Because it is precisely this pattern that creates a strong collective in which all benefit. In that sense, private vices lead to public benefits.

Self-interested morality is the most sacred value in this system, influencing all subsequent discussion in moral philosophy and political economy.

Obviously, the logic of the social system presented in the *Fable of the Bees* is not directly applicable to the more concrete questions of political economy, such as material wealth, money, the State and the market, because its form is not only too abstract but also comically exaggerated. It is not strictly a treatise, but an artistic piece with relevant content. So, we can ascribe to it categories of analysis such as spontaneous coordination behind the functioning of the law of value. The overall pattern of unconscious coordination of individual desires with social needs emerges from one single explaining factor: everyone struggles to fulfill their individual aims within objective limitations for free action. In that sense, we can think of the law of value as a natural mechanism. It floats above and directs the individuals, who believe they can act free from any ethical, moral, or religious interference.

The artistic and the scientific tones of the fable contribute to making the idea of a selfish society into something acceptable. Here we have also a connection between utilitarianism and the mundane matters of individual interests. Utilitarianism fits perfectly into the notion of a generic free individual who has an entirely subjective goal. The aims are determined by the agent him/herself. This is the basis for the further development of political economy in the epoch of the bourgeoisie. The liberty of the individual is constrained only by his/her own consciousness that he/she is part of a social body in which all others have the same individual rights as him/her. The next logical steps will take political economy to the turbulent waters of bourgeois socialism in its various currents. Later, Marxism will direct the flow towards a new stage of development for political economy.

What is Adam Smith's response to this depiction of the law of value behind Bernard Mandeville's poem? We find his position by relating two aspects present in *The Theory of Moral Sentiments*: first, the origin of ambition in chapter 2 of session III of part one, called Of the origin of Ambition, and of the distinction of Ranks (Smith ([1759] 1869), pp. 47–56) and, second, Smith's critique of other systems of moral philosophy in chapter 4 of session II of part seven, called Of licentious systems (Smith ([1759] 1869), pp. 271–278).

Regarding the origin of ambition and social distinction, Smith recovers a relevant question that appeared frequently in the thoughts of scholars when they talked about the pursuit of luxury and pleasure. Why does everyone seek to acquire power or money that goes beyond what is necessary to supply one's need for "food and clothing, the comfort of a house, and of a family" (Smith [1759] 1869)? What is the motivation for this struggle? It seems irrational since it surpasses the effort required to meet all fundamental necessities.

As mentioned before, ambition for Adam Smith is not necessarily related to the acquisition of material wealth. Material wealth, in the form of money and capital, is the propelling force of ambition in capitalism. But there are many other ways to the top other than just accumulation of wealth in this mundane sense. For Smith, the driving force for all individuals is an urge to be recognized by society. Fame and status is what we all seek, and there are various ways to achieve this, even though capital accumulation is the prevailing means to acquire status in a capitalist society. According to Smith, it is not the desirable object, in whatever form it takes, that satisfies our craving for more, but the respect we earn in society when we achieve our goals: "To be observed, to be attended to, to be taken notice of with sympathy, complacency, and approbation, are all the advantages which we can propose to derive from it. It is the vanity, not the ease or the pleasure, which interests us." (Smith [1759] 1869).

Thus, in Smith's view, the explanation for the infinite drive for more lies in the vanity of humankind. Accordingly, those engaged in profit-making activities do not really want more money to serve their needs or to increase their comfort and luxury. Rather, they are seeking social approval. To own more wealth, in the material sense of economic resources, is merely a specific method of acquiring the respect of fellow citizens. Now we can see that there is a close relationship between natural vanity and the behavior of the new character that personifies mercantile and capitalist logic. This new character is the merchant or bourgeois that initiates capitalist accumulation. He not only treasures wealth, but continually injects it back into the circuit of capital production.

I must warn that we are making here a sympathetic approach to Smith's world, which is not usual in the Marxist tradition. Obviously, it would be correct to point out right away that Smith does not distinguish between 'human being' and 'a human being that is inserted in a sociohistorical mode of production'. Our intent here, however, is to engage with pre-Marxian political economy in a positive sense because we need to comprehend the entire intellectual trajectory of the concept of the law of value.

We must keep in mind that Adam Smith remains faithful to his *Theory of Moral Sentiments* when writing *The Wealth of Nations*. If ambition always leads to social admiration, then it becomes much easier to direct private action towards the public good. What is the difference then between the two expositions? In *The Theory of Moral Sentiments,* we do not have a clear notion of the market as the concrete mechanism that makes this connection viable. *The Wealth of Nations* is a concrete analysis applying the general frame of the moral philosophy of sympathy to the real scenario of increasing labor division at the end of the 18th century in Europe.

Regarding other systems of moral philosophy, Adam Smith classifies Mandeville's system among the so-called licentious systems. He develops a careful critique, confronting the moral lesson to be taken from the fable of the bees. He argues that Mandeville's system is peculiar in one aspect: in general, all moral philosophers separated vices (negative) from virtues (positive), but Mandeville removes this distinction. Because of this, Smith writes that the system is "wholly pernicious" (Smith [1759] 1869). The dissolution of virtues and vices into one soup hides some truths that may trick the unskilled, i.e., the ordinary mind. This is the danger behind Mandeville's funny tale according to Smith.

In both systems, Smith's and Mandeville's, there is a struggle towards achievement. So, we can readily insert the argument for human ambition derived from vanity into Mandeville's world. This would bring the two author's thoughts into closer proximity, as indeed occurred in the development of the teaching of economic thought.

The extremely significant difference lies in the form the struggle takes. In the *Fable of the Bees*, success is to be obtained by any means possible, including trickery, deceit, and fraud. For Smith, the road to success must be travelled through socially accepted means. Merit is only secure if it employs socially appropriate actions. If someone achieves distinction based on Mandeville's morals, he/she will eventually develop a feeling of guilt. Why? Because he/she "is never to be satisfied, is full of jealousy and suspicion that we do not esteem him so much as he desires, because he has some secret consciousness that he desires more than he deserves" (Smith [1759] 1869). The situation of this individual is unstable because the social distinction obtained is fragile. It can fall apart at anytime; if the secret to success becomes public, the real judgement will take place. If socially despised means have been employed, the fall is certain.

Adam Smith goes further. In a case where someone looking for distinction with socially respected means has not yet reached the top, that person is at peace with him/herself. On the other hand, if someone has reached a high rank by socially condemned methods, that person is suffering. It is possible that society may never discover that this sufferer has achieved all his/her goals by unfair play. But there is nothing that prevents this discovery from being made someday. And this uncertainty again permanently disturbs the regretful knave.

It is important to recover the relationship between Adam Smith and Bernard Mandeville because their differences are almost entirely forgotten today. Moreover, it helps us to see that the law of value in classical political economy is conceived within a natural and harmonious system. Despite these differences, an embryonic invisible hand is present in both authors. It represents the impersonal mechanism that governs every individual in the same manner and in such a way that everybody is at the same time responsible for and victim of the mechanism.[6]

Finally, we see that this pattern of social organization is generated by the members of society themselves. There is nobody above. There is no judge in Heaven or any superior entity ruling others down on Earth. There is no separation and we ourselves are responsible for the rules of our society. All social relations are creations of the same agents that are bound by these relations. In this sense, the law of value appears at first in political economy as the most generic description of the nexus individual-collective without recourse to any *deus ex machina*. In the place of the unseen god, something else invisible must come. The invisible hand is the perfect analogy for the ideal functioning of the market society. It is like an orchestra playing without a maestro.

2   The Law of Value as Exchange of Equivalents

The law of value as the invisible hand is a philosophical concept. Now we investigate a more concrete definition of the law of value in classical political economy, which involves the quantitative parameter of equivalence between goods. In the physiocratic tradition, the concept of equilibrium from mechanical physics was central. This balance meant that the system was stable, and stability is fundamental for continuation. The economic system is a process of repetition and so the notion of equilibrium should also play a role here. The center of gravity for the movement of market prices must have a meaning in economic terms, just as equilibrium has a meaning in the terms of physics. What is the significance of the set of prices that puts the economic system in equilibrium? Here we think of the law of value as the rule of exchange of equivalents, which is the basis upon which the labor theory of value will grow.

Before classical political economy, there was already a long tradition of reflection about value. Briefly, we can state that there have been always two sides in the debate about how useful things are valued. On one side, thinkers focused on the efforts and costs of production. They wanted to explain value in terms of the obstacles to obtaining a useful item. On the other side, some authors stressed the aspects of consumption and utility. They wanted to explain value in terms of usefulness rather than the exertions and expenses

---

6 Marx pointed to close similarities between Adam Smith and Bernard Mandeville. He even states that Smith has almost copied Mandeville's description of the division of labor in the *Fable of the Bees*. See Marx ([1867] 2015), p. 256.

involved in the production process. We could simplify this opposition by call-
ing the first one the great strain of objective theories of value and the second
one the great strain of subjective theories of value.

Adam Smith's political economy was influenced by the physiocrats, who
focused on a purely objectivist approach to value theory when arguing that
all wealth must come from the soil. The soil (the usual example of the factor of production land/nature), however, can yield more of chosen products
through human action. So, Smith changes the focus to labor in the production
process. Smith's theory of value indicates clearly that nature plays a role, but
what matters for the analysis of human economic activity is what humans, by
commanding the forces of nature, produce. He dedicates most of his attention
to the objective side. We must also remember that his empirical observations
of workshops in the beginning stages of the Industrial Revolution were crucial for his idea that the driving force of incrementing productivity and wealth
lies in labor division. So, it must come as no surprise that labor appears as
the factor responsible for creating value. Labor division is the main source
of wealth, something that does not mean directly value, but nevertheless is
closely related to it.

Soon the idea that things with equal value/price could be exchanged with
one another developed into the notion that these things should require the
same amount of effort to produce. The quantitative equality between two
qualitatively different use values meant that both needed the same labor time
to be made available to society. Even things as different as water and diamonds
could have their value/price explained by this reasoning. So, the mechanism
was simple: adjusting the quantities of the compared use values to achieve
a relation of quantitative equivalence between them was just like balancing
chemical reactions. Both sides contain the same amount of a common substance. In the exercise of balancing chemical reactions, the common item is
mass and the law of conservation of mass determines the logic of recombi-
nation of elements. Labor plays the same role as mass (or energy) in political
economy.

Labor transforms inputs into outputs. So, even though water cannot directly
be transformed into diamonds, society can choose how much labor it should
allocate to the production of water and diamonds. These are options for which
society must choose how much effort should go into their production. There
emerges a quantitative relation between all possible outputs by comparing
how much labor society needs to employ in their respective production. Water
cannot be transformed into wine, unless the necessary material and energy-
related processes are at one's disposal. This shows that the quantitative relations between different goods must obey the limits of matter transformation,

and that this is the fundamental basis of all objective theories of value, such as the labor theory of value of Adam Smith and David Ricardo ([1817] 2010).

In modern society labor power is the most democratic ownership title— every human able to work possesses labor power, and thus is 'automatically' endowed with this property as long as he/she is not a slave. This created a new standard for justice regarding value/price. Equal quantities of labor must be exchanged in all commercial transactions, otherwise one of the sides (buyer or seller) will lose. The idea that the quantitative relations of exchange are governed by the quantity of labor became a strong component in the development of the theoretical core of political economy.

It is hard to indicate exactly when value theory became completely dominated by the element of labor. Labor as a category appears in many writings before Adam Smith (Ronald Meek [1956] 1973). Many authors who focused on the costs of production had already pointed to labor as the most relevant factor in the generation of value.

We emphasise that most of the history of value theory involves the opposition between two sides: production and distribution (circulation). In this sense, the most general form of controversy in value theory is the opposition between objective value theories and subjective value theories. This dichotomy goes back long before the publication of *The Wealth of the Nations*. All preceding works emphasized the question of production costs or consumption effects as the determining factor. If a value theory considered that the production process of a good was the most important sphere in the determination of its value/price, then it conflicted with value theories that focused on the consumption of the good.

On one side, all reasoning was directed to examining the transformation of inputs into outputs as it occurs when labor modifies nature. On the other side, all intellectual effort was focused on understanding how the produced good meets consumer needs. Both sides consider relations of value as pure natural relations. Even if the qualitative element for measuring quantity is different (labor and utility), both think of value as a relation of the kind human-use value. One side investigates how humans change nature to create useful items, whereas the other side investigates how human needs are satisfied by using those items. Thus, it is impossible to investigate the historical specificities of any mode of production.

The labor theory of value is one type of objective value theory. The sequence Smith-Ricardo-Marx-Marginalist Revolution represents its ascension, heyday and subsequent fall after the rejection of socialism by 'official' economists. The element responsible for creating value changes according to the economic conditions of each epoch because class struggle is always behind the validation of any value theory. It is not a matter of finding the one true element generating value, as if value was only a relation of the kind human-use value. Even when it is rational and empirically valid to explain the magnitude of value/price by analyzing the relation between humans and the world of use-values, this does not form a complete justification of a theory of value. A theory of value is not complete if it explains only quantity of value; it must also explain the quality of what value is made of. If we want to determine this qualitative element, it is necessary to study the relations between humans. The social relations of any mode of production interfere in the development of value theory and must be explicitly considered. So, besides the relation of the kind human-use value, there is also the relation of the kind human-human, which influences the construction of any theory of value.

The origin of wealth or value (the distinction was not properly developed then) was a matter of practical order until the 17th century. This means that no analyst was too worried about what wealth really is. All that mattered was to increase wealth, whose form was mainly that of precious metals. Accordingly, buying at a price and selling at a higher price was the core of both economic policy and political economy in the mercantilist era. But the continuous pursuit of greater quantities of wealth/value was already a fixed idea. The physiocrats investigated society by employing knowledge of the natural world—biology, chemistry, physics—and consequently directed their attention to the production process. Earth and human energy in the form of labor were already present in the physiocratic view. With the further development of capitalism and the profound transformations of the Industrial Revolution, the next generation of authors directed their attention to a new scenario created by the further development of capitalism. The separation between town and country became so great and the division of labor so specialized, that the idea that labor alone is responsible for creating wealth/value consolidated. The forces of nature act as media supporting the human action of producing, as auxiliary powers for human action.

Adam Smith presents the general plan of *The Wealth of Nations* in an introduction where he partly follows the teachings of the French physician-economists (the physiocrats) about the production and distribution of wealth among social classes. He also indicates the aims of each of the five books that constitute *The Wealth of Nations* and we see that the main goal is to reveal the processes that explain the economic power of a nation. His value theory is presented in the first book.

Division of labor is the first step in the sequence that leads to increased productivity and consequently wealth. The origin of the division of labor lies in the supposed propensity of human beings to exchange one thing for another.

We see that Smith pushes the intellectual boundaries of his age when he tries to associate exchange with the human ability to think and to talk, which he views as the difference between humans and other animals (Smith [1776] 1981).

Smith does not realize that there is a necessary precondition for sustaining the praxis of exchange. Useful things are being exchanged as private property, but what is the historical origin of this institution? The social phenomenon of private property, which is the necessary pre-condition for producing useful items that can be considered commodities, appears in Smith's system as if it were an eternal feature of humanity. For Smith, all human history is reduced to the history of a special human being who is born and lives in a market society. The market is treated as the natural, and the only way to organize the economy.

Although this is a grave mistake, which will be corrected by Marx in his *Critique of Political Economy*, there are relevant elements in this description that help us understand what the law of value is. Each individual acts according to his/her own will. At the same time, they all take part in the same social network of different task-activities that constitutes total social labor. The principle of exchange of equivalents guarantees equality and justice in accordance with the fundamentals of market society. How could there be inequality if the beautiful mechanism of supply and demand squeezes prices towards their fair levels? Prices oscillate around those indexes that signify the exchange of equal quantities of labor. Prices oscillate around values. This insight is one of the greatest merits of Adam Smith's analysis of the operation of the law of value.

Adam Smith is aware that the basic economic problem of every nation will not be solved by an idealized market, detached from reality. The increase in wealth enabled by rising productivity will only benefit everyone in society if there is an intelligent government that assures the good functioning of markets. Thus, Smith knows that there is no such thing as a market without the State. The political entity is decisive for enabling the markets to act in favor of all the population:

> it is the great multiplication of the productions of all the different arts, in consequence of the division of labour, which occasions, *in a well-governed society*, that universal opulence which extends itself to the lowest ranks of the people.
>
> SMITH [1776] 1981, p. 22, emphasis mine

Classical liberalism suffers from the humanist illusion of universal gains promoted by markets. Thus, we need to have a sensible approach and remember to consider its philosophical context given the progressive character of the bourgeois revolution. Neoliberalism, differently, is not exempt from vigorous attack. There are no excuses for returning to liberalism, which produced the tragedy of the World Wars in the 20th century. Smith knows that only a correct economic policy can direct the gains made as a result of labor division towards all groups in society. If this policy is absent, concentration of wealth might take place and the advantage of this kind of system for all might be questioned.

After presenting the logic behind the division of labor and its influence over productivity and wealth, Adam Smith presents the historical process that gave birth to money. Here we have another remarkable example of how the endogenous mindset of someone in bourgeois society leads to grave errors in the scientific analysis of the functioning of capitalism.

Smith argues that the logic of exchange of equivalents emerged naturally over time, because such a scheme would be beneficial to all involved in these kinds of transactions. For Smith it seems as if there was no violence involved in the destruction of communal economic systems. Barter exchange would have evolved first. Then a particular item would have been used as a general equivalent, to facilitate transactions and to solve the problem of coincidence of interests. What was this problem? If someone who has corn wanted shoes, and met someone wanting corn but who had only pigs to give away in exchange, there would be difficulty in satisfying the interests of both. The first person would have to take pigs as payment and then continue looking for someone who could exchange pigs for shoes. Money would have been invented as a facilitating tool since everybody accepts it. This tale became one of the most sacred ideas in economics and it is still widely used to explain how money was created.[7]

The problem with this explanation is not its logical coherence. Money does evolve from previous forms of value. Commodity, as a social relationship, must exist before money can develop, because logically, money is a commodity in a further developed form. Just as it is not possible to have certain forms of life before their supporting basis appears (for example, unicellular life forms precede multicellular life forms, etc.), the money form develops from the expansion of social relations based on private property, commodity and precisely quantified debts. So, the problem with Smith's thesis on the origin of money is of a historical and empirical nature, not of logical content.

There are two main theoretical currents that try to explain the origin of money. One of them argues that there is spontaneous creation of money through the expansion of the practice of barter exchange. This line of

---

7   For an extensive critique of Adam Smith's analysis of the origin of money from the perspective of anthropology and the political economy of mutualism, see Graeber (2011).

reasoning is strongly represented by an initial reading of Smith. The other view claims that money is created by the State through a political process, in which violence is employed to plunder and gain wealth, as well as to create new wealth by means of a military organization of labor. Chartalist theories of money are representatives of this last kind of explanation for the origin of money. Historical and empirical data show that money is created by mechanisms involving both sides of this controversy. On one side, the State does act to inject new money into the system by financing wars. On the other side, private agents can also interact with each other and generate new money by mutual agreement that will be eventually validated by the State.

Let us focus back on value and leave money for a later moment. As we have indicated, the problem of determining the quantity of value objectively or subjectively goes back to the pre-history of economic thought, because the regular phenomenon of exchange is a phenomenon prior to capitalism. The theory of value presented in *The Wealth of Nations* plays a decisive role in weighting this debate in favour of objective theories of value, especially the labor theory of value. Smith's perspective gained wide acceptance and led to a certain homogeneity around the theory of value that did not previously exist. It is as if Smith managed to consolidate his view as the mainstream in value theory. Almost all thinkers in political economy during the 18th and 19th centuries defended a labor theory of value in one form or another.

Now we come to the core of Adam Smith's value theory. He observes that the word "VALUE", written in capital letters (Smith [1776] 1981, p. 44), has two different meanings. So, every time we speak of value, we must distinguish between two concepts. The first meaning refers to the utility of the good under analysis, while the second meaning refers to the power of the same good for purchasing other goods. In other words, while the first meaning indicates how the good may be useful to meet a specific need, the second meaning is related to the capacity of that good to be exchanged for other goods. Smith calls these two entities 'value in use' and 'value in exchange'. It is a great advancement, because for the first time there emerges a strong consensus about the duality involved in the theorizing about wealth and value.

This duality behind the mysteries of value represents a long-standing dilemma for value theoreticians. It is the story about the contradiction in the relative values of water and diamonds. Smith takes up the challenge to explain why things which have the greatest value in use usually have little value in exchange and things that have low value in use can have enormous value in exchange. Water, for example, has evident utility for the material reproduction of any living organism and consequently, for the economy and society as whole. It is essential for survival. Where do diamonds, on the other hand, enter the in- and outflow of goods needed to meet various human needs? One cannot eat it or keep warm with it, and yet one can transform it into good food or even into housing. Smith warns the reader that he is initiating an investigation that is very abstract and that some obscurity may remain. We value theoreticians should celebrate his bravery for embarking on the topic.

Adam Smith's main effort from here on is to explain the difference between real or natural price and that price at which a contract is concretely sealed. There is a quantitative variation between these two entities. There is an adjustment along the way from the production sphere to the circulation sphere. Smith argues that whatever the price is in the concrete market, it must be connected to the objective realm of the production process.

But which single element of the production process should be held responsible for creating value? In Smith's analysis, the human being is the agent in charge of the transformation of matter. Since all agents organize the exchange of their products of labor by the quantity of labor they have employed privately, labor must be "(...) the real measure of the exchangeable value of all commodities". (Smith [1776] 1981). We see that the fundamental idea behind Smith's labor theory of value is that human action upon nature is the starting point of all economies. With this in mind, Smith justifies his position in the controversy between the subjective and objective value theories. All useful items circulating in the economy are products of human effort to modify nature and the possession of these items gives one purchasing power. Ownership of an item also gives, besides the power to use the item directly for immediate use value, a different kind of power: the power to command another's labor through exchange.

The duality of value shows that there are two dimensions of analysis. Value in use relates to the direct command by humans over goods. Value in exchange relates to the indirect command by humans over other humans. In this second case, humans command other humans' labor indirectly through goods. Both dimensions refer to the power of commanding something. But commanding labor is different from commanding a specific useful good, because, as we will see, labor has the potential to transform useful goods into other qualitatively different goods. It is potentially any kind of useful item, rather than a fixed form of wealth. It possesses the feature of abstract wealth.

What about the rules of exchange? Observation indicates that the pattern of quantitative relations governing the exchange of goods is not arbitrary. An individual transaction may happen as an outlier. For example, if someone buys a bottle of water for a sum of money sufficient to acquire an entire meal in a normal market environment (lucky seller). But most exchanges will take place at convergent prices, forming a regularity of prices for all items under negotiation.

Ideally, all members of society relate to each other as private owners of exchangeable goods. So, everyone recognizes and respects each other as formal bourgeois. We all are citizens of the same quality. The only difference is quantitative: how much labor do I command? Divisions of social class in a market society derive from different quantities of the same quality. This is the reason why justice in the traditional sense of the Bourgeois Revolution does not match the ideal of justice of the Proletarian Revolution.

The rule that makes different goods quantitatively equal establishes itself as the mechanism that guarantees justice to the exchange. All goods are exchanged with others according to the quantity of labor necessary to their production. Thus, all exchange acts are substitution acts of equivalents, of goods that have the same quantity of value. Each side of the transaction seeks the value in use of the opposite side, while maintaining its own value in exchange. So, Smith sees that the duality of utility and labor are present, but he chooses labor to be the qualitative element for measuring the quantity of wealth. From here on, Smith considers that the qualitative problem of value theory is solved and dedicates all his attention to the quantitative problem of value theory. He is aware that there is a quantitative discrepancy between value in terms of labor time and value in terms of what is realized at the market. Accordingly, he proposes some initial ideas on how to explain this discrepancy.

Smith recognizes the difficulties of his theory of value, but he looks for clever solutions. Marx thinks that this is one of Smith's most important contributions to value theory. Instead of throwing the law of value away, just because there is a systematic incongruence between value and price, Smith tries to understand this imbalance. By doing so, he conceives of the law of value as a regulating force that pushes and pulls market prices towards those indexes that refer to the average quantities of labor necessary to produce each one of all goods in an economy. The law of value is not a direct determination. It works as a tendency. Even if prices do not match value perfectly, they are always gravitating towards those ideal values that signifies the equilibrium of the reproduction system. Marx praises Adam Smith for not abandoning the law of value, because it is necessary to conceive the law as something that is not directly observable. Real prices are empirical indicators of the components needed to produce the commodity. In a perfect competitive market, the gravitational field would be uniform. Prices do not coincide with values just as the center of mass is not the same as the center of gravity.

To be rigorous, the debate on the transformation problem (of values into prices) should start with Adam Smith's classifications of different types of price. The systems of value and price, each one at opposite extremes, are connected through the categories of real price (price in labor) and nominal price (price in money). He correctly realizes that the identity between both sides is not perfect, but this does not shake his belief in the law of value. On the contrary, the movement up and down of prices in money, with its regularities and sometimes unpredictable moves, only reinforces Smith's insight that these movements must have a rationale to be found in the production process. Prices in money gravitate around prices in labor. There is an average line indicating the quantity that equilibrates this apparently chaotic movement, and this quantity reflects exactly the quantity of labor necessary to produce the good of which the price is under observation. We must remember that Smith is dealing with the simplest stage of the problem. He starts with simple commodity production. He tries his best to advance to the more complex issues of variation in productive sectors, capital reproduction and so on, but ultimately, he does not present a successful.solution.

The reasoning behind moving averages is like Marx's own approach to the transformation problem (of values into prices), and he corrects and details various aspects of Smith's scheme. What we must retain here is that we have for the first time a complete description of the functioning of the law of value. At the same time, we have a specific theory of value that captures intellectually this real phenomenon.

Adam Smith's labor theory of value strongly influenced the next generations of economists and eventually became the mainstream theory of value. His dominance in value theory only ended with the Marginalist Revolution one hundred years later, in the 1870s. Objective value theory, in the form of the labor theory of value, was consolidated as the scientific consensus in political economy. It was the most accepted theoretical apparatus to study and explain the law of value.

However, there was no blind acceptance of the doctrine. As in any other field of science, every theorization had to be critically reviewed. Moreover, the political and historical context of mature capitalism will begin to reveal that the theorization around the law of value is a battlefield of class struggle. The ambiguities and shortcomings of Adam Smith's theory were soon noticed, and new improvements were constantly added.

David Ricardo is one of the most famous economists who pushed Adam Smith's value theory further. He initiates his *Principles of Political Economy* exactly where the analysis about the difference between value and price stopped in *The Wealth of the Nations*. All the contradictions and imperfections in the theory become more and more evident, even though the fundamental elements in the description of the law of value remain stable. In short, the main problem is that the description of the market process does not fit the system of quantitative expansion of value. Increase of wealth (and poverty) is a permanent feature of capitalism. But this increase is not equal across all sectors of the economy. The dynamic of economic growth cannot be represented by the growth of a homogeneous mixture, which can expand and maintain the regularity of its proportions. Wealth is not simply the homogeneous concept of the domestic product in macroeconomics. It is not a sum of identical, homogeneous goods, which can be mathematically added as is the case when economists conceptualize it with the sign "Y". This is one of the aspects of the so-called aggregation problem. The irregular way in which the various sectors of the capitalist economy evolve make it extremely hard to apply Smith's theory of value in the study of all the complexities of the law of value.

Furthermore, there are two other issues, one of a quantitative and the other of a qualitative nature. First, almost all classical economists agree that the exchange of equivalents is a natural and eternal rule, which poses an obvious and yet complicated problem. Even in the case of a model of the economy as a homogeneous mixture (for example, Ricardo's corn model or macroeconomic models that focus on the growth of 'Y' and assume the aggregation is solved), we still must explain more precisely the origin of value, and consequently of surplus. What a challenge! Increase in value must be explained within the frame of the established literature in political economy, which states that all exchanges are exchanges of things of equivalent value. Legal equality between buyer and seller makes it difficult to see that there is a specific trade that might be responsible for the creation of more value. The second issue is related to the controversy about the qualitative aspect of value theory. The controversy about labor and utility still needs attention, as the consolidation of neoclassical economics will show later.

Even if utility is not the standard for measuring the quantity of value, as David Ricardo remembers by consulting Adam Smith, it is "absolutely essential" to exchangeable value (Ricardo [1817] 2010). The discrepancy between value and price is always there in Ricardo's elaboration. The labor required for production gives value to the produced item, but not absolutely. A product of labor which does not meet someone's needs will not be valued in the market according to the quantity of effort employed in the labor process. Ricardo tries to explain more accurately the quantitative aspect of Smith's labor theory of value and raises many problematic points. Ricardo presents a series of parallel factors that disturb the values that represent labor time. Despite all this, he maintains the Smithian basis according to which all products are the result of altering nature through human labor, and that, because of this, the most fundamental factor for determining the quantity of value must come from labor.

We should already be aware that the labor theory of value that we have here is a labor theory of value in the physiological sense. Therefore, it is comprehensible that this theory of value may also be entirely naturalized. Both Ricardo and Smith let the pre-capitalist economic agents act according to the law of value, as if there existed eternal forces of supply and demand in any mode of production. This naturalization of the labor theory of value is the path that non-Marxist socialists will later follow.

For David Ricardo, the law of value already appears surrounded by many question marks. But he does not abandon it. He separates the production sphere, where value is determined, from the circulation sphere, where this value suffers various pressures from different sources and may end up, as price, above or below the original value. Since Ricardo is too focused on these variations, which form the normal case of market and capitalist reality, he fails to explore the issue of value creation in a perfect equilibrated environment. Consequently, he fails to explain the origin of surplus value and to maintain the logic of equality in exchange.

The sacredness of the exchange of equivalents is in question. Appearance and essence do not coincide. It seems that all members of modern society are equal, but essentially, all thinkers know that huge concentrations of resources and inequality are taking place. On one side is wealth, on the other poverty in all its manifestations (even in the form of a healthy young person who happily travels every day to work in a comfortable underground train listening to music on an iPhone without ever noticing the scale of his/her indebtedness, as is often the case nowadays). From the 1820s onwards, this contradiction is investigated more seriously. The law of value, which was until then conceived as a natural, harmonious, and perfect thing, also has its dark side. Theories of value fight openly to bend the law of value according to the various material interests that constitute a class society. The task of scientific political economy since then is to reveal these connections, which will ultimately increase class consciousness and contribute to the control over the law of value by the working class.

The decline of classical political economy is intimately related to the finding of various contradictions between the law of value and the prevailing theory of value (the labor theory of value of Smith, Ricardo and subsequent authors who could not solve or even grasp the transformation problem of values into prices). The systems of value (production) and price (circulation) have an intricate nexus that seems to refuse the idea that value is created by human labor. Thus, the labor theory of value needs to solve this problem if it intends to remain in the official arena of economic thinking.

By the beginning of the 19th century, socialism as a real political movement was already causing great transformations and political economy was also affected. The quantitative problem of value had to be solved as a necessary condition for sustaining the powerful theory that proclaims that value and wealth are created only by those who live from their labor. If the attempt fails, other theories of value will develop with the aim of justifying ideological patterns of distribution that suit the interests of the proprietors of the means of production. Value theory is the realm in political economy where class struggle expresses itself most blatantly.

The quantitative problem of value is a matter that can be solved without leaving the framework of classical political economy. The qualitative problem of value, on the other hand, requires an advancement that only becomes possible within the framework of Marx's materialist conception of history. I argue that Karl Marx tackles both problems in the theory of value (quantity and quality) and that failure to make this distinction creates unnecessary confusion.

3 The Law of Value as Contradiction between Value and Price

The third form in which the law of value appears in classical political economy is the explicit acknowledgement that value is not the same as price. More specifically, the law of value here intends to elucidate that this difference is conceptually important. As mentioned, value and price were already understood as separated concepts. Both Adam Smith and David Ricardo understand that value and price are in different dimensions, but connected as if through a tunnel or a wormhole. Although value and price are usually treated as synonyms, they are separate entities. Prices do not always reflect value as a perfect image in the mirror. Distortions are the norm and the contradiction between value and price should not shake the firm belief in the labor theory of value.

Since William Petty ([1690] 1996), labor is the decisive element in the explanation of wealth (and value) creation. Empirical prices always reflected the quantity of labor required to produce the negotiated good. *Quantity* is not an issue and it is easy to show that labor functions well as the standard by which to value useful things in any economic system. The 'Robinson exercises' show this clearly as we will see in the next chapters. The idea in these is that there is one unique logic arranging the total amount of labor in a society to produce the necessary items that guarantee economic reproduction.

In classical political economy, it is already known that the law of value must operate not only in a simple commodity society, but also in a fully developed capitalist society. This makes things more complicated for even the simplest form of the labor theory of value. We saw that it is easy to describe the law of value as the invisible hand or as the exchange of equivalents. But now we must find out how the law of value makes value and price dance together in a coherent framework. The real economic system has many productive units or sectors that employ very distinct productive powers. Units or sectors producing the same use value compete directly, but units or sectors producing different use values (and many different use values at the same time) do compete also, though indirectly. Every sector has a specific period for its reproduction cycle.

We can think of many other variations to bring in the notion of complexity that is necessary to address the relation between value and price. What matters here is that, in the market, use values confront each other as commodities in the competition process. So, on the surface, the consumer is not interested in knowing which producer had more difficulty in supplying a certain good. A comparison between competing goods does not involve knowledge about the circumstances in which they have been produced. Ideally, if competing goods have the same features (they are equivalent use values for satisfying a human need), they will have the same price. So, despite having different values, because one of them may face disadvantageous conditions in production, the empirical price in the market is one and the same for identical items from the perspective of the consumer. This indicates that labor time is not sufficient to answer the question. 'Socially necessary labor time', as proposed by Marx, is an attempt to alleviate the pressure on the crude notion that the price of each single commodity indicates exactly how much labor was employed in the production of that commodity.

This is a brief introduction to the initial stages of the transformation problem of values into prices, as it was debated at the end of the 19th century. The difference between value and price opened the way for a systemic attack against the labor theory of value. Decades later, due to mathematical formalizations of the classical models, the transformation problem established itself in the specialized literature as a formal controversy.[8] The law of value as a

---

8   In Camarinha Lopes (2019) I argue that the history of the debate on the transformation problem of values into prices can be divided into three phases. The first phase begins in 1885 with Engels's challenge presented in the preface to *Capital* book 2 and ends in 1906 with Bortkiewicz' (1907) proposal for correcting Marx's solution to the transformation problem. The second phase embraces the years from 1907 to 1971, when Samuelson (1917) published his famous *voilá* paper on the eraser-algorithm. This second phase is what I call 'the traditional transformation problem'. The third phase began in the 1970s, when the paradigm of the Sraffa shock was popularized by Steedman (1977). I call the third phase the 'critique of redundancy' of the labor theory of value. See also Camarinha Lopes (2013b) for an explanation about how the critique of contradiction against the labor theory of value turned into the critique of redundancy of the labor theory of value.

contradiction between value and price is the most developed form of conceiving the law of value within the framework of the classical approach to value theory. It appeared first in a few passages in the works of Adam Smith and David Ricardo, and then more systematically in *Capital* by Karl Marx.

In the preface of *Capital* book 2, Friedrich Engels ([1885a] 1985) explains in detail the problem surrounding the theorization of the law of value. It was necessary to show how the law of value related to the formation of an equal rate of profit for all sectors, regardless of their organic composition. Given that the division between constant and variable capital in each sector is unique, there must be a mechanism that elucidates why all these sectors move towards a general rate of profit that is valid for the economy as a whole. Engels's challenge represents the highest contradictory point of the pre-Marx labor theory of value.

What was this problem? If value and price, as quantities, must coincide, where does this original quantity come from? And where does the additional quantity, i.e. the surplus value come from? In other words, if the law of value holds, how do we explain the augmentation of value and the creation of surplus value? If the law of value can be thought of as a law of conservation of energy or mass, the question would be where does energy or mass come from? It is the problem of creation *ex nihilo*.

Marx formulates an answer after careful study of all preceding authors who tried to explain the origin of surplus value. The prerequisite for an acceptable answer is to maintain the established consensus that the law of value acts as an invisible hand and as a force of gravity pushing every price towards their average indexes, expressed as values. The trajectory of Marx's study is archived in the *Theories of Surplus Value*.

The *Theories of Surplus Value* is part of the preparatory material for *Capital* and it was written between 1862 and 1863 (Marx [1862–1863] 1968). It contains Marx's notes while he was studying bourgeois political economy (both reactionary and progressive in the form of utopian socialism). It begins with a general remark that indicates what underlies Marx's critical reasoning towards political economy.

What does he say? Economists make a common error of not examining surplus value in its pure form, but only in the form of the various incomes in the circulation process of the market. These various incomes deriving from ownership of the means of production (and not labor power) receive specific names like profits, interest, rent, etc. The main idea developed throughout the *Theories of Surplus Value* is that we must dismantle the natural vision that economists have about the pattern of distribution implied in income deriving from property in general. Based on this, Marx explains the specific process through which surplus labor is controlled and extracted in the capitalist mode of production. Exploitation, which is a normal feature of every class society, has its specificities in capitalism.

In addition to this, *Theories of Surplus Value* also investigates the quantitative problem of value. The concluding remarks indicate that it is necessary to make minor adjustments in the prevailing labor theory of value of classical political economy. The category 'labor' is not adequate to serve as the basis for a solid theory of value. 'Labor power', on the other hand, seems to fulfill this role much better, since Marx already perceives that we must think of everything in terms of the entity 'commodity'. The expression 'labor', as used by labor value theoreticians in the 18th and 19th centuries, does not refer to something that can become a commodity. Why? Because it refers to the process of altering nature itself and not to the potential embodied in the human organism to make this alteration.

How does the quantitative problem of value show itself in *Theories of Surplus Value*? Here we notice that the quantitative discrepancy between value and price distracts the theoreticians. They look away from the decisive point where the creation of new value takes place and focus only on the distribution of value that has already been created. Of course, the problem of distribution is also important. But without solving the mystery of the origin of this mass of value that is only distributed among different entities, we will end up with a partial theory of value that deals with half of the issue. Marx's intention is to solve both problems: distribution and production. However, to resolve the issue of value and surplus value creation, it is necessary to address the quality side of value theory, something that no economist had done before.

It is important to notice that one aspect of Marx's contribution is merely a continuation of classical political economy, while another aspect of his theory is new terrain. We must have this in mind because the relationship between Marx and political economy is extremely complex and should not be tackled in a superficial way.

The quantitative difference between value and price had already been discussed by James Steuart in the 18th century. According to Marx's notes in chapter 1 of *Theories of Surplus Value* ((Marx [1862–1863] 1968), pp. 220), there are two very distinct aspects for James Steuart regarding the quantitative increase of value. One of them is what he calls 'profit upon alienation'. The other is what we may call 'positive increase of wealth'. The first one refers to the augmentation of the value of someone's property due to market circumstances of price above value. The second one refers to a situation where new value is created and inserted in the economic system. In other words, while the first one is only a redistribution of previous existing total value in the economy (forming commercial profit), the second one is a process in which more value appears and increases the total stock of abstract wealth in the economy.

James Steuart concludes that if every commodity were sold by its real value, there would be no surplus and every profit would be reduced to individual profit coming from the appropriation of previous existing value that is in circulation. This is how the mercantilists used to explain surplus value. Marx gives an especially important warning here that, even when value and price coincide for all commodities (when there is no transfer of value among different entities due to circulation), profit, surplus and exploitation still exist. After this warning he proceeds to the next stage in the history of value theory, to physiocracy.

The school of economic thought known as physiocracy developed in parallel to the mercantilist school and it has a complementary function to the ideology of mercantilism. Mercantilist economic policy represents the concrete action of every modern State to expand its dominance over the world market, in accordance with the private interests of capitalist agents of the respective nation. The physiocrats, by contrast, spread the idea of *laissez-faire* and counterpose this against all economic policies of protectionism. Both schools reflect the hypocrisy of leading capitalist economies, which on the one hand try to convince every nation in the world about the advantages of liberalism and, on the other hand, practice all the mercantilist repertoire in the competition arena of the global economy.

According to Rubin ([1928] 1987), the social context in France in the 18th century explains the particularities of physiocracy. With respect to value theory, this philosophical current of economics has made a great contribution to the understanding of value and wealth creation. The physiocrats claim that the site of the origin of value is in the sphere of production. This moment is important because it breaks with the lasting idea that value could be created in the sphere of circulation. However, physiocracy has its own social historical conditions that constrain the further development of value theory. For the French economists, value is only created in those activities that involve agriculture. Therefore, the element of nature is assimilated merely as earth. Their view is too narrow and every laboring activity in the urban area is left out of their theory of value. Marx announces in *The Theories of Surplus Value* the main confusions in physiocratic thought, such as its inability to distinguish the analysis of social relations from the analysis of material balance behind a society's economic reproduction. Moreover, the connection between exchange value and the quantity of use value is so close that wealth is mixed with value. Abstract wealth and concrete wealth are treated as the same thing. Consequently, value is conflated with use value.

Concerning the contradiction between value and price, physiocratic thinking was fundamental in establishing the schemes of reproduction that sustain the notion of 'natural prices'. Technical coefficients of production, which describe the quantitative relations of the transformation of inputs into outputs, act as material pillars for both the notion of equilibrium and the material balance of a reproducing economic system. Because of their emphasis on the technical aspects of production, they shift attention away from empirical prices towards those ideal values that assure a balanced material reproduction of the expanding economy. Adam Smith surpasses both mercantilism and physiocracy by focusing on the relation between these two entities (value and price), in his search for a way to maintain them tied together. The gravitation of empirical prices around those values that the physiocrats call natural prices is his final draft on the operation of the law of value.

According to Marx, Adam Smith made one of the greatest advancements by enunciating that the contradiction between natural prices and empirical prices at the market has its own logic. Smith should be praised for struggling to connect the analysis of superficial exchanges in the market with the profound basis of the production process. Here, Smith is impelled to move from simple commodity exchange to a special kind of exchange: the exchange between capital and wage labor (Marx [1862–1863] 1968, p. 245).

Smith was aware that this was a critical point and realized that there was something wrong with the law of value. As we have indicated, the law of value had established itself in a double sense: it is an invisible force stemming from the social nexus of bourgeois individuality and it follows the rule of exchange of equivalents. The crux of the matter is that, at this level of analysis, the total quantity of value in the economy is fixed. It is not allowed to vary. But where did this fixed quantity come from? And if the total quantity of value in the economy increases (as every economist knows is the normal case due to the growth paradigm of the capitalist economy), how does it occur?

Adam Smith's thinking follows the capitalist logic of workshops and manufacture. This stage of industrialization indicates that it is no longer possible to acquire surplus value with ease by merely transporting commodities around the globe. It is necessary to explain where the value that is only distributed in circulation comes from. Fortunately, the continuous expansion of productive capital in comparison to merchant capital will facilitate this explanation. Now, the theoretical apparatus of the law of value, which already takes into consideration the two previous aspects (invisible hand and exchange of equivalents), must include another feature that shows explicitly how new value is launched into the circuit.

We are at a critical point in Adam Smith's comprehension of the law of value. The challenge is clear: he must show how the quantity of value increases without violating the law of value. Marx acutely observes that Smith's strength lies in his identification of the contradiction and that his weakness is his lack of confidence in the concept of the law of value. Another way to appreciate this critical moment is to remember that the concepts of incorporated labor and commanded labor also resemble the challenge to explain how labor can at the same time be responsible for expanding the total quantity of value in the system and be exchanged in the labor market according to the rules of equal exchanges. In chapter 4 of *Capital,* Marx ([1867] 2015) announces that the issue is indeed challenging, but that he has found a solution.[9] How is it possible for someone to acquire surplus value if we neutralize profits deriving from the difference between value and price (profit upon alienation)? If we maintain the system in an equilibrated state, where no one can capture value from anyone else in distribution, how is it still possible for someone to acquire surplus value?

When Marx observes the quantitative aspect of value, he knows that the law of value cannot be abandoned because of the analytical obstacles in the exercise of linking empirical prices to the technical coefficients of production. It is necessary to establish a strong bond between the real prices appearing in each negotiation between buyer and seller and the values referring to the physiochemical transformations of inputs into outputs in the production process. Why does Marx insist so intensely on the law of value to explain the motion of capitalism?

The law of value must not be understood only as an automatic mechanism of markets or as the rule of trade between goods of the same value. The law of value must also encompass a third function, which ascribes to everyone the fixed praxeological behavior of looking for maximum abstract wealth. The law of value also transforms each agent into a formal capitalist agent because all decisions and actions must follow the incessant circuit of capital accumulation. This third function indicates that the law of value must fit the standard procedure of the sequence of buying and selling to regain the initial stock of value with added surplus. But how can someone buy, sell, and obtain an increment in value if the rules of exchange in the market maintain the stability of

---

9   When facing the challenge, Marx announced: *"Hic Rhodus, Hic salta!"* (Marx [1867] 2015, p. 116), which is a proverb meaning "prove what you can do, here and now". One must explain how value is created on the very basis of the law of value, and not based on something alien to it. This is the challenge.

the total value stock? There must be a special trade in which the exchange of equivalents occurs and new value is added to the circuit at the same time.

Marx became anxious about the fact that Smith and Ricardo are uncertain about the validity of the law of value in the case of expanded reproduction. If the law of value is valid in simple commodity circulation, why should it not be valid in the capitalist mode of production? After all, capitalism is rooted in the market, so these two entities (market and capitalism) should not be in contradiction. Smith and Ricardo are unsure about the discrepancy between value and price. But giving up the law of value would open the door to superficial theories that try to explain value creation in the circulation sphere. There must be a way to maintain that value is created in production and only distributed in circulation.

Failure to tie the value system with the price system in a single theoretical framework results in the separation of production and distribution in economic analysis. However, the task of connecting the value system with the price system is a complex one. Above all, the value system and the price system represent conflicting political positions, related to two antagonistic sides: labor and capital. Given this acute difference between value and price, economists thought they had to choose either one or another way and this made the very notion of the law of value disappear.

Those who followed the price system looked only to the surface of all capitalist phenomena. All their attention was taken by the circuit of exchange at the tip of the iceberg and all relevant features of production were forgotten. Jean-Baptiste Say may function as an early example for this current of thought. He was one of the most prominent vulgar economists, in Marx's classification, because he did not want to investigate further the true origin of value and surplus value at the work place as the labor theory of value prescribes.

However, the other economists who eventually chose the other way and focused on production did not think further about the rules of capitalist distribution. Consequently, they defended the law of value but could not connect it to the reality of the equalization of profit rates across sectors. I refer here to Ricardian socialists like Thomas Hodgskin, John Francis Bray, John Gray and Percy Ravenstone. So, although this second current is politically progressive (because they stay on the side of the wage worker whose scenario is the fabric and the labor market rather than on the side of the bourgeois consumer whose scenario is the market of goods), there is also vulgarity in their research in political economy, yet of inverted signal. Their approach implies that the law of value is like the normative standard that distribution should follow and so they are unable to solve the contradiction between the labor theory of value and the distribution of surplus value according only to the magnitude of capital, regardless of how labor intensive the individual enterprise under consideration is.

Classical political economy reaches a contradictory peak precisely because it fails to unite production and distribution in a coherent theory. Production and distribution are presented as two parts of the economy that are entirely independent of each other. This leads to the grave error of concluding that production is governed by natural laws (since it seems to be the process of human action upon nature) and that distribution is governed by social laws (since it seems to be the process of allocating the results of human action on nature among members of society). This is exactly the thesis defended by John Stuart Mill ([1885] 2009), who represents a last attempt to sustain the theoretical system of classical political economy. Mill's efforts to maintain the structure initiated by Adam Smith were not enough. The contradictions in the theory of value were fueled by political forces that were fighting each other fiercely. Tension was too high. From here on, there were two opposite currents in economic thought that shared a common mistake. Each believed that its value theory will stand based on production OR distribution.

Thus, we must also understand the law of value as the discrepancy between value and price. The incongruence between production and distribution in an economic system that combines these two sides through the impersonal mechanism of commodity relations should be no reason to abandon the very concept that brings rationality to a self-organizing entity.

CHAPTER 3

The End of Classical Political Economy
Value or Price?

The idea that economic self-adjustment is a real phenomenon grew gradually with the development of classical political economy. Authors used the expression 'law of value' to refer to this mechanism. So, the law of value is not the same as the theory of value. The law of value is the real phenomenon, while the theory of value is the mental process through which economists assimilate this real phenomenon.

The existence of an objective phenomenon called the law of value was a matter of consensus among authors of the 18th and 19th centuries. They disagreed only on minor aspects about how the law of value was to be formalized in a theoretical system. Nonetheless, most of them believed that a labor theory of value was the best candidate for the job.

Even though the labor theory of value was well accepted, there was a major challenge ahead. The statement that the price of a commodity indicates the exact quantity of labor needed to produce that commodity is a simplification of a more complex idea. Empirical prices oscillate around an average labor time that society needs to spend on the production of a certain useful item.

There is no automatic identity between the exact quantity of labor and the price of a given commodity, say a specific and concrete umbrella offered in the market. The price on the label does not correspond one-to-one to the volume of labor involved in the production of that unique specific item. It is only an approximation, an average of items of similar complexity. Value and price therefore do not coincide. Price gravitates around value. Classical political economy draws on physics to describe this movement. They often refer to the law of value as a gravitational force pulling market prices toward their curves of production costs. Two celestial bodies that attract each other do not collapse into one and the same trajectory but sustain a regular movement of orbit around each other. Similarly, prices and values behave in such a way that they are connected by an objective logic but are not the same thing. The constant self-adjustments would lead to that ideal state of equal profit rates all around. It is like a state of perfect equilibrium, where both celestial bodies revolve around each other undisturbed in a stable system. If prices are too high or too low with respect to values, there is a force that pulls them towards the average line that guarantees the equal profit rate in every sector. In this sense, the quantitative disparity between value and price is not a big problem, because there is a mechanism explaining why value and price do not permanently coincide. The only thing that is fixed is the process of adjustment that brings subjective evaluations of consumers to the objective dimension given by the technology. Thus, labor time, and more specifically, quantities of concrete labor as expenditure of energy are the ultimate determinant in the formation of prices. Moreover, what matters is not the mathematical formalization that would transform values into production prices, but the description of the distribution pattern of surplus value that leads to an equalization of profit rates between all sectors. The fundamentals of capitalist competition would then be rigorously demonstrated. Similarly, what matters is to apprehend the logic behind the allocation of labor in the economy.

The quantitative divergence between the index of labor time needed to produce each good and its respective empirical price is a concrete challenge. In the second half of the 19th century, economists were still trying to solve this weak spot in the labor theory of value. The most important thing is that we should not give up the law of value just because there is an obstacle in the relationship between the value system and the price system. It is correct to try to make sense of the deviations of prices from values because these deviations are rational. There is a mechanism explaining the discrepancies and it must be unveiled. Adam Smith and David Ricardo did their best to discover this mechanism. Marx and Engels thought this effort should continue. If we fail to relate value to price, we fail to capture the law of value as the totality which integrates production and distribution in market economic systems. Consequently, there is an important continuity between classical political economy and Marx's economic theory on this point.

Marx (in *Theories of Surplus Value* [1862–1863] 1968) and Engels (in the preface to *Capital* book 2 [1885a] 1985 and in *Law of value and rate of profit* [1895–1896] 2003) argue for a solution to the contradiction between the worlds of value and price in order to preserve the connection between production and distribution. If there is no connection, one might think that production and distribution are unrelated, as if the rules of distribution were independent of the social relations of production, as John Stuart Mill argues in his *Principles of Political Economy* from 1885. A solution for the incongruency between value and price for the individual commodity is necessary to preserve this connection. The analytical separation of the institutions of wealth distribution from the social relations of production must be avoided because it breaks the complex, yet necessary, bridge between the spheres of natural and social scientific inquiry.

We should not forget that the rise of neoclassical economics was provoked by political reality. Classical political economy and its theory of value were fundamental tools for the progressive development of socialist ideas. It helped to identify the acute contradictions of capitalism. The great paradox was that the tremendous production of wealth was not eliminating poverty. In fact, both wealth and poverty were increasing in the Industrial Revolution. This was shocking for those who upheld the ideal of human progress towards peace, prosperity, and equality. The reality of class struggle could not allow political economy to continue as if everything was alright.

There were basically two major explanations for this paradox. On one side, thinkers argued that poverty was a permanent condition of humanity. They claimed that no matter how much and how fast wealth is produced, humans will always exhaust the resources and return to poverty. It is as if material scarcity were a natural phenomenon that could not be changed, like a law of nature. It would be impossible to eradicate it, just as it is impossible to eliminate the light of the Sun or revoke the law of gravity. Poverty is an immutable condition and people should give up ideas of overcoming it.

On the other side, many economists were realising that the dynamic between production of output and human needs was radically changing with the immense progression of productive forces. So, the permanence (and increase) of poverty was not a natural condition, but one involving social institutions. The economic problem of scarcity could no longer be viewed as a technical issue, because of the huge advancements in productivity. As a result, economists had to acknowledge that poverty was a social issue. The paradigm of scarcity changed to the paradigm of scarcity *within abundance*.

So, it is true that the disintegration of the classical school of economics is related to the contradictions between the capitalist utopia and the reality of poverty accumulation. However, we want to focus on the theoretical core of political economy. As regards value theory, the end of Adam Smith's hegemony is represented by the bifurcated focus on value or price. If Thomas Malthus (1766–1834) is the main representative of the political decay of the classical school, because of his naturalization of poverty, Jean Baptist Say may represent the main value theoretician who broke with the solid tradition of the classical theory of value.

The Russian economist Isaak Rubin ([1928] 1987) explains the disintegration of the classical school by saying that economists no longer tried to relate value (essence) to price (appearance). They did not look further for a scheme which would relate value to price. They thought there were two mutually exclusive paths. If value is chosen, then they paid no attention to price. Conversely, if they wanted to investigate price, then they did not think any longer about value. It is as if they stood before a bifurcation. On one side there was value, and all fundamental elements of labor and production. On the other side, there was price, and all the superficial aspects of market phenomena.

Following Marx, Rubin argues that vulgar economists focus on price to avoid the true and harsh reality of exploitation in production. My approach here is to explain that the opposite side to vulgar economics is not yet Marxian political economy, but another vulgar form of economic science, namely that of Ricardian socialism. The difficulty here is that this form of vulgar economics was progressive rather than reactionary in Marx's time. Accordingly, vulgarization of economic science is not exclusive to capitalist apologetics. It may also lead to labor apologetics. Marxist scholarship in economics ignores this fact. This is why it is important to present the critique of political economy in the manner I propose in this book. It is a critique of both vulgar forms of economics (pro-capital and pro-labor) in the sense that it reveals that they naturalize their respective value theories.

Let us take a closer look at the bifurcation we are discussing. Isaak Rubin ([1928] 1987) presented in his book *History of Economic Thought* an explanation for the end of the classical school of political economy. For Rubin, the core idea of classical value theory was the connection between the two systems of the economy: on one side, production, on the other side, distribution. Value and price are connected, and the examination of this linkage was a fundamental feature of the analysis. Economists had an acute understanding of the fact that, even though value and price are not equal, they belong together. Both entities form one single totality of economic reality. What is the logic of the bond between price and value? There is a real and impersonal mechanism determining the the price of each commodity. There is something indicating that commodities' prices do not move freely as if the preferences of buyer and seller had no restrictions. There are objective limits to the movements of prices, and they are given by the structure of production. The quantities of labor in the production process restrict and pull prices toward specific trajectories. The law of value was the name given to this mechanism of connection between value and price.

In classical political economy, both parts of the economic system, production, and distribution (which are abstractly represented by the value system and the price system respectively), were theoretically connected. The law of value was the concept used to describe the ongoing adjustment of the regular mismatches between supply and demand. Classical economists knew that there is no coincidence in the realm of reality. Equilibrium is a process, a movement, rather than a stationary concept. So, they wanted to explain the difference between the so-called labor values and empirical prices. If empirical prices contain information about the possibilities of economic gain and all agents act in the same way as capitalist subjects, then their investment and consumer decisions lead to a specific pattern of how social labor is employed in the economy. To summarize this idea, it is said that labor allocation is guided by the law of value in market economies.

The law of value brings coherence and order to the erratic individualist system of commodity relations. The law of value is the unique dictator that rearranges inputs periodically to sustain the infinite growth of capital. If the working class does not take control over it, capitalism will continue to exist indefinitely. As Marx has pointed out, capital is only limited by itself. There are no external barriers to the eternal spiral of capital accumulation. As we will see later, the law of value may lead to a fully planned economy in which the fundamentals of commodity and capital production still exist. Consequently, it is not correct to oppose market to planning in the same way we oppose capitalism to socialism/communism. The law of value is a preliminary indication that a fully planned capitalist economy is possible, at least in theory.

But if the law of value is the real phenomenon and theories of value are only the mental sketches capturing this concrete economic fact, we have a new way to investigate the core of economic science. Every economist is also a value theoretician. And his/her value theory is unique, according to a series of factors including the most relevant factor: his/her position in class society. However, since every theory of value has the same object of investigation, namely the law of value, they all have a common feature. Critics of value theories must be aware of this, otherwise we will end up repeating the same mistake of separating what must be united into a single theory. A complete theory of value must make sense (i) of both value and price [quantity] and (ii) of the meaning of the magnitude of value and price [quality].

According to Rubin ([1928] 1987), the disintegration of the classical school of political economy began when an alternative understanding of the relationship between value and price gained popularity. In this new view, value and price do not belong to the same framework. They become two alternative theories to explain the totality. So, instead of looking for ways to insert both value and price into the same theory, economists thought it was necessary to choose between value or price. Value and price were no longer seen as two aspects of the same entirety, but two mutually exclusive alternatives. It is a bifurcation that led to the end of the classical approach.

Consequently, the expression 'law of value' disappeared from the texts. From here on, treatises on political economy focused either on value and the labor process or on prices and market fluctuations. On some occasions, the connection between the two sides appeared again. However, there was no explicit mention of the terminology used by the classical economists who departed from the physiocratic materialist basis to investigate later the subjective evaluations of individual agents in the market. Alfred Marshall ([1890] 1985), for example, worked to find a synthesis. But the project to integrate both value and price in one single theory that would explicitly deal with the phenomenon of the law of value was abandoned. The conceptual difference between value and price was no longer relevant. Classical political economy was over, and two main currents of value theory replaced it.

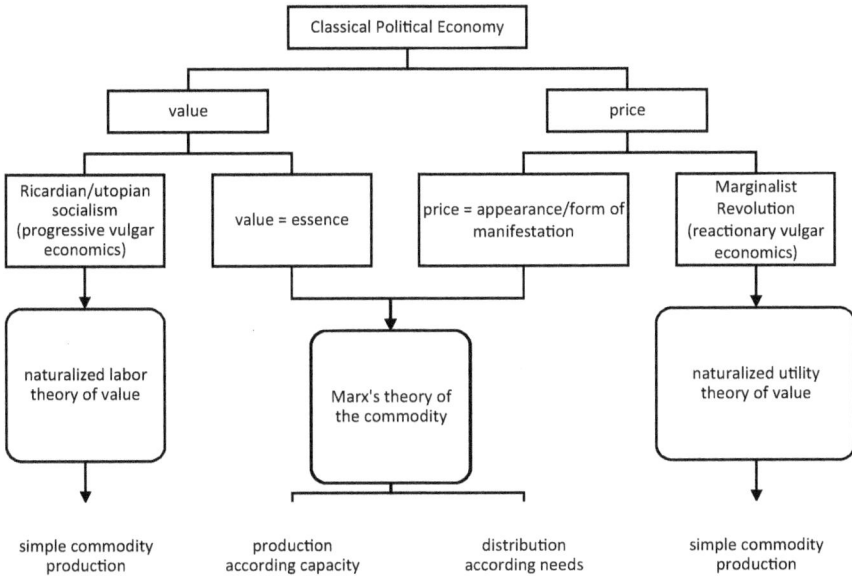

FIGURE 1   The end of classical political economy in a bifurcation[a]
            a The bifurcation leads to the opposing currents of value theory that are
            described in the boxes as Ricardian/utopian socialism (progressive vulgar
            economics) and Marginalist Revolution (reactionary vulgar economics). I use
            a flexible terminology to refer to these currents along the book. For Ricardian/
            utopian socialism (progressive vulgar economics) I employ the expressions
            non-Marxian socialist economics, progressive non-Marxian economics, pre-
            Marx socialists, etc. For Marginalist Revolution (reactionary vulgar economics)
            I employ the expressions Neoclassical economics, utility value theory,
            mainstream economics, etc. There are many subdivisions within both major
            strands. Besides indicating the splitting between value and price, this figure
            resembles Samuelson's Family Tree of Economics, presented in various editions
            of his textbook *Economics*. It visually presents the end of the Classical Era. For
            an analysis of how the Family Tree changed along the editions, see Backhouse
            (2016).

Figure 1 is an illustration of the argument to be developed in the following chapters. It starts with classical political economy at the top. Then it shows that value and price became detached. This division generated the two main currents of value theory we will analyze in chapters 4 and 5. Both currents, following their own path, eventually arrive at the system of simple commodity production, an idealized representation of bourgeois equality. They conclude that the dynamic of exchange value is the unique and natural way to organize the economy: in other words, pure commodity fetishism. Figure 1 then indicates in the middle that Marx's theory of the commodity criticizes both currents of value theory, opening the way for the communist principle of organizing production and distribution.

Marx's method does not lead to a simple combination of both sides. It is a dialectical synthesis that overcomes the limits of the contradictions between them.[1] The scientific strength of classical political economy came to an end when authors opted for one of these divergent ways. Since the 19th century they either investigated the superficial phenomena of market or the essential elements of the economy in the production and labor process.

The price path led one group of economists to the Marginalist Revolution. It recovers the once heterodox principle of marginal utility as the foundation of exchange relations and establishes the intellectual headquarters for defending bourgeois ideology. In that sense, this path is regressive. The value path took another group of economists in a progressive direction, when we look from the perspective of class struggle. This group will turn political economy into a manageable tool in the hands of the waged working class. As we know, the labor theory of value will be of extreme importance for various demands of the organized proletariat. However, this group is a victim of the same error made by marginalist economists. When we consider all non-Marxian labor theories of value, there is no effort to merge value with price. There is no integration between value and price. Value and price remain separated as if enemies. It is a melee. Although it resembles a real war of capital against labor, there is too much confusion in this simplistic approach to the relationship between value theory and class struggle. Because of this, neither side is able to progress and win.

So, the two sides represent two great currents of thought in value theory. And both are doomed to a dead end. Why? Because the concept of the law of

---

1 My methodological approach to relating Marx's political economy with non-Marxian political economy is guided by the works of Oskar Lange. For an overview on Oskar Lange's strategy for dealing with non-Marxian economics, see Lange ([1959] 1963), Lange (1971) and Lange (1935). For a historical contextualization of Oskar Lange's intellectual and political trajectory, see Kowalik (1964), Kowalik (2018), Toporowski (2014), Lampa (2011) and Lampa (2014).

THE END OF CLASSICAL POLITICAL ECONOMY

value vanishes when we look at one side only. Even if authors avoid this concept, it follows them because, as we saw, the law of value is a real phenomenon in market economies, regardless of whether the economists are aware of it or not. In that sense, the law of value comes to seem so natural and idealized that vulgar economists (from left and right) cannot analyze it adequately. It is as if any conscious action to counteract the forces of the law of value were in the wrong direction because the law of value appears as both the natural and desired aim. It is as if engineers refused to build an airplane, because the craft should be designed to dig in towards the center of the Earth, towards the gravity forces that pulls everything down. What kind of economy will we have if economists put all their energy into a project that reinforces the logic of the law of value? If we want to understand what the law of value is and how we can free ourselves from its dominance, we need to follow Marx's critique of political economy. Marx's contribution is the only one which accurately criticizes both antagonists' naturalized theories of value. It is not enough to criticize the economic thinking of the 17th, 18th, and 19th centuries. We also need to unveil the theoretical core of political economy in the 20th and 21st centuries according to Marx's guidelines. Marx's economics is the first stage to recovering the lost project of connecting value and price correctly. The methodological suggestion here is that these two blocked roads should be surpassed by a superior synthesis. As argued, this synthesis is not a horizontal combination of two equal sides, because each side of the battle always represents either labor or capital. We will explore this synthesis in chapters 6 and 7. But before that, we need to dedicate our attention to each of these parallel tracks. We need to better understand two different theories of value: the theory of value of utopian socialism and the theory of value of the Marginal Revolution. Then we will be able to better comprehend Marx's approach to the law of value.

CHAPTER 4

Value

The Naturalization of the Labor Theory of Value in Utopian Socialism

1   **Appropriation of Political Economy by the Labor Movement**

The pre-Marxian labor theory of value is a naturalized form of value theory. This means that its justifications for selecting input labor as the responsible factor for creating value are rooted in the use-value analysis. Inasmuch as this is ultimately an analysis of how humans relate to the natural world, the concept of human labor is close to that of work in physics. According to Marx's critique of political economy, this foundation for a theory of value is not adequate because it tries to make the justification that labor creates value by means of the physical and chemical relations only, instead of viewing human labor as a complex process in which nature is modified by humans who live in societies and establish social relations among themselves. Social relations are cultural creations only framed by the material world, not determined by it. In utopian socialism, human labor is a relatively simple concept that indicates how much energy human bodies put into the production process as if there were no human-human exploitation. The only exploitation here is of the kind human-nature. So, despite being correct as a value theory for describing the quantitative dimension of value (exchange value), it is unable to decipher the qualitative dimension of value (substance of value). Utopian socialism is in accordance with this naturalized form of value theory and its result is the model of simple commodity production.

Political economy is the science of wealth production and distribution. It contains crucial truths about how workers can improve their conditions, understand the economic system under which they live, and even change this system according to their own interests. Since the 1820s, we can say that socialist thinkers struggle to command political economy. The difference between socialist economics in general and Marx's political economy is of great importance for the social sciences in general and for economic science in particular. The non-Marxist socialist current of economic thought naturalizes the labor theory of value. As we will see later, one of Marx's most significant warnings is that no theory of value can be explained by natural phenomena only. The social institutions in concrete space and time where humans labor cannot be disregarded. The scientific approach to value theory must be a coherent integration of all complexes of human-nature and human-human relations. It must consider both the laws of matter transformation described by natural sciences and the social laws that derive from human culture. Thus, in class societies, the class struggle must be explicitly considered when we develop a theory of value. From the standpoint of the human-nature process, all theories of value are equally valid. No argument based on natural character can win the battle against competing value theories.

Because of this, we cannot understand the traditional battle between two opposing theories of value (the labor theory of value on one side and the marginal utility theory of value on the other side) from a quick and superficial examination. This clash does indeed express the fundamentals of the political struggle around value theory since the end of the 19th century. However, we need to look deeper. When we investigate the battle between these two theories of value in the literature, we see that neither of them can impose itself as the sole dominant theory of value in economic science. This is because every theory of value is equally valid from the analytical perspective of the relationship between humans and nature. Both labor and utility can be used as starting points to clarify these relations, as the 'Robinson exercise' shows by examining a single agent in the world-island of use values to explain the quantification of abstract wealth.

Robinson Crusoe is the title of a novel published by Daniel Defoe in 1719 (Defoe [1719] 2004). It tells the story of a sailor who survives on a desert island after a shipwreck. This bestseller of the 18th century created a literary genre called 'Robinsonade', 'desert island story' or 'castaway narrative'. Works of this genre are always about an individual or a small group that must survive isolated from their original civilizations. Economists took the opportunity to use it as a powerful, yet very problematic, didactic tool. Robinson Crusoe must perform the same tasks as in any other society (we all need to eat, find water, protect ourselves from weather, etc). The only difference is that he is alone, so all social relations normally involved in the organization of these tasks disappear.

I am an enthusiast of using the 'Robinson exercise' to teach economic science. However, this tool must be employed with great caution.[1] This exercise has serious limitations. For example, it is not possible to have an adequate concept of capital based on the political economy of Robinson Crusoe unless we think that capital is a relation between human and nature. If capital is considered

---

1   For an inspiring review of Daniel Defoe's Robinson Crusoe in the sense I am proposing, see Hutnyk (2020). For an analysis of Daniel Defoe's political thinking in the context of his lifetime, see Schonhorn (1991), who indicates that the "Lockean" Defoe is a myth that should be critically interpreted.

strictly as a means of production that aids labor in its transformation of nature, then the model can serve. However, capital means more than this. Capital signifies that the means of production and everything else serves one perpetual circuit of value expansion. This is not the case in Robinson Crusoe's economy. Survival and the improvement of life conditions by mastering wild nature are the real aims of the stranded. Money is useless, or more precisely, money does not exist. Logically, the accumulation of money, and hence capital, is alien to the reality of the isolated Robinson Crusoe. The infinite expansion of wealth can only be considered if we suppose that he will behave on the island according to the social institutions of the civilization from which he came. This assumption artificially transfers the dynamics of capital to a non-capitalist economy in the form of infinite use value accumulation. This is a serious error.

Before making any rash judgement about the superiority of the labor theory of value over the utility theory of value (or vice versa), we must first comprehend the limitations they share. Frequently, Marx's theory of value is presented by progressive economists as a minor addition to Adam Smith's and David Ricardo's work on the theory of value, in opposition to the marginalist approach. Likewise, Marx's work is often presented by Marxist scholars as something totally different from that of Adam Smith and his followers. The average economist is not taught how to distinguish Marx from classical economists, especially when introductory lectures on political economy emphasize that they all spoke in favor of a labor theory of value and against a theory of value based on value in use. The differences between them are too complex and have repercussions on the development of economics after the 19th century. In particular, this topic is crucial for a correct understanding of how political economy and Marxism relate to each other. Features of continuation and rupture between classical political economy and Marx's critique of political economy coexist. I am drawing attention to the fact that we need to be careful when relating Marx to economists. This is a turbulent relationship involving critique, but also admiration and appropriation. It is not a matter of the rejection of a model and substitution by another one. We need to bear this in mind in order to politically influence the teaching of economics in the future.

Marx's critique of political economy is not as simple as it seems at first glance. Marx has a complicated challenge ahead. He must explain why the labor theory of value arises and is consolidated during the 18th and 19th centuries (and not in any other period in the history of economic thought). Specifically, he must clarify that the labor theory of value is not a natural law, but the ideological shape of a particular value theory based on one of the many use values in an economy that have become a commodity, namely labor power. At the same time, he must present himself as a defender of this theory, because of the class-related character it has already incorporated. The dual nature of his task is one of the sources for the controversy about the continuity and rupture between Marx and the classical economists.

Let me repeat this point because it is extremely important for my approach. Marx must deal with two limitations in economic thought, specifically regarding the theory of value. First, he must show that the labor theory of value is not an eternal entity that is independent from the socio-historical specificities of a mode of production. Second, when dealing with this first limitation, he must place himself at the side of workers in the defense of 'their' value theory. So, at the same time he must criticize the classical labor theory of value and defend it. It is a rather tricky move and every effort to make meaning of it will help us better understand how Marx thinks about both the law of value and all theories of value.

The socialist movement of the beginning of the 19th century became stronger and stronger. The working class took various ideas and concepts from political economy to defend its cause. Obviously, the labor theory of value seemed a perfect weapon to use in support of their pledge for a better future. But the form in which the labor theory of value further developed in utopian socialism entirely missed the point of Marx's main contribution to political economy. Utopian socialism chose the path based on labor, production costs, and working process. However, it also employed the naturalization of social relationships in its method of analysis. All quantitative relations of exchange between different goods were explained by quantities of human physical labor. If labor counts only in this energetic sense, why should work performed by animals and machines not count also? It did not problematize why human labor is the right quality to measure the quantity of value. And when it did ask the question, the answer was to naturalize the explanation. Instead of admitting that the choice of labor is a political choice, authors tried to justify the labor theory of value through technical reasoning based on the relations of the use value world. In the end, labor value theoreticians of utopian socialism met the Marginalist Revolution in the final stage of the market labyrinth. Simple commodity production indicated that even the most progressive development of classical political economy cannot overcome the limits of commodity fetishism.

In this context, political economy ceased to be a research field restricted to a few thinkers isolated from the crowd. More and more people were socialized through money. Primitive accumulation through separation of the worker from the means of production created the waged working class. Now, this huge and violent historical transformation did not go unnoticed by economic thinkers. Economic science was appropriated by the socialist movement. In other words, all the knowledge presented by Adam Smith and his followers began to be assimilated by minds who were sympathetic to the causes of the working class.

One of the main aspects here is the confirmation and radicalization of the idea that the theory of value must be constructed based on production and more precisely, on the labor process. All economists of this current of thought continued, with their own specificities, to associate value/price with labor. The labor theory of value became a sacred pillar of the political economy of socialism.

If we consider the dichotomy between value and price as previously explained, we can affirm that this current directed all its attention to value. The entire reasoning here was that exchange relations must be determined by the quantities of labor employed in the production of each good being purchased and sold. The law of value should be the central mechanism that turns the quantities of labor, measured in time, into the quantitative indexes that make up prices in the market. The quantities of value are the expression of the quantities of labor necessary to produce commodities, and no other interpretation is viable. The meaning of the quantities expressed in exchange relations is an unambiguous quality: human labor measured in time. No other thing can be used to measure the quantities of useful objects. For this current of thought, human labor is not merely the socially recognized standard for the measure of wealth, but the ultimately true standard that does not even depend on the recognition of society itself. Accordingly, the labor theory of value here is an ahistorical institution. It exists detached from and above any specific mode of production.

At first glance, the notion of an absolute theory of value seems attractive. If physics has its own theories that must encompass all corners and dimensions of the universe, why shouldn't political economy have its own theory of value that is valid for any economic system whatsoever? Is it not the correct procedure in scientific investigation to find general laws of specific partial systems?

The problem is that all theories of value have the same pretension to be the unique theory of value that explains the matching of supply and demand based on the same system: the market. It is not wrong to look for a general framework that explains how production and distribution are organized according to the fundamentals of human society's metabolism with nature.[2] What is not adequate is to think that every conceivable economic system must obey the rules

---

2   For a detailed explanation of the distinction between general economic phenomena (common to all modes of production) and socio-historically specific economic phenomena (which exist only when very precise cultural institutions are present), see Oskar Lange's separation of general and specific economic laws in chapter 3 of *Political Economy* (Lange ([1959] 1963), pp.55), and in chapter 3 of *Introduction to Econometrics* (Lange ([1961] 1967), p. 170). Looking for a theory of everything in political economy leads necessarily to the materialist

of a phenomenon that is specific to capitalism. Commodity production is not the central mode for most economic systems in the history of human civilization. It is only an appendix in some societies that developed private property relations. When economists give their theories of value universal validity, they are in fact affirming that the law of value cannot be under human control and that every economy is a commodity producing economy. If they were aware of the alienation process sustaining the law of value, they would say that commodity fetishism is technically impossible to overcome. This is a huge mistake.

Now we can look further into some of the works of authors who first gave voice to workers in their treatises on political economy. These economists must be studied with greater attention than usual to avoid jumping too hastily from classical political economy into the critique of political economy. This is why I will still present the views of marginalist economists after talking about the Ricardian socialists. A rapid change of focus from Adam Smith and David Ricardo to Karl Marx is precisely what facilitates the creation of two erroneous interpretations of Marx's economics: the 'continuist' interpretation (which thinks that *Capital* is a mere continuation of Smith and Ricardo) and the 'rupturist' interpretation (which thinks that *Capital* has no single line of connection between the bourgeois political economy and its Marxist critique).[3]

An unqualified defense of the labor theory of value may harm the scientific orientation of the communist movement. This is why it is imperative to apply Marx's method of critique to all types of the theory of value, and not only to the mainstream, marginal utility theory of value.

2   The Laborer's Theory of Value of Utopian Socialists

Pre-Marx socialist economists argue for fair exchange based on the labor theory of value. They do not question the act of exchange itself, but only its quantitative deviations from a level that they consider just. When they occasionally think about the foundation of exchange, which is the establishment of a quality that allows quantitative comparison, there is no doubt that this quality is

---

conception of history as first sketched by Marx ([1859b] 1977) in his *Preface to a Contribution to the Critique of Political Economy*.

3   Napoleoni (1970), with his influential work *Smith, Ricardo, Marx* may be seen as contributing to this rash leap which leads economists to think that the relationship between Marx and classical economics is a trivial one. This kind of approach created the illusion that there would be either continuity OR rupture between Marx and the classical school. As I argue, however, both elements coexist.

human labor. On one side it is a progressive theory, because it supports work-ers' demands for improvement against capital oppression. On the other side, it is also a limited theory, because it does not recognize that anything may serve as the qualitative element to measure quantities.[4]

Here, the law of value refers to the notion of exchange of equivalents, one of the fundamental interpretations of the law of value in classical political econ-omy, as seen previously. If all exchanges followed the rule of the labor theory of value, as pre-Marx economists think, then there would be no exploitation and no surplus value. According to them, the reality of exploitation and sur-plus value production violates the labor theory of value and something must change. They do not recognize that it is perfectly possible to have identity between the value and price systems and at the same time to have surplus value production. If the total surplus value produced is ideally distributed among all sectors, and within each sector in the same proportions between all inputs, then we have a systematic increase of the quantity of value without violating the equivalence between the value and price systems.

So, instead of looking for an explanation in which exchange of equivalents and production of surplus value is possible, they recover a normative argu-ment. Of course, this is a scientific retreat. All theories based on the separation of what is and what ought to be are important to illustrate what must change, but they do not concretely indicate what to do. Here, the worker offers a cer-tain quantity of labor, but he/she receives in return just a part of this total quantity. This exchange relation is not normal according to the ideals of equal exchanges: one side is gaining and the other is losing. One could even say that it violates the law of value, because it seems to be an unequal exchange.[5]

---

4 According to Marx in chapter 1 of *Capital* book 1, standards of measure are various and, from the standpoint of the world of use-values, all of them fulfill the function of measuring equally well: "Every useful thing, as iron, paper, etc., may be looked at from the two points of view of quality and quantity. It is an assemblage of many properties, and may therefore be of use in various ways. To discover the various uses of things is the work of history. So also is the establishment of socially-recognized standards of measure for the quantities of these use-ful objects. The diversity of these measures has its origin partly in the diverse nature of the objects to be measured, partly in convention. Marx ([1867] 2015), p. 27."

5 I know that the identification of labor with labor power is a grave error in classical political economy. However, the correction of this error cannot turn into a political attack against the laborer's theory of value. It cannot become a complex discourse that oppress the naive idea that surplus value and exploitation is robbery. We must remember that the natural-ized theory of value we are dealing with here was, and still is, the easiest theory of value to be incorporated into the day-to-day struggle of workers. This is why I argue that Marx has quite a complicated challenge ahead. The laborer's theory of value must be at the same time encouraged and criticized. On one side, it must receive our political support and sympathy. On the other side, we must criticize it for naturalizing commodity production. When we

The laborer's theory of value (as I like to call the labor theory of value to emphasize its political position) is represented by a rich variety of authors from various countries. All these authors oppose the official trend in economics, according to which every production factor (and not labor alone) should have its income. So, they share the belief that all products of society should be appropriated by labor alone in the form of a wage. They refuse to acknowledge that any other kind of income, such as profit, interest and rent, is just or has a place in the systems of rights based on natural law.

One of the pioneers of the labor theory of value was the English philosopher John Locke (1632–1704), whom we have already talked about when dealing with the theory of the State. Locke argues in many passages that all goods are the result of labor. In his work about the origins of the labor theory of value, Ronald Meek ([1956] 1973) explains how labor became more and more central in the theoretical conceptualization of the production process. The physiocratic notion that goods are the fruit of the land lost power. Labor and land may have the same status, as Marx recalls William Petty's idea that they are like the father and mother of material wealth. But even so, labor plays the active role over passive earth, revealing that labor has become the most important element for describing the origin of wealth.

After John Locke, Adam Smith (1723–1790) takes the labor theory of value to the next level. His research for writing *The Wealth of Nations* led him to conceive a strong bond between labor division and productivity; no longer a simple bond, but an unbreakable connection. This helped Smith propose a reasonable solution to the water/diamond paradox.

David Ricardo (1772–1823) in his *Principles of Political Economy* reaffirms the idea of two kinds of value (value in use and value in exchange). He indicates that labor time is the most important component in the determination of the quantity of value. Still, he raises many questions that challenge the basics of the labor theory of value. Discrepancy between value and price is a common feature among the various labor theories of value and Ricardo tries to explain it.

---

make the distinction between labor and labor power too hastily, we risk losing an audience and weakening non-Marxist economic schools of thought that are part of the socialist movement of the 21st century. I am aware that we could solve the problems of the utopian socialist labor theory of value right away, but this will not contribute to the graduated education of scientific socialism among progressive economists. Political education requires openness and humility. Most economists trained in capitalist countries are indoctrinated to replicate the oppressor, and the way out of this is to promote critical pedagogy, as proposed by Freire ([1968] 2015).

The significance of Adam Smith and David Ricardo as proponents of a labor theory of value is that they are ambiguous sources for sustaining the theory of exploitation, because they represent the economic thought of the capitalist ruling class. An unambiguous labor theory of value must lead to the conclusion that all output must be appropriated by workers. However, Smith and Ricardo never take their reasoning to this logical conclusion. They defend a labor theory of value but did not develop a theory of exploitation (at least not explicitly). If workers want to have a full theory of value in their own interests, then they need increased influence over the development of political economy.

The ambiguities of the economic theory of the capitalist class became more and more evident. John Stuart Mill (1806–1873), one of the most successful popularizers of David Ricardo's system, is a symbol of the last attempt to reconcile the antagonistic classes of capitalism. Mill's theory contains all the contradictions of bourgeois thought together in concentrated form, because he tries to combine the ideals of justice and equality with the increasing opposition between capital and labor. According to Oskar Lange ([1959] 1963), Mill presents an eclectic compromise between socialist economic thought and capitalist economics. This kind of mixture between socialist economics and capitalist thinking had already begun with other authors, such as Jean Charles Léonard de Sismondi (1773–1842).

Socialist and capitalist principles coexisted for a while before Marx's contribution to political economy. Many authors, who investigated not only economic matters but also politics, philosophy, and social aspects were behind the formation of socialist thought.

François Noël Babeuf (Gracchus Babeuf) (1760–1797), for example, explains in the *Manifesto of the Equals* (1796) that the revolution in France needed to continue, if equality were to be achieved. Babeuf ([1796] 2016) argues for the common good in a clear contrast with the interests of private property. He calls the proposed new society the Republic of the Equals, where the masses could find happiness through independence, freedom, and equality. The Manifesto explicitly announces that the principles of formal equality do not coincide with real equality, indicating that the French Revolution was not completed according to its own ideals.

Claude-Henri de Rouvroy or Comte de Saint-Simon (1760–1825) is another memorable name among socialist dreamers. Saint-Simon presents his view of society in two texts from the turn of the 19th century. In *A dream* (*Un Rêve*) from 1803, he reports that he has elaborated a vision where society is organized around councils of scientific experts. Saint-Simon considers Isaac Newton an example and intellectual guide for all humans, who should follow a new religion that promotes the progress of the human spirit. It is a curious dream, in which scientific knowledge is invested with the power of a religion to direct the new society. It is interesting to notice that Saint-Simon emphasizes that every human being will work in this society (Saint-Simon [1803] 1980, p. 33).

In *Parable*, from 1819, Saint-Simon imagines two situations: one in which every wise man, artist and artisan of France has died and another in which ten thousand proprietors, nobles and State authorities have lost their lives. For Saint-Simon, the first hypothetical situation would be a serious problem, while the second would be merely an emotional problem. Why? Because he considers it quite easy to replace the men in the second case. He clearly contrasts the useful members of society with the useless ones by pointing to the division between exploiters and exploited. Productive individuals often let themselves be dominated through violence and slyness (Saint-Simon [1819] 1980, p. 37). As a result, incapable men receive the task of managing capable people and there is a total inversion of moral hierarchy (the immoral educate, the unjust are the judges, etc.). It is implicit that the domain of science and praxiological competence should be paramount in setting the new parameters of the hierarchy of power.

Apart from these broadly socialist thinkers,[6] there are other writers whose works are more related to the issue of value. They all represent an intermediate step between the classical economists and Marx's critique of political economy. They are defenders of the labor theory of value and are thus attacked by the reactionary forces. The struggle between opposing value theories is already taking place.

One of the first books to make a systematic defense of the labor theory of value is *Labour Defended against the Claims of Capital* by Thomas Hodgskin (1787–1869), published in 1825. Hodgskin understands that the terms of the debate need to be reframed. The debate between David Ricardo and Thomas Malthus corresponds to the fight of the landowners against industrial capitalists, two distinct factions of the capitalist class. In value theory, this corresponds to a contrast between the components of earth/land and equipment/machinery. Now, when land is integrated into the means of production in the form of capital, only the element of labor remains as antagonist to every other input in the production process. The struggle now is between labor and capital (i.e. all inputs that are not labor). Hodgskin warns that the context of his research is this battle. He concludes that every advantage that is attributed

---

6 Other figures besides Babeuf and Saint-Simon are the revolutionary conspirator Louis Auguste Blanqui (1805–1881), and Charles Fourier (1772–1832) who did not see himself as a socialist but envisioned a society based on the pleasure of collective association.

to capital derives from the coexistent and skilled labor (Hodgskin [1825] 1986, p. 309).

Against the attacks of capital, Hodgskin defends labor in a very coherent way. Capital-allied economists argue that if capital contributes to production, then it creates the opportunity to claim a part of the total output referring to this partial contribution. However, Hodgskin says that if everything is created by labor, as political economy asserts, then it is necessary to reject all theoretical reasoning that capital has the right to receive an income. The existence of interest contradicts the labor theory of value. Hodgksin's text has the merit of being noticeably clear on this. It does not allow any ambiguity regarding the law of value founded on labor and the structure of interest, rent and profit. He is critical towards post-Ricardian authors, such as John Stuart Mill, because the attempt to reconcile capital and labor leads to blatant contradictions. One of the results of such an endeavor would be that capital 'works'. Hodgskin's strict logic deduces that if labor is the only true source of wealth, then only one result is possible: we will only achieve justice when the worker can have his/her output at his full disposal.

Another defender of the labor theory of value was Johann Karl Rodbertus (1805–1875). He is one the authors of this group who came closest to Marx's theoretical developments. However, Rodbertus has an alternative interpretation that takes him far away from other economists struggling at the side of the workers. Rodbertus does not conclude that 'undeserved income' (the normative expression for interest and all other non-labor incomes) and private property should be abolished. He proposes, instead, that all proprietors should be integrated as participants in the production process. These agents should carry out necessary tasks according to the demands of the national economic system. This shows that if owners of the means of production do not have any productive assignment, they will be left out of the new system. Rodbertus thinks that these proprietors have technical ability that contributes to production.

Despite this obvious retreat, Rodbertus's advancement, by comparison with the other utopian socialists, is that he treats interest systematically in association with the theories of Adam Smith and David Ricardo. Böhm-Bawerk ([1921] 2010, p. 56) indicates that, in the history of economic thought, Smith and Ricardo have become indisputable authorities on the construction of the labor theory of value. So, strategically, from his point of view, one must show the ambiguities of the idea that value is an exclusive result of labor. Böhm-Bawerk ([1896] 2007) in his work *Karl Marx and the Close of his System* realizes that the only way to counter the labor theory of value is to cling to the quantitative incongruence between value and price. This is the path he follows in his attempt to destroy Marx's system at the beginning of the 20th century, taking as his opportunity the lack of a solution to the transformation problem of values into production prices.

So, we see that since the early writings of political economy, labor increasingly assumes a place of honor in the determination of value. As bourgeois revolutions take place in Europe and the Industrial Revolution proceeds, value theory does not remain as an abstract concept connected to the objective inputs of the production process; rather, value theory becomes a political instrument that supports the material interests of the workers. This is why it is no longer merely the labor theory of value; instead, it could be called more accurately the laborer's theory of value.

3   The Right to the Full Results of Labor

The fundamentals of value theory of the Smithian system provoked a double effect. It not only established the sacredness of the invisible hand concept, but also of the notion that every single price must have its source traced back to quantities of labor. The right to the full results of labor derives almost directly from Adam Smith's and David Ricardo's theories.

If we think of the social output as the total social wealth, this means that 100% of this sum should go to those who work. Renewal of the means of production should also be paid with part of this output. However, there should not be a rent to pay the private owners of the means of production. This kind of income is not related to labor, but to the property title only. The fight to acquire the full payment of labor is in this sense a fight against financial incomes that have nothing to do with the real contribution to the production of new wealth. So, to put it simply, the right to the full results of labor means that labor should receive 100% of the economy's total income. This would correct the injustices of unequal exchange in the relationship between labor and capital.

It is important to notice that, at this stage, we are investigating the theory of value without addressing the crucial questions raised by Marx. This means that, although there is a clear distinction between a labor theory of value and a utility theory of value, we have not yet systematically explored the motives behind the choice of these two different elements (labor and utility) that constitute the quality of value. Here, we are temporarily setting aside the qualitative investigation and focusing on quantitative issues only. We know that these two opposing theories reflect labor and capital in class struggle but, as indicated before, we still need to understand what their common mistake is. This is extremely important, because the entire line of critique inaugurated by

Böhm-Bawerk ([1896] 2007) cannot be addressed either by defending the labor theory value of the utopian socialists or by saying that Marx's labor theory of value has nothing to do with classical political economy. A correct solution to the paradox of rupture and continuity must guide our approach. What is important is not to show in a neutral manner that labor is the sole element responsible for creating value, but to indicate that the power to create value is assigned to an element by the theoretician. The theoretician is the non-neutral agent here. The theory is not the agent who has a political position, but the theoretician. Both abstract labor (the question of quality in value) and the traditional quantitative exercise of price formation are necessary factors to consider in an analysis that can overcome the dichotomous view of rupture or continuity in the relationship between classical economists and Marx.

When we set aside the qualitative side of value and focus only on quantity, it becomes clear why the ideological discourse in favor of full payment of labor is so intense at this stage. Pre-Marxian socialist economists thought that quantity was the only thing to investigate in political economy, i.e, they thought it was all a matter of how high or low labor was priced in the market. Wage labor is the only kind of labor they observe. They do not question the fact that labor (or labor power, to be consistent with Marx's terminology) has a price. They do not question the fact that it is a commodity and exists only within the social institutions of the market. All they do is to argue that labor must be paid its fair price. And what is the fair price of labor? Since labor is responsible for 100% of society's wealth, it must receive 100% of the economy's total income. This position is coherent with the strict logic of the classical labor theory of value. It fits well with the wishes of the worker to receive what he thinks is fair for his/ her labor. However, it cannot be sustained. This is so because such reasoning remains only socialist, it does not develop further into communism. It stops in the middle of the road. The argument in favor of a total distribution of output towards labor signifies only that the means of production are not the property of those who work.

Lack of investigation of the quality of value is also a shortcoming among these economists. Even so, the quantitative issues are of great importance for the development of socialist and communist political economy. The quantitative problem of value should be studied in close association with economic planning. The quantitative approach to value deals with plain allocation of resources. There is no philosophizing about the settings of the allocation problem to be solved. Of course, the aims of the allocation game must be set by someone. But once this is established, the quantitative relations arise automatically. Economic calculation, as a pure relation between means and ends, is a common feature of every mode of production, from Robinson Crusoe to the ultimate commune on a global scale. The quantitative problem appeared first in the question of the adequate remuneration of labor. Utopian socialism never rebels against the wage system, but this does not mean that it has no positive advancements. Economic calculation does not disappear in communism, so it is imperative that we maintain all quantitative questions aligned with the qualitative approach.

In the pre-Marx system, the law of value is almost a synonym for the labor theory of value. It is, however, a mistake to believe that they are the same thing. In progressive vulgar economics, the law of value is just a guide to the political economy of injustice. From the standpoint of theory, it has little constructive to offer. It is almost entirely focused on denouncing the poor pay of labor. However, there is an even more serious shortcoming than this. The ideology of equal exchange prevents any author in this tradition from ever thinking outside the bourgeois pattern of production and distribution. The best they can do is to imagine the harmonious and illusory society of simple commodity production, where all are equal and can use the results of their own individual effort. Within this system, which does not break the spell of commodity fetishism, distribution is organized according to the maxim of each according to his/her effort. So, effort and reward are connected through individual accountability. The separation between income and output remains. In other words, parts of the output become special social forms which are transferred to individuals according to social laws that appear as if they were natural laws. The right to use the output is attached to the individual contribution to the common good. More precisely, the right to appropriate part of the social output is directly connected to the individual property ownership of the items that enter production. On this basis it is no surprise that progressive vulgar economics is not able to recognize and praise the rise of a new organizing principle of the economy, i.e., that according to which each one dedicates his/her individual capacities to construct social wealth and withdraws from the collective fund only what is necessary to attend his/her needs.[7]

---

7   Marx explained in the *Critique of the Gotha Programme* that the communist principle is different from the socialist principle of production and distribution: "In a higher phase of communist society, after the enslaving subordination of the individual to the division of labor, and therewith also the antithesis between mental and physical labor, has vanished; after labor has become not only a means of life but life's prime want; after the productive forces have also increased with the all-around development of the individual, and all the springs of co-operative wealth flow more abundantly—only then can the narrow horizon of bourgeois right be crossed in its entirety and society inscribe on its banners: From each according to his ability, to each according to his needs! (Marx [1875] 1970)"

4   The Naturalization of the Labor Theory of Value

Despite its progressive political attitude, there is a grave theoretical error in the pre-Marx socialist system of political economy. This represents a remarkable challenge for value theoreticians struggling at the side of the working class, as already mentioned. It is necessary to both support and criticize the authors who defend the classical labor theory of value. It is a delicate operation. It is necessary to show that, although the labor theory of value expresses the working class character of a specific value theory, it is also wrong when it tries to sustain itself based on neutral and natural reasoning. Instead of openly admitting that it represents the material interest of workers *and* is technically sound, authors try to justify the labor theory of value only with empiricist approaches to relate labor value to market prices.

All theories of value are expressions of a position in class struggle with the pretension of resting on neutral reasoning. The crux is that neutral reasoning works for every conceivable value theory. Moreover, neutral reasoning leads to the notion that the law of value operates in any conceivable mode of production in history. The historical specificity of capital relations of production is lost when authors seek to defend their value theories based on the relation human-nature and not human-nature-human.

Pre-Marx socialist economists (as well as reactionary vulgar economists) think that economic output and commodity are the same thing. The truth is that the commodity is a specific social form of the economic output. Due to this mistake, they are not able to see the special circumstances that allow the development of the economic output into the forms of commodity, money, and capital. Consequently, they fall into the idea that labor in general has the capacity to create value. This kind of thinking leads to the naturalization of a phenomenon that is essentially socio-historical. This type of approach to political economy is a point of convergence between socialist and bourgeois reformists.

We need to understand how the labor theory of value is naturalized, and why this is a mistake. To do this, it is necessary to follow the double trajectory of the rupture and continuity between classical political economy and Marx's system.

The production process (also known as the labor process) is the usual expression in political economy to refer to human activity over nature to sustain the material reproduction of society. Hunting, gathering, farming, etc., are all tasks of the social body that can be described by natural sciences, when we remove the social frame in which humans live. Now, when we observe the production process in this pure form, that is, when we set aside the social relations that are specific to a certain period of history in a certain region, there are only three fundamental elements. Marx calls them "[t]he elementary factors of the labour-process (...) 1, the personal activity of man, *i.e.*, work itself, 2, the subject of that work, and 3, its instruments." (Marx [1867] 2015, p. 127).

The combination of these three elements transforms inputs into outputs. Economic output is the concept of the entire result of this transformation, which can be used in different ways by society. To sustain society materially is the most basic motive of this basic movement. At this level of analysis, economic output can be thought of as a general category of economic science. Every mode of production must perform the physical-chemical modification of matter through human intervention to initiate its reproducing cycle— whether it be Robinson Crusoe isolated in an island, a peasant family, or someone who is part of the social whole interacting exclusively through the market. Every economy must reproduce materially the conditions that allow society to continue existing.

Marx classifies both the instruments and the subject of work as means of production. Labor, the third element remains isolated. This is a trivial observation when we describe the production process through the lens of natural sciences. In this perspective, as is the case with all preceding economists— including anti-socialists such as Böhm-Bawerk ([1889] 1985, pp. 123–145) and Ludwig von Mises ([1949] 1998, p. 133)—labor is the only element in the process that has the power to activate the circuit of matter transformation that results in economic activity. If human activity is absent, all other elements remain integrated in nature. Everything remains out of the reach of humans, and there can be no talk about economy in the sense we use the word to refer to human social organizations. Other living beings also reproduce themselves by changing the environment they inhabit, but we do not call the result of these changes economic output as we can infer from Engel's argument presented in his essay *The Part Played by Labour in the Transition from Ape to Man* (Engels [1876] 1934).

Thus, human labor assumes a central position. Labor is the name for how humans struggle to survive in the world, not only in the writings of pro-labor value theoreticians, but also in the treatises of the enemies of workers. But while for socialists the concept of labor is used as political tool to vindicate their claim for better conditions for workers, capital-allied economists merely acknowledge that it is a mechanical force which can be executed by humans. Right-wing economists even admit that humans are the starting point in the long process of the modification of nature. Untouched earth, raw material and all intermediary stages until the final output form a long sequence that was once initiated by bare hands that shaped the first stone tool. The importance of labor to produce useful stuff is unquestionable. However, this is not the true reason for grounding a theory of value in labor. Meeting needs is also of utmost importance for the purpose of making useful things. Why should a theory of value not be designed based on utility instead of labor? The human-nature perspective that naturalizes every conceivable theory of value has the paradoxical result of enabling the justification of any theory of value. This is why the classical labor theory of value and the neoclassical utility theory of value have the same status and must be criticized in parallel.

Adam Smith had merged all the mercantilist and physiocratic theories of national wealth into the same system. Political Economy had a new look, perfectly suitable for the economic interests of the British Empire in 18th century capitalism. Moreover, the new system placed labor in the highest position. Without labor, there can be no production, and no wealth. The continuation of this solid argument led to the notion that all economic output, and therefore, all wealth is due to labor. It is self-evident that labor must be the basis of values and prices, as any other natural phenomenon that appears to be so obvious that no one can contest it. To criticize such an idea is to go against nature itself.

However, as we are arguing, no natural foundation for any theory of value can solve the issue. When we limit the analysis to the relation human-nature, any theory of value will be valid for any mode of production in history. This method of constructing a value theory does not allow us to discover that capitalism is just another social arrangement of relations of production besides many other possible architectures. In any society human labor, as potential energy liberated by the organism in a purposeful direction, is "expenditure of human brains, nerves, and muscles" (Marx [1867] 2015, p. 32). So, there is no gain in information about the specificities of capitalism when we adhere to the labor theory of value, as it was envisaged by classical economists and pre-Marx socialists. The labor theory of value is not the essential aspect that gives superiority to Marx's theory, as Lange (1935) explained to professional economists. It is not right to elevate the labor theory of value to a sacred status, even if it feels necessary when it is brutally attacked by capital-allied economists.

The description of the labor theory of value in its physiological sense is obvious for any serious thinker.[8] We must be aware that Marx himself views

---

8 In a letter to Ludwig Kugelmann in 1868, Marx ([1868] 1928) explains why he uses the labor theory of value and appeals to this reasoning. My approach implies that Marx could not sustain his theory on this argument only, because this is the same argument used by all labor value theoreticians before him. There must be another element atop the physiological to explain why labor, among the huge number of candidates to function as a standard of measure for the quantities of useful objects, must be chosen. Indeed, in my perspective, a labor

the labor theory of value in this partial sense. He admits that, for the quantitative aspect only, it is possible to begin with the construction of the labor theory of value of the classical economists. Of course, this has significant limitations. But once we remove the qualitative mysteries of value, it is a perfectly suitable theory of value to play the value-price game of pure quantitative matching. The problem of the classical labor theory of value is not in the quantitative dimension. The problem is in the qualitative dimension. The labor theory of value in the classical system suffers from what we call 'naturalization', as if value were only determined by the interaction between human and nature.

It is perfectly possible to replicate the quantitative relations between use values in the world of Robinson Crusoe. Because of this we tend to think that it is possible to develop a general theory of value, i.e a theory of value based on the relationship human-nature. But this is only a mental experiment that shows that resources must be allocated, combined, used, etc. in any kind of economy, without breaking the laws of nature. The main difficulty lies in the fact that commodity fetishism leads us to think that the eternal movement of value expansion must also exist in non-capitalist social settings. Poor Robinson Crusoe and all hunters, fishers, and savages!—for they are presented as if they expand their needs infinitely. If they all have free access to the means of production, why would they live just to work? *Homo economicus* must logically have insatiable needs.

How human is it to have insatiable needs? The naturalization behind this also infects the labor theory of value when it is based on the pure physiological sense. Even though we can count value using labor time in any mode of production, this is not the reason why *the* theory of value must necessarily be a labor theory of value. To count value is to measure the quantity of use values, and there have been many other socially recognized standards to fulfill this function through history. The problem of the naturalized labor theory of value is not that it works to count value. Its problem is that it takes as a natural fact

---

value theoretician does not have to convince an audience that it must pick labor. What he/she must do is to reveal that the choice for labor reveals a political position in class struggle. For a full analysis of this passage about the labor theory of value and the law of value in Marx's letter to Kugelmann, see Pilling (1972), who criticizes Dobb, Meek, and Lange. I agree with Pilling's acute distinction between Ricardo and Marx. However, I do not think that the question 'why did Marx choose labor as the basis for his value theory?' is out of place as he argues. I do believe that the question must be posed. The problem is not with the question, but with the answer. See the debate between Pilling (1973) and Meek (1973). Pilling correctly indicated that quantity and quality must have unity in a coherent understanding of the law of value in Marx, however he fails to unfold the commodity correctly into the various levels of dialectical contradiction. For a proposed correction, see Figure 4.

that labor quantity is the way to measure concrete wealth, as if no other standard could be employed.

In its physiological sense, the labor theory of value shows that the most
valuable items demand a greater quantity of labor time to obtain. The interaction between exchanged goods in the perfectly idealized market reflects
the degree of difficulty in their production. This is precisely what makes the
'Robinson exercise' possible, where everyone exchanges their products of labor
in an environment where money does not even exist. The true advancement
made by pre-Marx socialists was to simply make a political use of this reasoning in order to demand the full payment of labor.

The result of the production process is a mass of useful stuff that assumes
the abstract form of money, which is then distributed in different forms of
income. What prevents workers from receiving 100% of this sum that constitutes national wealth? There are social constraints guaranteeing that non-
workers have the right to own everything that goes beyond what is necessary
for survival. Surplus is reserved for the class of exploiters. Here, the economic
confronts the political and the dispute around the surplus shows how the distribution of the output does not fit well in the labor theory of value. This conclusion marks the end of the harmonious system inaugurated by Adam Smith
and the further development of economic science must necessarily follow the
trail opened by Marx's critique of political economy. Before we proceed to that,
we still need to clearly comprehend what is the final scheme of the political
economy that naturalizes commodity relations of production, from the side of
socialist economics.

5   Desideratum of Utopian Socialism: Simple Commodity Production

Socialist economics is a daughter of classical political economy. It is time to
describe the final stage of this progressive line, which nonetheless remains
non-Marxian. As we have argued, since utopian socialist economists naturalize
social relations as neoclassical economists do, it may come as no surprise that
non-Marxian socialist economics arrives at exactly the same idealized economy as the reactionary line: simple commodity production.

Socialist authors defend vehemently the principle of equal wage for equal
work. They also defend the end of all privileges. But is this not what lies behind
the ideology of the free market world? For those who believe that the French
Revolution did not fulfil its aims, certainly this remains to be achieved. However,
for those who know that the revolution only used the working masses to defeat
the Ancien Régime and to stem the flow of History at the stage of bourgeois

jurisdiction, a new principle is required. Accordingly, economic science must replace the supposed egalitarian pattern of production and distribution based on markets by a higher dictum.[9] Marx's *Critique of the Gotha Programme* is one of the first systematic works to dissect the differences between socialism and communism.

If we want to understand how the theoretical system of pre-Marx socialists leads to the trap of the simple commodity production society, we must analyze how Proudhon understands the labor theory of value. Consequently, we need to understand why Marx dedicates so much energy to criticizing Proudhon's political economy. Proudhon represents the contradictory peak of socialist politics founded on the social relationship commodity.

Pierre-Joseph Proudhon (1809–1865) noticed the polarities at stake and realized that 'official economists' were blocking the advancement of socialist ideas. He observed that their maneuvers laid bare all the contradictions between the logical conclusions of political economy and the class interests that supported this same political economy for decades. In his work *The Philosophy of Poverty*, which is also called *System of Economical Contradictions*, published in 1846, Proudhon argues that the observed economic system operates through acute contradictions. They reveal the irrationality of the economy given all its technical potentialities for solving the economic problem of humankind (Proudhon [1846] 2007).

Proudhon's text asks many profound philosophical questions that show how he proceeds from concrete themes (such as hunger, production and consumption) to abstract ones (such as the existence of God, forms of thought and the logical system of the apprehension of truth). Social matters underpinning money, value and human relations in general are inserted in this all-encompassing treatise, well equipped with the latest findings in the fields of politics, history, political economy and even philosophy (when we ignore the highest level to which Marx has taken Hegel's system). For those who have accompanied Marx and have surpassed with him all the conundrums of Feuerbach's courageous critique of Hegel, it is quite difficult to follow Proudhon and his *System of Economic Contradictions*. He is involved in a philosophical puzzle to which Marx has already found an answer. Proudhon is deluded by speculative philosophy according to Marx's letter to J. B. Schweitzer (Marx [1865] 1969).

The incompatibilities of antagonistic elements are present in each line of Proudhon's work. He correctly describes how the socialist idea contradicts

---

9 For a colorful presentation of how the historical movement transforms the revolutionary bourgeoisie into a reactionary class, see Hobsbawm ([1977] 2014), p. 111.

many of the reactionary novelties in political economy, especially those which pretend to justify property incomes. All these incomes come from sources other than performed labor. In chapter 1, session 2 of *System of Economic Contradictions*, he investigates the origins of the logic behind lending and borrowing money (usury) and indicates that this phenomenon seems to be a spontaneous happening, close to a natural event, because its source rests in the deepest part of human nature:

> Undoubtedly—and I am the first to recognize it—the rent of land, like that of money and all personal and real property, is a spontaneous and universal fact, which has its source in the depths of our nature, and which soon becomes, by its natural development, one of the most potent means of organization.
>
> PROUDHON ([1847] 1888), p. 30

Furthermore, he understands that usury, or the practice of lending money to receive it back with a surplus, is not restricted to the most liquid form of property, namely money. In the most obvious case, a proprietor allows someone else to use his/her money and charges a surplus, which in this case is called interest. But this practice is not limited to money and may be extended to any property that can be used by a non-proprietor during a certain time. So, the renting of land, or of a machine, etc. yields similar 'interests' but under other terminology such as rent. All these elements (money, land, equipment, etc.) accrue more value as time passes, when they operate as capital. This means that capital is productive in the sense that it has the capacity to bring more value to its proprietor. Moreover, Proudhon thinks that this standard is so common that it has been one of the most powerful means of economic organization.

Despite this naturalization in the explanation of interest, Proudhon does not forget that it sharply contradicts the fundamentals of political economy as it is understood since the time of Adam Smith. He clearly illustrates the bifurcation in political economy. The notion of capital productivity behind the phenomenon of interest conflicts with the theoretical notion that all value is created by labor. However, to correctly assert what is at stake is not enough to take political economy further. The socialist movement had long shouted against the status quo. Now it needs to know how to change this reality. Political economy must replace this spontaneous and universal fact by something else. Otherwise, social constructs, which appear as natural forces, will continue to control the working masses as if these social institutions really were immutable laws of the universe.

Instead of reaching the conclusion that this contradiction expresses the antagonistic, irreconcilable material interests of two social classes, Proudhon struggles to find an intermediary solution. He asks:

> How, then, reconcile the theory of farm-rent or productivity of capital— a theory confirmed by universal custom, which conservative political economy is forced to accept but cannot justify—with this other theory which shows that value is normally composed of wages, and which inevitably ends, as we shall demonstrate, in an equality in society between net product and raw product?
>
> PROUDHON ([1847] 1888), pp. 30–31

Proudhon understands that socialists have taken the tools of political economy to defend their cause. These authors argue in favor of the right to the full results of labor. Still, he feels that this is a fragile justification for the general theory of value because the phenomenon of non-labor incomes must somehow find a place in the theoretical system of the political economy of the future. This is the final limit, not only of the pre-Marx labor theory of value, but of all socialism based on French politics and English economics. Proudhon does not see a light at the end of the tunnel. A third pillar is missing: the German philosophy of Hegel surpassed by Feuerbach, Engels, and Marx.

The conciliatory alternative leads to an unsustainable system. For Proudhon, there must be a midway between the extreme positions of capital (interests, rent, profits, etc.) and labor (wages). This in-between principle would reconcile them into a genuine advancement in theory. But neither socialists nor economists can produce such a theory. Proudhon criticizes socialists because they abandon the principle of indemnity. Consequently, they go for universal expropriation. They go for production and consumption in common. They go for communism.

According to Proudhon, this solution is not enough, because he thinks there must be specific and clear lines of how such a system could work. According to our reading, he is trying to say that without the establishment of the social rules for organizing the communist economy, it will remain as a utopian movement never able to build itself in the real world. Clearly, this means that the usual principles of exchange do not fit in the communal economic system. Proudhon logically draws the right question: given the contradictions of society, how should the new social system work? For him, who consistently thinks inside the philosophical dimension of contemplation, before proceeding with the expropriation according to the general concept of public interest, it is necessary to have a full and detailed plan of this new society.

Like Marx, Proudhon looks in political economy for the elements of of the society of the future. He describes the contradictions with precision and calls for a search for a broader rule capable of reconciling the conflicting theories of capital and labor. Without such a rule, Proudhon believes that socialism will fail. It is very curious that he is worried about escaping from utopianism. This means that he is aware that he is within idealism in terms of Marxian philosophy. In any case, given this limitation, the economic solution would come from the theory and not from the real practical movement that constantly solves the problems that appear day after day.

Bourgeois economic thought and radical egalitarianism merge into an impossible puzzle under Proudhon's pen. And he knows it. The combination of the labor theory of value with the observed structure of income (interest, rent, profit, etc.) is untenable. At this point, the option for the labor theory of value is already a matter of political choice in the struggle and no longer a speculative search for the origin of value.

It is very well known that Marx rejected Proudhon in his text *The Poverty of Philosophy* (Marx [1847] 1955). However, the idea that Marx and Proudhon are light-years apart from each other gives the impression that there are no points of contact between them. Moreover, this distancing may have contributed to the belief in a sudden rupture between utopian and scientific socialism that must be revised according to my approach. In fact, there are many aspects of similarity between them which should be stressed to call attention to the economic calculation problem. We cannot see Marx's relationship with all non-Marxian socialists as just a breach. Marx's method is one of appropriation and transformation.

What about the labor theory of value? Proudhon comes close to the great questions behind the alienation process of commodity production in chapter 2 (Of Value) of *System of Economic Contradictions* (Proudhon [1847] 1888, p. 38). He hits the heart of the problem by correctly verifying that the duality of value in use and value in exchange has an acute contradictory characteristic. This indicates that the individual agent in the market system is trapped in the collective, so private production and appropriation are conditioned by social production and appropriation. The private and public spheres are connected through a subtle scheme that creates a powerful illusion. It seems that everyone is entirely free, as if there were no bonds with the social group. Proudhon realizes that the social system under investigation works only within exchange relations and that exchange presupposes private property. Accordingly, labor creates both value and the right of private appropriation as if it were its natural property.

Proudhon then courageously asks in chapter 11 about the origin of this social norm. It is the "problem of property" (Proudhon [1846] 2007, tomo II, p. 169). Here he stands before a philosophical precipice. Proudhon tries to explain property and.argues that philosophy has, over three centuries, produced the right tool to investigate any idea. Proudhon wants to analyze the entity of private property with this tool and concludes that "the property is inexplicable outside of the economic series". (Proudhon [1847] 1888 and Proudhon [1846] 2007, tomo II, pp. 169–196, especially p. 190). Property appears as eternal. But the real political movement demands its abolition. How can economics continue outside the economic series? It is the end of political economy framed by the capitalist mode of production. It is the last moment of the naturalization of commodity social relations.

So, how could society achieve equality without leaving the rule of property? If the right to property was equally extended to every member of society, would this not be the ideal solution? This is the desideratum of simple commodity production.[10]

Proudhon realized that the generalization of property was also a false outcome. For, in this case, who would be excluded so that private appropriation could exist in the first place? At the same time, he insists on the maintenance of two irreconcilable sides. Accordingly, he draws absurd conclusions such as these: the greater is the decline of the institution of private property, the farther away communism seems to be. Proudhon is fully aware of all these absurdities when he writes that,

it is not by becoming common that property can become social: one does not relieve rabies by biting everyone. Property will end by the transformation of its principle, not by an indefinite co-participation.

PROUDHON [1847] 1888, p. 243

---

10   I use the concept of simple commodity production to emphasize the idea of equality. My concept of simple commodity production includes what I call 'expanded equilibrated reproduction'. It is a state of expanded reproduction in which total value increases but the proportions of the various use values that constitute the input and output matrices remain the same. So, we achieve a uniform pattern of value expansion where all agents have the same level of economic power. Here it becomes clear that exploitation is not a direct relation between two agents only, but the result of alienation among all private proprietors who exploit themselves through competition. For a detailed analysis of the concept of simple commodity production, see Rakowitz (2003) and Chattopadhyay (2018). For a computational model to test the validity of the law of value in a simple commodity economy, see Wright (2008). For a critical engagement with the concept of simple commodity production in a historical sense, see Milonakis (1995).

In the end he resigns and admits that socialism is just a wish. This means that people do not know how to construct it and, logically, it is necessary to give it up. What an end!

Proudhon's withdraw or retreat from the debate had a strong effect over the communist movement that remains up until the present. His strength dissolves negatively into anarchism. The dichotomy between wish and impossibility reproduces itself since then in the circles of the petite bourgeoisie and even among members of the waged working class. In that sense, socialism is locked in the safe of utopianism. This is the reason why Marx dedicated so much energy to fighting Proudhon.[11]

Finally, after its dominance in the mainstream of the economics of the 18th and 19th century, the labor theory of value was expelled from the official arena. The idea that labor alone was responsible for all creation of wealth had to be countered. As we have indicated, anti-communist forces had to theoretically defend private property with all the instruments that economic science could offer. Since the objectivist approach to value theory could not satisfy this adequately, the subjectivist approach was employed with greater success. However, as is implied in our thesis, both approaches are making the same mistake of naturalizing a specific social relation of production. Marxist economists usually treat the Marginalist Revolution of Menger, Jevons and Walras with disdain. But we must deal with it in the same way Marx dealt with classical political economy. We need to dedicate time and effort to unveiling all the details of neoclassical Political Economy. The critique of political economy is not only targeted on the past, but also on the present and future of economics. By giving an equal treatment to both strains of non-Marxian political economy after the end of Adam Smith's system, we will finally be able to overcome the dichotomy of the 'rupturist' and 'continuist' readings of Marx as a political economist.

---

11   The continuation of Proudhon's political economy leads to left libertarianism and the anarchist current of political economy called mutualism. For a contemporary introduction to mutualist political economy, see Carson (2004).

CHAPTER 5

Price

The Naturalization of the Utility Theory of Value in the Marginalist Revolution

1 Seizure of Political Economy by Capital

Like utopian socialism, the Marginalist Revolution also develops a naturalized form of value theory. Instead of adopting labor as the standard of measure, it chooses utility. The explanation for picking utility to be the qualitative element by which to measure the quantitative relations of exchange between use values is based on an analysis of the natural world. So, it is also incomplete, since it can indeed describe why commodities have the prices they do (quantity) but cannot explain concretely why what they are measuring must be utility and nothing else (quality). This strand of the naturalization of value theory is a key basis of neoclassical economics and its result is also the model of simple commodity production.

The neoclassical utility theory of value follows an opposite and yet parallel road to that of the classical labor theory of value. The typical Marxian political economy literature correctly points to the grave mistakes in the naturalization of capitalism that lies behind the homo economicus paradigm of the marginalist approach. Despite these errors, however, we want to draw attention to the fact that that it also makes a positive contribution in its investigation of the details of price determination at the surface level. Even though the expression 'law of value' vanishes from its written works, nevertheless, the movement of prices still has something to do with the interaction between production and circulation. There still exists a unique logic governing the movement of prices. What should we call this movement, if not the law of value? My point here is not about terminological differences, but about recognizing that every school of thought in value theory deals with the same objective phenomenon, regardless of how it is named.

Considering the traditional standpoint of Marxian political economy in the West, it may seem strange for a Marxist to claim that there must be something useful in the Marginalist Revolution. Strongly influenced by the qualitative philosophical reading of *Capital*, Marxists economists in the West typically believe that the Marginalist Revolution and the vulgarization of political economy are one and the same process. It is true that there is a close connection between them, but it is important to separate science from apologetics in the works of political economists, as indeed Marx himself demonstrated. Our approach is based on the view that that such a separation should not only be applied to authors of the past, but that it is also possible to extract valuable scientific contributions in all branches of non-Marxian economics today.[1]

Socialists directed Adam Smith's system toward essence, to value. On the opposite political side, economists moved away from a focus on production and paid attention to the phenomena of the surface level. The socialist movement of the first half of the 19th century dominated the field of political economy and showed that a new phase of class struggle was influencing the elaboration of value theory. Workers contested the justice and right to exist of forms of income other than wages. The classical theory of value was seen as too sympathetic to labor by reactionary forces, who looked for alternative theories of value. Soon they found a path in what was to become the Marginalist Revolution. The works of Menger ([1871] 2007), Jevons ([1871] 1988) and Walras ([1874] 1954) served as the starting point for a new consensus for surpassing Adam Smith's theory and all its labor-friendly derivatives. According to this consensus, the concept of value was no longer centered on labor, but rather on utility.

Left-wing historians of economic thought usually interpret the Marginalist Revolution as a pure ideological defense of capitalism. It is common to hear the argument that Ricardian socialism may have caused panic among capitalists. Logically, it would not be irrational to affirm that capital-allied intellectuals who grasped the relations between the social sciences and class struggle purposefully acted to design another theory of value, that is, to bury the labor theory of value and replace it by something else.

We do not deny that some authors in the Marginalist Revolution may well have been aware of the political fight behind the theoretical core of economic science. However, we must recognize that various changes within the scope of what is called the Marginalist Revolution are not directly politically driven. Formalization and mathematization, for example, are necessary developments that can enhance the explanatory power of any theory in any field of knowledge, if properly employed. It would be reductive and inaccurate to claim that all those involved were primarily motivated by class-conscious

---

1   See Lange ([1959] 1963), p. 274, footnote 323. Lange gives as an example of this approach the text *A Characterization of Economic Romanticism* by Lenin, who analyzes Sismondi in the history of economic thought. The idea is that Marx's method absorbs the systems of economists by separating what is a real investigation from what is only propaganda for specific economic interests.

political aims and indeed this kind of approach can impede a more nuanced understanding of the Marginal Revolution and its contribution to the development of the theory of value. We want to call attention to this aspect of mainstream economics in order not to personalize social material relations of struggle that interfere in the development of political economy. The simplistic transposition of class struggle to the ideological sphere where economists express their ideas may lead us to a *cul-de-sac*. A representative author who denounced the Marginalist Revolution as a pure ideological defense of capitalism was Piero Sraffa. Sraffa argued that changes in the prevailing ideas of economic science begin with a deliberate action, politically motivated, and end with the appearance of a neutral modification.[2] He understood what was going on when the mainstream abandoned the surplus approach and celebrated the rise of a theory of value that supported the idea of capital productivity. He worked more than 30 years to publish an incisive attack against this theory of value. However, in my view, his attack failed precisely because he did not consider this subtle element in the art of war: the enemy cannot be defeated by such a direct assault. Formal logic is not enough to overcome vulgar economics. The internal critique of the marginal theory of value is important, but it will not do the job alone.

Sraffa studied the deep foundations of the theory of value in classical political economy. He investigated its physiocratic inspiration and its decline with Ricardo's school. He concluded that, by leaving the surplus approach behind, neoclassical economics opened the way for the marginalist perspective to spread to value theory. What he may not have realized is that marginalism is the opposite and complementary side of utopian socialist economics. In this sense, marginalism also plays the value-price game, though in a quite different manner. Value is no longer synonymous with labor, but with utility. Divergences between prices and values are interpreted as divergences between the subjective perspectives of the economic agents. The terminology is somewhat new, it is different, but it also functions to describe the quantitative movements of exchange relations between use values. From this perspective, utility value theory is as valid as the classical surplus approach. Both theories work fine for describing the movement of prices, though they employ different terminology and represent opposing political views.

---

2   See Sraffa's notes entitled *16 Lectures in Michaelmas Term 1928–1929 Advanced theory of value* (Sraffa (1928–1931)), and the comments by Bellofiore (2008), p. 71 and p. 86.

According to the methodology I am proposing, every theory of value is trying to make sense of the same real phenomenon of prices formation. Even if
they do not recognize it, all theories of value have the same object of investigation: the law of value. So, the empirical observation that useful things have
their values measured by prices must have an alternative explanation in the
marginalist approach in comparison to the classical labor theory of value.

In the marginalist approach, prices correspond to the forces of supply
and demand that equilibrate the relation between the effort (pain) and
reward (pleasure) of individuals. So, economists with this approach try to
relate empirical prices to internal aspects of another kind of essence. In
classical political economy, appearance is circulation and essence is production, whereas in neoclassical political economy appearance is exterior
and essence is interior. The external world is connected to the internal
world of the agent, who subjectively values useful things. Instead of considering production and circulation of the whole system as the two halves
of the economy, the neoclassical authors think in terms of the connection
between the individual and the society. We have a different dichotomy. It
is another kind of pair of complementary entities that oppose each other
dialectically. Nonetheless, the dichotomy exists, and we must find the law
of value in this new scheme.

How should we identify value and price in this scheme? How do their
reciprocal repulsion and attraction appear here? At first sight, the marginalist
approach leads to the abandonment of value in favor of price, at least, this is
how the story is told from the traditional critical perspective on the Marginalist
Revolution. However, if we take a more sympathetic approach, we will see that
the price theory of the capitalist surface also contains something deeper. What
is the meaning of such quantities? In classical political economy and its utopian socialist derivative, these quantities refer to the quantity of effort in the
form of labor employed in the production. So, labor works as the quality to
measure the quantity of abstract wealth. In the Marginalist Revolution, these
quantities refer to the magnitude of consumer satisfaction. So, utility works as
the quality to measure the quantity of abstract wealth. Thus, the marginalist
approach also has a qualitative aspect to value theory, and also has the same
problem as the classical labor theory of value in that this quality is naturalized. Both labor and utility are thought of as processes of interaction between
humans and nature.

So, the great failure of the marginalist approach is this naturalization of
the qualittative aspect, and not that it abandons value in favor of price due to
the complicated matter of transforming values into production prices. This
is the usual explanation that goes back to Engels and even Marx himself. Of

course, to leave a hole in the process of transforming values into prices is a serious weakness because economists are desperately trying to replace all Smithian terminology for dealing with the law of value with other concepts. The class-related character of this maneuver was correctly anticipated by Marx and Engels, and most Marxian economists emphasize it in their critical evaluation of the Marginalist Revolution (like Sraffa, who served as an example).

However, we must not forget that the Marginalist Revolution does not come out of thin air. Classical political economy is the soil in which any theory of value grows. It is true that the utility theory of value develops as an alternative to Adam Smith's political economy, but it is also a fact that it maintains many of its foundation stones, such as liberalism, harmony, and equilibrium. The dream of a perfect world based on the institutions of private property are kept as sacred maxims. Just as utopian socialism did not entirely break with its past, so the Marginalist Revolution is not an absolute rupture with classical economics. Consequently, neoclassical political economy must also contain relevant insights hidden in its theoretical core, and it is these that need to be found and translated into the system proposed by Marx. The Critique of (Classical) Political Economy is also the critique of neoclassical political economy.

Considering this, where should we look for truths that are hidden behind layers of capitalist apology in mainstream economics? We must contextualize the meaning of a utility function. Subjective elements also influence the definition of empirical prices. The classical approach and the labor theory of value only consider the objective side. Dialectical unity requires that both objectivity and subjectivity are integrated into any theory of value that claims to be complete.[3]

I am aware that this is a rather unorthodox approach for the standard literature on Marxian political economy. But since my intent is to show that Marx's critique of economic science strikes both classical and neoclassical economics in the same manner, we need to show how both non-Marxian theories of value (utopian socialist labor theory of value and utility theory of value) are equivalent and opposite systems. This will facilitate our understanding that Marx's work is not directed at any specific epoch or system of economic thought, but

---

3 During the 20th century, non-western economics has attempted to make sense of the neoclassical mainstream tools of price determination from a Marxian point of view. Economic planning may benefit from it, as various concrete historical examples show. I want to invite all western Marxian economists to at least consider these approaches, before discarding Marginalism with disdain. Apart from Lange (1971), whose work and approach strongly influence my approach, see also Horvat (1970) and Horvat ([1982] 2020).

can be used to criticize any system of political economy that naturalizes the construction of a theory of value. Engaging constructively with the neoclassical framework is a necessity if we want to influence mainstream economic thought today.

Regarding the theory of value, it may be better to try to find useful aspects in the neoclassical framework than to try to destroy it. Value theory is the theoretical core of political economy. Class struggle and all material conflicts are condensed in it. The complexities and divergences are too great to employ standard strategies of critique. A direct assault does not lead to victory, because the variables involved are too many and the struggle is dynamic. A more subtle, flexible procedure is necessary to engage in the arena of competing theories of value.[4]

---

4 After studying Sraffa's critique of economic theory and the Cambridge controversies, I recognized that it is not possible to simply delete the marginalist paradigm. I believe today that, even in the case of a strategical alliance between Marxians and Sraffians to fortify Sraffa's program against Marginalism as I have proposed (Camarinha Lopes (2013a)), the utility theory of value cannot be destroyed. According to my research, Oskar Lange's strategy seems to be more robust than Piero Sraffa's project for dealing with the marginalist approach in particular, and vulgarization in economic science in general. Keynes' attack against the Marshallian system and the classical school (for Keynes, classical economists are those who accept Say's Law) was a collective effort in Cambridge, England. Piero Sraffa, Joan Robinson, Richard Kahn, Nicholas Kaldor and Richard Goodwin were some of the leading participants. In this respect, we can interpret Sraffa's project as another current in a broader attempt to overcome the marginalist paradigm. See Pasinetti (2009). There are huge differences between Marx's and Keynes' critiques of classical political economy. The main difference in my view is the following: Marx argues that classical economists naturalize the capitalist mode of production. Keynes argues that classical economists build their models on the notion of equilibrium behind Say's Law. Sraffa was part of that collective endeavor under the leadership of Keynes, and, although his influence as a full independent thinker became evident after the publication of his masterpiece, *Production of Commodities by Means of Commodities* in 1960, his methodological attack against neoclassical economics may be contaminated by Keynes's weak critique of classical economics. Oskar Lange contributed to the formalization of Keynesian economics in terms of traditional curves of supply and demand and had with a different method for dealing with mainstream neoclassical economics. Despite their differences, Piero Sraffa and Oskar Lange are two fine exemplary Marxists who put all their creativity into shaping economic science in the 20th century according to the needs of the working class. They did not disdain and ignore the world of non-Marxian economics. They engaged with it seriously and critically. Sraffa and Lange were befriended probably since the late 1920s, when they must have met in England. Lange helped Sraffa with bibliographical information about the Polish publications of David Ricardo's work (Ricardo (1951)) and Lange welcomed Sraffa in his home in Warsaw in 1954, when Sraffa was returning from a trip to China (Lazzarini e Brondino (2019)). Further research is necessary to find out the content of their communication, specially regarding how to deal with non-Marxian economics.

2   The Consumer's Theory of Value in Jevons, Menger and Walras

The Marginalist Revolution caused an important change in the history of economic thought. It marks the transition from political analysis and historical
description to a new standard. Previously, economic thinking was a multidisciplinary field, which systematically connected matters of material interest with
politics, society, philosophy, and natural sciences. Now, a much more formalized structure began to dominate political economy. Abstraction and mathematics invaded the pages of the treatises. They no longer found their starting
point in questions of national well-being and wealth, but with the choices of
the consumer at the market.

    In this new framework, the individual is the starting point of analysis. More
accurately, the individual in the role of a consumer at the market is the starting
point of analysis. The fact that the consumer must also be, at some point, the
worker is almost completely forgotten. This figure does not appear explicitly as
the one who works, but only as the producer. In other words, when marginalist
economics remembers it must also say something about production, it evokes
the agent who has the power over the production process. It does not consider
the worker, but the proprietor of the means of production who buys various
factors of production, including labor. The political conflict behind wealth creation is left aside. After all, the producer need not be someone who uses his/
her hands to move matter but may be idealized as someone who combines all
factors of production through his/her purchasing power. All attention is centered on what happens in the circulation sphere, at the market. In the neoclassical standard textbooks, the complexities of production and labor are left to
further chapters when the reader is already educated to approach economics
from the standpoint of the commodity consumer.

    The individual chooses how he/she spends money to acquire useful things
at the market. By observing this, it is possible to design a theory of value. The
theory describes the rationality behind these choices and provides content for
interpreting the relations between useful things. Accordingly, the explanation
of value lies in the subjective evaluations of how commodities, as use values,
meet individual needs.[5] The foundation of value became value in use and not
value in exchange. Consequently, the bond to labor, which determined the
capacity of a useful item to be exchanged by another useful item, was cut.

---

5 It is important to remember that in neoclassical language there is no meaningful distinction
   between value and price. This distinction has been left aside and all attention is directed at a
   single set of exchange relations that guarantees equilibrium. Thus, the terms value and price
   are used interchangeably within neoclassical mainstream economics.

There are three main authors whose work represents the consolidation of the consumer's value theory since the 1870s. There is no consensus interpretation of this episode in the history of economic thought, except that it marks the beginning of a new era (between 1871 and 1874). Stanley Jevons, Carl Menger and Léon Walras, despite being usually presented as a homogeneous group, each have a view with different specific characteristics. It is worthwhile recalling these differences, because from a radical point of view, many dismiss all mainstream economics without ever considering the details.[6]

In the preface of the first edition of *Theory of Political Economy* from 1871, William Stanley Jevons (1835–1882) contextualizes his work in the scenery of economics of the 19th century. In his view, there was a feeling of conclusion to the development that had been initiated by Adam Smith. There was nothing that could be added to the system. For Jevons, after the contributions of Malthus, Senior and Ricardo, it reached a peak with John Stuart Mill and then it seemed that nothing new could be included. Because of this, Jevons believes political economy must take another path, departing from a different starting point for the theory of value. His intention is to challenge the standard labor theory of value by presenting an alternative economics based on the calculus of pleasure and pain (Jevons [1871] 1983, p. 3–4).

Accordingly, it is an approach that diverts from the mainstream economics of the 19th century. It seeks to analyze the concrete phenomena of markets from a different perspective. Instead of following Adam Smith in the water-diamond paradox, Jevons wants to defend the view that value is determined by the utility of goods and not by the labor required in their production. In parallel to this, Jevons argues that it is necessary to insert mathematical techniques into the traditional qualitative studies in political economy. Natural sciences are making huge progress and Jevons is excited to use certain of its techniques to deal with economic matters. In particular, he is influenced by physical mechanics, which already has a coherent theory for explaining all movements of bodies. Political economy is also a study of things moving. Why should it not benefit from the application of mathematical tools? According to Jevons, the qualitative considerations around utility, labor, capital, and value

---

6 My presentation derives from a direct reading of the original works of Jevons, Menger and Walras. My aim is to distinguish the particularities of each one, in the sense that they are not only a coherent trinity, but also three different value theoreticians with individual characteristics, as Jaffé (1976) argues. For interpretations of this turn in the history of economic thought, see Collison Black, Coats and Goodwin (1973), Clarke (1991), Milonakis and Fine (2008) and Kaldor (2020).

need to reach a degree of precision that is only possible with quantitative analysis framed by the rigor of mathematics.

It is interesting to note that until the end of the 19th century, political economy was a field that was relatively distant from formal structures. In fact, all fields of scientific research were closer to the usual philosophical approach, where reasoning and the accumulation of knowledge are led by the investigation of great fundamental questions. Mathematical formalization is a result of massive labor division in scientific research, and it also reached the field of political economy. Complex mathematics was almost absent in political economy until the second half of the 19th century. In the 17th and 18th centuries, William Petty ([1690] 1996) and François Quesnay ([1758] 1996) had indeed started to elaborate theories capable of receiving an organized quantitative analysis, but economists were content to use the simplest methods of accounting based on the four basic mathematical operations.

Arithmetic was enough to deal with all quantitative phenomena in political economy. Sometimes, authors used the concepts of growth rate when the observation of variables in time enabled the identification of a pattern. Economic output, productivity, the decline of profit rates, all had a certain tendency. The dynamics of rates of growth were important in the debates around Malthus's work. The size of the population and the total quantity of resources had specific dynamics of change that had to be considered to achieve adequate conclusions about the economic problem of humanity. Diminishing returns of scale was a broad phenomenon that could well be described with differential calculus. But the emphasis on pure mathematical reasoning decisively penetrates the core of political economy only after the Marginalist Revolution.

Jevons's preface shows that the mathematical approach already existed, but it was excluded from the mainstream discourse in Smithian style. The complexities of a quantitative analysis were present in the writings of various writers and part of Jevons' aim is to recover these works. These mathematical works in political economy were marginalized during the hegemony of Adam Smith. Jevons's *Theory of Political Economy* presents an appendix with a detailed list of books, essays and other works that focused on the mathematical approach to political economy. This list covers a period from the beginning of the 18th century to the end of the 19th century and it continued to be expanded by Jevons's family after his death in the subsequent editions of the *Theory of Political Economy*. The list is a collection of works that describe the lineage of the marginalist theory of value. It tells the parallel story of economic science apart from the tradition of Smith, Ricardo, Malthus, and John Stuart Mill. Jevons thought this heterodox current was fertile ground for the development of political economy and should be better known.

We must understand Jevons's advice. As I have indicated, my approach to the neoclassical School is quite different from the traditional Marxist reading. I am looking for useful and positive things outside the Marxian School. Here, I think Jevon's argument about the importance of mathematics is valid. Progressive vulgar economics is usually wary of mathematics. The critical and radical development of economic science, which followed the path of utopian socialism and not that of the Marginalist Revolution, became more and more distant from the use of mathematics applied to political economy. By contrast, the Marginalist Revolution became more and more distant from history and social philosophy. This structural deficiency on each side demands our attention. On the one hand, the abandonment of quantitative tools by one side allowed the dominance of right-wing economists over the techniques of quantitative analysis. On the other hand, the abandonment of the qualitative analysis of history and politics by the other side contributed to turning economics into a hard-sciences field, as if it dealt with a system without human beings.

The problems in Adam Smith's and Ricardo's theory of value are real and Jevons wants to find a solution. Due to the capital apologetics employed by reactionary vulgar economists, the longstanding tradition of marginalism (which reaches back in time to a period where there was no open conflict between capital and labor, as was the case from the 1820s onward) is discarded right away by the usual Marxian economics discourse.

The utility theory of value is not entirely a result of the political reaction against the spread of the labor theory of value. It also contains correct elements that were taken up later by political forces during the Marginalist Revolution. The fundamental core of the reactionary development of political economy already existed before the 1870s. Subjective evaluation has always been a candidate for explaining prices/value but it was not the mainstream theory of value.[7] Adam Smith's materialist perspective was undisputedly the most accepted approach to value theory. This gave the objectivist approach to value a greater advantage over the subjectivist approach.

---

7   Hermann Heinrich Gossen (1854) is considered the pioneer of the marginal utility theory of value of mainstream neoclassical economics, but the origins of this current of value theory are prior to Gossen His work is entitled *Die Entwickelung der Gesetze des menschlichen Verkehrs, und der daraus fließenden Regeln für menschliches Handeln.* [*The Laws of Human Relations and the Rules of Human Action Derived Therefrom*]. For an overview of the lineage of the subjective theory of value see Kauder (1965). For an introductory presentation on the shortcomings of the standard story of the Marginalist Revolution around Menger, Jevons and Walras, see Ekelund and Hébert (2002).

At first sight, Jevons seems to be following the apologetic path of Malthus and Senior. It is important to remember, however, that the consumer's theory of value is not born with the Marginalist Revolution. It only receives definitive support to dominate the mainstream of economic thinking because of the political context of the second half of the 19th century. Accordingly, we need to both criticize and be sympathetic to the consumer's theory of value, as previously with the theory of value of non-Marxian socialists.

The transition from the classical era of economics to the neoclassical era is tumultuous and full of significant changes. One example of an important change is Jevons's proposition, in the second edition of *Theory of Political Economy*, to replace the name 'political economy' by the single convenient term 'economics' (Jevons [1871] 1983, p. 6). He calls it a 'minor alteration', but it certainly has a huge significance. The widespread use of this modified name is consolidated by the massive adherence to Alfred Marshall's textbook some decades later. Such a small adjustment of the nomenclature for economic science synthesizes what the Marginal Revolution means. Instead of dedicating attention to the broad aspects of social philosophy, history, ethics and politics, the economist is now a specialist in the abstract art of describing the phenomena of market exchange without ever questioning the institutional prerequisites for the existence of private property and capital production. The economist observes the market agents gambling to increase abstract wealth. The perspective of the consumer at the market is the normal, natural case and all the world is viewed through these lenses. Jevons argues that this new narrow focus for economic science contributes to organizing the chaotic and confusing state in which political economy finds itself. Jevons's recipe is simple: leave politics, philosophy, and all complicated social matters to other thinkers. For him, 'subdivision is the remedy' (Jevons [1871] 1983, p. 7).

Obviously, not everybody agrees with Jevons. Many argue that the economist still needs to be a complete social thinker and scientist. The idea that the economist must deal with all the complexities of society as whole is a strong one. Whatever position one may have on this, it is important to recognize that there already existed an alternative tradition to Smithian economics prior to the Marginalist Revolution of the 1870s. Many authors worked with mathematical formalizations and wrote very specialized treatises whereas the bestsellers of political economy were reasonably accessible to the average reader. Jevons wants to popularize this alternative approach to political economy, (which seems reasonable if it is not just an apologetic move to defend capital). He knew that focusing on only one of the two sides (quality/totality or quantity/partiality) would never fully solve the problem. But ultimately his work did not escape the destiny set out by the marginalist turn: the craving to destroy the classical theory of value was so great that his contribution was also used in the movement to leave classical political economy behind. Instead of integrating both sides into the same set, mathematics and formal abstractions gained almost all terrain.[8]

We should never forget that the effort to dismiss the labor theory of value is real. Jevons is on the side of Senior and Malthus against the Ricardian School. He openly states that he wants to get rid of 'the mazy and preposterous assumptions of the Ricardian School' as well as of the strong connection between labor and value by affirming that 'there is no such thing as absolute cost of labour; it is all a matter of comparison.' (Jevons ([1871] 1983), p. 18, 21, my translation)

The marginalist critique of Adam Smith's and Ricardo's system also has a duality that we usually overlook. Mathematics can certainly be an ally of political economy. But there is also a negative element in the Marginalist Revolution, fueled purely by the need to politically discredit the labor theory of value. It is important to recognize such duality, otherwise we will always repeat a superficial interpretation of the Marginalist Revolution that impedes a correct interaction with mainstream economics from a Marxist standpoint.

The will to throw the labor theory of value away is a decisive weakness in the marginalist turn. The classical labor theory of value was the best tool for holding all the pieces together. This law of value was a coherent concept tying circulation and creation of wealth together into one rationally organized scheme. There was an objective logic behind the apparent chaos of the market. This logic, called the law of value in the classical system, seems to be discarded in the neoclassical system.

It is more accurate, however, to say that the law of value is signified anew. The logical basis for deviations from the equilibrium is no longer between production and circulation, but between an internal and an external dimension. The divergence is one between individual and social evaluation. Despite this difference in perspective, the concrete phenomenon of the adjustment of forces between the two antagonistic sides of purchaser and seller continues to

---

8   As a result of this imbalance, the German historical school emerged to combat the Austrian group of the Marginalist Revolution. The Methodenstreit (battle of methods in economics) was the debate in Germany and Austria at the turn from the 19th to the 20th century between historical and logical analysis in economics. The historical approach formed the German historical school (Gustav von Schmoller, Werner Sombart, Friedrich List and others). The logical approach formed the Austrian School (Menger, Bawerk, Mises, Hayek and others). For a presentation of the original debate between Menger and Schmoller, see Louzek (2011).

exist. Just because we adopt a different point of view it does not mean that the observed item has changed its nature.

Many argue that there cannot be a theory of value based on psychological subjectivism. But it is too easy to counter this kind of critique by indicating that extreme objectivism is equally problematic. Again, dialectics demand that both objectivity and subjectivity find their places within the unity. It is true that there must be a choice of priority, otherwise we will not find a way out of the contradiction towards dialectical materialism and the philosophy of praxis. But one cannot directly reject a theory of value just because it begins the journey from a standpoint which is not our own. Both Isaak Rubin and Oskar Lange reject the marginalist approach not because of its internal analytical errors (as Sraffa does), but because it is totally incapable of recognizing that it is mirroring the same mistakes as the non-Marxian labor theory of value. They disagree with the idea that it is possible to surpass the objective theory of value based on labor just by replacing it by the subjective theory of value based on utility. Replacing objectivism by subjectivism (or vice versa) will not lead us far.

To return to Jevons, what is his particularity as a marginalist value theorist? In comparison to other adherents of neoclassicism, Jevons makes every effort to integrate the mathematical language into the traditional discourse of political economy that culminates in John Stuart Mill. He wants his text to be accessible to all non-mathematicians. The principles of marginal utility are presented in a very didactic way inasmuch as every quantitative consideration is accompanied by long qualitative descriptions. He takes care to show that there is no gigantic gap between the quantitative and the qualitative approaches.

And what does Jevons share with other authors within Marginalism? He retains something from Adam Smith that is of extreme importance for uniting political economy under Marx's critique. The utilitarian calculation for balancing pleasure and pain in Bentham makes his treatise a study of an abstract human being in his/her struggle for survival. It is as if the hunter or fisher from Adam Smith's and Ricardo's theory had their behavior described using all the logic of marginal substitution. Jevons theorizes an abstract economy for Robinson Crusoe where every agent has a unique utility function, but in which everybody needs to make exchanges in an idealized market. This feature ensures that his approach naturalizes every aspect of the capitalist economic order. We find the same error in the other exponents of the Marginalist Revolution. This is the particular kind of error that we should focus on when criticizing the neoclassical school. To aim at specific features such as the utility theory of value, the focus on the consumer rather than on the laborer, or the mathematical language, is to miss a critical strike opportunity. The problem of neoclassical economics is not that it has other peripheral concepts that replace the classical concepts in Adam Smith's and Ricardo's writings. Its problem is that, just like the classical economists and the non-Marxian labor value theoreticians, it naturalizes the social relations of commodity, money, and capital.

The second author behind the rise of the consumer's theory of value is Carl Menger (1840–1921). His work, *Principles of Economics,* was published in German in 1871 in Vienna, Austria. The original title, *Grundsätze der Volkswirtschaftslehre,* employed the German expression for political economy, which is closer to 'national economy' than the English 'economics'. Jevons' starting point was the treatment of economics as a calculation of pain and pleasure, focusing on the perspective of the individual economic agent instead of the economy of the whole nation. Menger is even more explicit about focusing on the subjective perception of the individual. Even though the work's title in the original language points to the social and collective dimension of the economic system (Volkswirtschaft), Menger is an enthusiastic defender of methodological individualism.

According to Menger, Adam Smith's system was deficient on specific unexplored points that could be helpful to relate abstract theory to empirical observation. For Menger, the traditional sciences, such as chemistry, should inspire methods of studying political economy. Due to the great distance between natural and social sciences, it would be necessary to find the links connecting empirical facts with the generalizations of political economy. Menger is influenced by the illuminist tradition, which over-estimated the objectivity of natural phenomena. The elaboration of a theory should strictly follow concrete data. He intends to employ such a procedure of investigation in political economy. He announces that his work is constructed based on the empirical method of natural sciences and that it will hopefully succeed in demonstrating that 'the phenomena of economic life, like those of nature, are ordered strictly in accordance with definite laws' (Menger [1871] 2007, p. 48).

One of Menger's main concerns is to identify the regularity of political-economic phenomena from which we can derive principles of economic action. In his vision, this would avoid the normative bias that dominates political economy. When politics is embedded in economics all authors feel authorized to propose, in his/her own name or in the name of a group or a cause, what should be done in terms of economic policy. The philosophy of laissez-faire liberalism is a strong influence on Menger's thought. He thinks that individuals are free to select which economic activity they prefer. Accordingly, the economist should only observe the choices individuals make in order to find out the fundamental principles of economic science. His quest is to discover what explains why people act in one way and not in another. Political economy should not be a normative science of announcing how the economic organization of society should be, but a science of describing what it is based on the factual decisions and actions of the individuals.

It is easy to identify here a clear distinction that is common to neoclassicism. Normative considerations, both at the household (micro) level and national (macro) level are excluded. The task of the economist is to gather material data and to describe the choices being made. Menger proposes a hardcore positivist economics, eliminating everything that represents the proposition of economic policies. The economist is not allowed to interfere. Similar to Jevons, who proposed a name change from 'political economy' to 'economics', Menger argues that politics must be expelled from pure economic analysis.

Regarding the theory of value, Menger is remarkably close to Jevons, but he reaches the conclusion that value is founded on the utility of goods by a different route. In Jevons, the quantitative calculation of pain and pleasure was like a weight balance of high precision. It indicated at each instant a specific and determined quantity of utility that the individual 'possesses' given his/her concrete situation (represented by a basket of goods that could be lined up in an indifference curve when they accrue exactly the same quantity of utility). The utility function is defined for every conceivable combination of goods, and continuity is a strong feature. In Menger, we do not find the techniques of differential calculus used to solve the problem of programming the maximization of utility. Menger presents the principles of choice restricted by various conditions through a qualitative approach. Thus, one of the main characteristics of Menger's work, by comparison to that of the other exponents of the Marginalist Revolution, is the absence of quantitative tools in his book.

Mathematical calculation of definite quantities is not to be found in Menger's system. Here, all reasoning to describe the formation of value/prices derives from a qualitative development. Menger explains how goods are valued according to how well they meet human needs, that is, the value/price of things refers to their use values, more specifically, to how well the concrete properties that constitute the use value of things meet a certain human need.

In Menger's book we do not find a single mathematical exercise of comparison that expresses the magnitude of two distinct stocks of utility. Why not? The reason is that here it is only possible to classify an order of preference, without being able to calculate the distance between the baskets of goods that serve as reference points. Moreover, classification is a purely individual process that impedes any generalization of calculation of the type presented by Jevons. In Jevons' system, the calculations of individual welfare can be aggregated into a calculation of social welfare. It is possible to apply the principle of utility maximization to the whole society. This is the reason why Austrian economists will fight against the standard neoclassical theory of value with such ferocity in the socialist economic calculation debate. In Menger's framework, it is not possible to conceive a principle of utility maximization for the collective, but only for the individual, because there are no objective bounds that permit the transposition of the individual evaluation to the public sphere.[9]

Menger's presentation of the utility theory of value is influenced by a cartesian vision of cause and effect. The consumer is at the center, and everything exists in relation to the consumer, the point to which every item must move. This is the Austrian perspective that sees the entire chain of external goods that make up the economy from the point of view of the internal psychology of the consumer. The satisfaction of this consumer is the great dogmatic principle behind Menger's system. The means of production constitute only a transitory step on the path to meet the immediate needs of the consumer. The means of production are never thought of as the aim of the economic process. The concept of capital here, as in the rest of the neoclassical school, is always a means to something and not an end in itself. There is a hierarchy of all goods that end up in the possession of the consumer, the king of the economy. Say's law underlies Menger's entire work, since he does not admit that capitalism is an economic system whose purpose is not to meet human needs but rather to expand capital accumulation endlessly.

Among the first theoreticians of the Marginalist Revolution, Menger is important because of the ideological opposition towards socialism that has been derived from his system. His greatest follower, Eugen von Böhm-Bawerk, is a self-declared anti-socialist militant and is considered the founder of the Austrian school of economics. This current will eventually become separated from the neoclassical mainstream along the socialist economic calculation debate. I argue that this happened mostly because of a clever strategy of isolating the apologetic elements in the Marginalist Revolution during the calculation debate. Oskar Lange was one of the authors who contributed to the construction of such a strategy.[10]

---

9   The background to this divergence between Jevons and Menger is the controversy over the concepts of cardinal and ordinal utility. This is one of the distinctions between neoclassical mainstream economics and the Austrian school. See Angeli (2014) for an explanation of this distinction. On convergences and divergences between the cardinal and ordinal utility, see Mata (2007).

10   See Lange (1936) and (1937). The socialist economic calculation debate became a scholarly controversy after Mises (1920) argued that the socialist economy could not perform rational economic accounting. The first attempts to respond to Mises were made by Karl Polanyi, Eduard Heimann, and Bukharin (Boettke 2000). Then, another group of authors, including Taylor (1929), Dickinson (1933), Lerner (1934) and Knight (1936) tried to rebut Mises based on the neoclassical theory of price formation. They were following previous

León Walras (1834–1910) is the third and last member of the movement that brought the transition from classical to neoclassical political economy. His main work title is entitled *Elements of Pure Economics or the theory of social wealth* (in French, *Éléments d'économie politique pure, ou théorie de la richesse sociale*). It was published in 1874, three years after the books by Jevons and Menger. It is a compilation of Walras lectures while he was a professor at the University of Lausanne in Switzerland. The book is a compendium of what Walras thought would be an elementary course in pure rational economics that demands only a basic knowledge of mathematics, such as geometry, algebra and the first notions of analytical geometry in two dimensions. What distinguishes Walras from the other authors in the Marginalist Revolution is his abstract treatment of what he calls a 'pure' or 'rational' form of describing the economy. It is an economic model abstracted from all friction and disturbances that exist in the real world. Everything is conceived as forces interacting in an ideal system where there are no distractions to the determinant elements of the quantitative exchange relations of all goods which guarantees total equilibrium. Thus, while Menger remains distant from mathematical formalization and Jevons seeks to open the way to quantitative analysis by leaving room for qualitative description, Walras' methodology immediately passes from descriptive sentences to algebraic expressions.

Mathematics, a strong characteristic of neoclassical economics, is thus an outstanding feature of Walras' political economy. While Menger had put all his effort into a qualitative approach, Walras focuses on quantity only. Among the sacred trinity of the neoclassical revolution, only Jevons showed concern for combining both quantitative and qualitative analysis. It is important to notice that Walras is responsible for popularizing the notion of decreasing utility based on infinitesimal calculus, which requires mathematical functions with specific properties. It is a new level of formalization that abandons the intuitive explanation for the decline in the increase of utility accrued by one more unity consumed.

---

works by Walras ([1874] 1954), Pareto ([1906] 2014) and Barone (1908). Taking this line of reasoning to the ultimate level, Oskar Lange showed that Mises had to make a choice. He had either to admit that rational accounting under socialism was possible or to leave the arena of mainstream economics. Since Mises' followers were not willing to accept socialist ideas, they were expelled from the mainstream neoclassical School and formed the Austrian school of economics (Camarinha Lopes (2021b)). This was one of the most remarkable victories of Lange in the war against the capital apologetics that proliferate in economic science. I call Lange's strategy 'Langean anthropophagy'.

Walras' system is clearly ahistorical. It does not exist in any specific time or space. There is no relation to a concrete economy such as the economy of a particular nation in a certain epoch. It is a systemic view, which resembles in many aspects the theory of the physiocrats. His use of the term 'pure' to refer to his system means that he treats the economy in abstract generality, as an ideal system of useful items that are exchanged and that return as inputs for another round of the production process.

It is possible to notice some incongruencies just by pointing out minor divergences between the three authors of the Marginalist Revolution. Jevons and Menger had a view centered on the individual or consumer. Walras' conception of the totality of the system is clearly superior in this respect. Standard introductions to neoclassical economics do not start with the totality of a self-reproducing economic system, but with an abstract human being acting within an imaginary framework. S/he is alone and surrounded by natural factors of all kinds (land, water, plants, animals. etc.), *Homo economicus* struggles to survive according to the basics of mathematical optimization. There is no discussion about the choice of what must be maximized. Since utility is the basis of value, it is obvious that this Robinson Crusoe must act to increase his utility endlessly.

Jevons' and Walras' description of this game worked well because their program only had one individual. However, the economic reality is not one single castaway on one single island. In fact, we have millions of them. On one side, each one of them is isolated in his/her private sphere. On the other side, they are all connected in space and time through the entity called market. How should we transfer the individual calculation of minimizing utility loss and maximizing gains to an economy where the population is trapped in the same net of commodity social relations?

This is the question behind Walras' challenge. In other words, how should one present in mathematical language the notion of general equilibrium that is supposed to replace the old invisible hand of Adam Smith? Imagine millions of Crusoes exchanging their private products of labor with each other in a virtual environment. Since everyone goes through an identical process (we only have differences in quality, not in quantity), the system achieves a stability that cannot really exist. What matters here is that Walras is not concerned with any specific Crusoe, but with the totality of the interactions between all Crusoes. This systemic character of Walras is important because it intends to show that individual struggle to fulfill self-interest necessarily leads to the construction of the common good. This is precisely one of the main theses of the classical system.

The utility theory of value has an element of social support in Walras' system that is not as clear as in Jevons' (whereas in Menger's system the social or public dimension is entirely left aside, and all attention is directed at the private sphere). Because of this, the consumer's value theory in Walras has a different flavor. Its explicit consideration of the totality of the economy makes it easier to see that the consumer is at the same time the producer. Moreover, the liberal credo of the invisible hand can easily be related to economic planning. As a matter of fact, there is a curious resemblance between the perfect competitive scheme and a fully planned system. Many decades later, the socialist economic calculation debate showed that there is a formal similarity between the capitalist and socialist economies when we describe them in the pure language of balance equations. Input-output economics, which was developed and expanded through the works of Wassily Leontief, demonstrated the universality of such approach. The Walrasian auctioneer is the mirror-image of the central planner. Every individual action is in conformity with meeting the collective goal of increasing the value of some social utility function. The thesis of formal similitude revealed by the socialist economic calculation debate is another way to recognize that both paths of economics outside Marx's political economy (utopian Ricardian socialism and neoclassical economics) are parallel roads that later converge into a dead end: the idealization of a perfect society based on the commodity social relationship.

To summarize, the work of each one of the key authors in the Marginalist Revolution triad has its own distinctive characteristics. Jevons, Menger and Walras presented at the same time new systems for theoretical political economy and influenced the future development of the field. It is also important to consider their common features as well as their individualities. The exercise of de-homogenizing their work has the purpose of showing that the Marginalist Revolution is not a simple transformation. It involves many more authors and views that we cannot deal with here. Furthermore, there are complex elements of technical and political order behind the Marginalist Revolution that should be studied with greater caution.

From the standpoint we defend, the neoclassical current should not be rejected because of its intensive use of mathematics, the methodological individualism, Bentham's utilitarianism, or because of any isolated characteristic that illustrates superficial changes in the classical system. Of course, we may criticize all these non-essential features and so strengthen the heterodox vision of economics in opposition to the mainstream of economic science that was consolidated in the 20th century. But if we want to construct a coherent framework for economics at the side of the working class, it is essential that we unite both the classical and neoclassical eras of economic thought in the same sample when we present Marx's contribution to political economy. We need to replicate with the neoclassical authors the approach that Marx took towards the classical authors. Thus, we must identify the common ground between these two groups before entering the world of Marx's *Capital*.

3 Output as a Relation between Human and Nature

Between the end of the 19th century and the Second World War various authors developed the works of Jevons, Menger and Walras further.[11] The naturalization of the specific social relations of commodity production became more and more evident. Moreover, the focus on price and not on value made it more difficult to deal with the issues of production. Consequently, all relevant questions around exploitation were left aside. Reactionary forces knew how to seize this opportunity.

One of the first and most influential theoreticians in the expansion and consolidation of Marginalism is the Austrian economist Eugen von Böhm-Bawerk (1851–1914). He tries to create a theory of interest to negate the conclusions of all socialist economists. His attack also targets Karl Marx. What is his project? Taking his cue from the Marginalist Revolution of the 1870s, which had diverted attention from production towards the market, and building on Menger's theory, Böhm-Bawerk presents a system in which the concept of capital is totally unrelated to social relations. Other marginalist authors and the classical economists also had a similar notion of capital as a tool. But Böhm-Bawerk makes it explicit that capital is a relation of the kind human-nature and not a relation of the kind human-nature-human. The political corollary of this project is to make it much harder to connect capital incomes to any asymmetrical social relation of power. Moreover, this new perspective implies a tremendous change regarding the surplus approach. It is true that the physiocrat legacy of the surplus approach had already been forgotten by the early marginalists. Nonetheless, depending on how one conceives the utility theory of value, material and objective determinations can still find their place in the system.[12] This is why Böhm-Bawerk needs to widen the rupture with

---

11   Authors from this period who contributed to the consolidation of the new theory of value in economics are Eugen von Böhm-Bawerk, Friedrich von Wieser, Alfred Marshall, John Bates Clark, Irving Fisher, Knut Wicksell, Philip H. Wicksteed, Vilfredo Pareto and Enrico Barone.

12   For an approach that unites the subjective and objective approaches to value theory, see Hagendorf (2014), who merges the utility and labor theories of value. A fusion of these

the physiocratic surplus approach by promoting the subjectivist system of Menger. His goal, however, is not easy to achieve. How can he reject the surplus approach, the perspective on production and labor, without falling back on the mercantilist concept of profit upon alienation that was unable to explain the creation of new value?

When we see the conditions of Böhm-Bawerk's problem, we realize the complexity of the task. There are at least three challenges. First, production must be considered and have its place in the theory. At the same time, exploitation of humans by other humans needs to be erased. This requires a kind of description of the production process that is far from the empirical reality of capitalist production. Böhm-Bawerk's consideration of the labor process is thus wholly disconnected from historical and empirical facts. It is a presentation that is entirely focused on the logical connection between an abstract human being and his/her natural surroundings.

Second, if capital is to exist, it is necessary to present the phenomenon of interest rates as a strictly natural phenomenon. Accordingly, political economy should no longer deal with society, but with nature. Political economy becomes the science of the relation between human and nature and not a science of how humans modify nature within a specific social setting of cultural and religious institutions. Of course, this was already present in the earliest stages of the Marginalist Revolution. Indeed, classical political economy always tended to naturalize the capitalist mode of production. But now, Böhm-Bawerk explicitly admits that the aim of political economy is not to understand how different social institutions lead to different economic systems, but to describe how a 'rational' human interacts directly with nature.

Third, it is necessary to destroy the theory that labor creates value. The labor theory of value held by the pre-Marx socialists was so strong that it was considered natural that labor created value. In fact, I am in agreement with Böhm-Bawerk in this third task, although for the opposite reason. It is indeed necessary to denaturalize the notion that labor creates value. But while Böhm-Bawerk wants to do this to weaken the working class and to replace a naturalized theory of value by another naturalized theory of value, I want to do it to explain that there cannot be a natural theory of value of any kind. In sum, Böhm-Bawerk's challenge is to defend interest from the socialist rage by erecting a system based upon the most fetishistic form of the commodity social relation, namely interest-bearing capital.

---

two theories is possible due to their common characteristic of naturalizing social relations of production.

How does he do it? Böhm-Bawerk believes that the correspondence between the three factors of production (labor, land, and equipment) and its respective revenues (salary, land rent and profit) allow a unique concept of capital. For him, every increase of value in the financial sphere would be the result of adopting superior indirect methods of production. But capital is not only a synonym for the means of production. There is another aspect that productivity theories, as he calls a whole branch of theories of value, do not consider. Capital is also like a gravitational force that attracts value, regardless of its direct contribution to production. Böhm-Bawerk departs from the empirical fact that capital 'acts like a magnet, drawing a portion of the national product to itself, and delivering it over to its owner'. He concludes that capital 'appears, in a word, as the source of Interest' (Böhm-Bawerk [1889] 1930, p. 1).

Instead of separating appearance from essence, Böhm-Bawerk follows the immediate forms of capital and opens the way to conceptualize them as forces of nature. In the end, time will be decisive and the ultimate determinant of interest, exactly as Marx anticipated. There is an absolute and complete naturalization of the commodity social relation. Nonetheless, the foundations for this naturalization seem solid. Why? By not questioning the institutional social and historical circumstances, the analyst is forced to theorize economics from the standpoint of Robinson Crusoe.

Because of this, there is no internal logical incongruity in Böhm-Bawerk's discourse. The problem is that all socially determined categories overlap with the general categories in any economic system. For example, output and commodity become synonymous, as well as means of production and capital. Output and means of production are general categories of economic science and can be applied to any mode of production, whereas commodity and capital are specific social forms of these general categories that exist only within the frame of a special manner of producing and distributing. The concept of capital based on time comes from this conflation. Robinson Crusoe invents tools and becomes more and more distant from nature in progressive stages. Robinson Crusoe no longer needs to produce using his bare hands because he can use a stone, then a knife, then a fishing rod, then a computer and so on. We could say that the greater the productive forces, the greater is the force of capital. The problem of Böhm-Bawerk's system is not its internal logic, but its inability to distinguish the cultural institutions that allow the emergence of capitalism in time and space from the mathematical optimization that describes the pure movement of capital.

It is interesting to note that in Böhm-Bawerk's system capital is the result of a certain action. This action is preceded by an idea of how to use a new method of interaction with nature to obtain an output. Böhm-Bawerk thinks that technological innovation in a capitalist society is the result of individual minds who have first discovered innovations, as if each member of society worked alone.[13] It is clear that the historical aspect of the development of the productive forces is entirely replaced by the purely logical aspect of this progress. The social network and division of labor necessary to boost the scientific revolution are absent in Böhm-Bawerk's scheme. Idealism is present in every line of his work. 'Economy' and 'capitalism' are conflated—a common feature that unites classical and neoclassical political economy. Böhm-Bawerk actively adopts this error as the baseline of investigation.

In its initial stages, the Austrian school (represented here by Böhm-Bawerk) ignores the concrete trajectory of human civilization. It invents a myth to explain the origin of capital. In fact, both classical and neoclassical approaches do not investigate how capital emerged historically, but only logically. This is a huge deficiency if we want to understand that capital is not only a movement of value increase, but also a social order that came into existence in time and space.

One of the explanations for the dramatic separation between the historical and logical perspectives is the strong influence of the so-called Methodenstreit, the battle of methods in economics. This separated the German historical school from the Austrian economists and created a great division between economists who focused on history and economists who focused on logic. The Marginalist Revolution became dominated by the logical-deductive approach and all consideration of the concrete phenomena of human history was discarded as being the domain of heterodox economics or economic history (and not economic theory). Böhm-Bawerk's presentation of the concept of capital shows precisely the general problem of naturalizing a social setting that is historically determined. In other words, Böhm-Bawerk's system indicates how classical and neoclassical political economy are the same when they think of the economy as if it could not be anything other than capitalism.

If we set aside the social relations that govern production and distribution, we can say that the aim of any economy is to provide the means for the material reproduction of society. Accordingly, Böhm-Bawerk thinks about capital as a pure means to achieve the goal of material reproduction. So, capital and all

---

13   For a provocative discussion of the relationship between technology and capitalism, see Cockshott's (2019), especially chapter 5. Cockshott argues that the initial technological novelties behind the rise of capitalism come from non-mercantile environments. This is an important point because it emphasizes the conscious processes that lead to scientific discoveries and their application in production, in contrast to what the traditional/ Eurocentric historiography of Marxism says about the scientific revolution in modernity.

equipment are thought of as purely the means used to meet human needs, as if capitalism were an organized economic system with the purpose of fulfilling the utility functions of the members of society. But, unlike other theoreticians of utility value theory, Böhm-Bawerk argues that capital is not just an instrument of production and that it does not act independently. It does not move if humans do not act. Thus, he recognizes that we cannot talk about the productive forces of capital or about its capacity to create.

The active element of wealth creation lies in humans. Capital is a mechanism for capturing natural and human forces and for accumulating them through time. Thus, Böhm-Bawerk concludes, in opposition to the thesis that capital also works, that capital is not autonomously productive. This is important because it clashes with the traditional view of neoclassical economics, which is that capital functions in the same way as labor. The standard vision of mainstream neoclassical economics is that all factors of production have the capacity to create value, and that it is possible to know how much each of them has contributed to the total production of wealth.

So, what exactly is capital for Böhm-Bawerk? In chapter IV of *The Positive Theory of Capital*, called The Theory of the Formation of Capital, Böhm-Bawerk pictures 'some Robinson Crusoe thrown on a lonely shore without either tools or weapons' (Böhm-Bawerk [1889] 1930, p. 101). To survive, initially, he has only the direct forces embodied in his organism. He must use his own hand, for example, to gather fruits. He develops this scenario to present what is a very peculiar idea about how capital emerges as the result of a rational choice from the perspective of the economy of resources.

When all effort is needed just to survive, there is no possibility of rising above subsistence level. Then, Böhm-Bawerk supposes that there emerges a new possibility. For some reason, Crusoe does not have to employ all his energy in the struggle to survive. So, he now has some extra time. This new scenario allows him to make a choice regarding the size of his economy.

Crusoe has now two options: either he can gather fruits for 10 hours a day and guarantees himself a decent supply of food or he can do the same task for only 9 hours and acquire the amount needed so as not to starve. In this last case, he could use 1 hour to dedicate his energy to the construction of utensils, such as a bow and arrows. Reduction in consumption and increase in investment lead to an accumulation of forces inside the means of production. Lithic flake marks the first stage of capital formation. According to Böhm-Bawerk, this technology was invented after a rational decision to reallocate energy away from the production of the means of subsistence towards producing the indirect means to increase those means of subsistence. Capital formation is presented as a conscious, autonomous, and individual process related to human

rationality regarding the economic use of resources. Improvement of the indirect means to obtain the necessary items for survival generates a future superior stage for Crusoe. As the productive forces develop, he can obtain more
output in a shorter period. We could say that necessary labor time diminishes
and productivity increases. In Böhm-Bawerk's terminology, this effect shows
that capital is being formed. Here, capital is not a social form of organizing
production and distribution, but the pure logic of productivity augmentation
behind the infinite logic of capital accumulation applied to a Robinson Crusoe
kind of economy.

It is interesting to notice that the concept of labor is always present in Böhm-
Bawerk's example. The active element of the production process lies with the
human being. Capital may be understood as a mere instrument mastered by
this human being. How did this human being do it? By adjusting his own consumption over time to achieve more highly developed stages of productive
forces. It is a tale of the origin of capital based on pure logical reasoning. No
consideration is given to the empirical data that assert that humans have never
lived alone, but always in herds, in collective groups. Böhm-Bawerk's extreme
individualist perspective shows that the fundamentals of capital formation
can be told as if it was a purely deliberate choice by a conscious individual.
This clever Robinson Crusoe has learned that he can increase his own productivity by adopting certain behaviors and creating tools. It is as if capital formation has the concrete purpose of facilitating life on Earth. The abstraction from
reality leads to an idea in which capital is not a history of power and control by
humans over nature *and* other humans, but a story of power and control of a
single human over nature only.

The focus on the individual and his/her subjective preferences was already
strong in the Marginalist Revolution. Böhm-Bawerk takes it to the next level.
Political economy is no longer concerned with the study of societies, but with
the study of the oikos of a single agent in the wilderness. All the realia considered by previous authors, such as overseas trade, manufacture, labor division, industrial revolution, population growth and concentration, disappear.
The overwhelming interdependence of a massive number of salary workers
simply vanishes when Robinson Crusoe becomes the standard for analysis.
Methodological individualism is too far from the real facts of human history
and it cannot explain how capital was formed. Nevertheless, it can describe
how the abstract economic system of the *Homo economicus* would behave
under the logic of the infinite expansion of value.

In Böhm-Bawerk's world, there is total coincidence between the general
economic laws and the specific social norms that frame a real economy in
determinate rules. While general economic laws refer to all normal natural

laws that production and distribution must obey, specific social economic laws refer to the traditions and cultural institutions constructed by humans in concrete space and time. A certain quantity of bread can feed only a certain quantity of humans because of the constraints imposed by the laws of nature. One cannot produce wine with only water as input. Biology, chemistry, and physics govern all processes of the real economy.[14] The other side of the economy has to do with social rules of appropriation and labor division. People modify them through a historical process that enables new economic systems. Thus, while general economic laws cannot be violated in any mode of production, specific social economic laws are different according to the mode of production involved. Non-Marxian economics merges these two different sets of economic laws into the same framework and therby generates much confusion (Lange 1935).

Is it possible to separate these two sets and rescue positive contributions from utility value theories? If we remember that non-Marxian socialist economics also tend to fuse these two different dimensions of economic analysis, why should we discard (vulgar) utility theories of value and embrace (vulgar) labor theories of value? At this level of investigation, both are equally limited and erroneous. So, if it is acceptable to take elements that are true from one side, it must be acceptable to take elements that are true from the other side as well. The relation between human and nature is fundamental for any economic theory. We must never forget, however, that individuals act and think within a definite social system that has grown through time in a concrete region.

---

14   Likewise, there cannot be transformation of matter without the passing of time. Some authors develop the utility theory of value towards a time theory of value. For this group, value becomes almost identical to time. Note that the magnitude of value is not related to *labor* time in this framework, but to time alone. Böhm-Bawerk was one of the pioneers of this kind of theory of value. According to this view, time preferences are behind capital and interest rates. In the end, interest exists because time passes and money becomes strongly associated to time (See Marx [1894] 2010, pp. 230, *Capital* book 3, Chapter 21: Interest-Bearing Capital). Time has always been considered in the classical tradition, but only because time is necessary for production. Friedrich von Wieser ([1889] 1893) Knut Wicksell ([1893] 1954), Irving Fisher (1930) and Hayek ([1941] 2009) continued to develop a theory of value based on time. For an insightful critique of this strand of the utility theory of value, see Lange (1936b), who explains that interest rates cannot be a purely time-based phenomenon. Marx had anticipated that a time theory of value could emerge from the naturalist approach to economic science. There are internal controversies among time value theoreticians, but it is sufficient to conceive of them as a uniform group within the strand of the utility theory of value in this book. For alternative approaches to the Austrian paradigm of value, see John Bates Clark ([1907] 2013) and the works of Frank Knight, who responded to Lange's critique (Knight (1937)).

The complete picture of the *Homo economicus* forgets that Robinson Crusoe is only a didactical resource to explain the basics of resource allocation. If we are aware that neoclassical economists never question the infinite movement of expansion—because of methodological limitations, or even because they are class-conscious defenders of the capitalist order—there is interesting material that can be appropriated. All quantitative relations between variables and even the qualitative differences between distinct alternatives can be described through the ahistorical and naturalistic approach of neoclassical economics.[15]

But if we are looking for a solid methodological basis on which to distinguish capitalism from other modes of production, we need to look elsewhere. Theories of value based on utility or subjective evaluation, which focus on the individual acting in the market, do not allow us to think outside the commodity social relation. Accordingly, commodity and output become the same thing, which appears as the result of human action over nature, as if there could be no other system of organizing the economy except through the market. All historical and social institutions, such as private property, are viewed as given. Robinson Crusoe is a *Homo economicus* inside the matrix: he/she cannot see the code behind the program in which he/she lives. Commodity fetishism dominates everything.

4   The Naturalization of the Utility Value Theory

The Marginalist Revolution is not a homogeneous process of change. The work of each marginalist author has unique features when we consider all the details as part of the history of economic thought. Accordingly, despite all the similarities that justify the view of the Marginalist Revolution as homogeneous, there is a scenery full of variety after the end of classical political economy. Just as classical political economy was not formed from the work of a homogenous sample of authors, so also the neoclassical economic era is full of various economists that converge in some respects but diverge in others.

Neoclassical economics is not properly a school of economic thought, but a period in the history of economic science when most economists agree with some methodological approaches. For our purpose, we need to identify what is the common ground between classical and neoclassical political economy.

---

15   For a study on Robinson Crusoe as a method common to both pre-marginalist political economy and neoclassical economics, see Karagöz (2014).

By doing so, we will be able to show that Marx's critique of political economy is not directed only at the economic thinking of the 19th century and earlier, but to all economic thinking that naturalizes and justifies the status quo of any given economic organization.

The core of any investigation related to material interests must lie in a theory of value. Let us expand the description of classical and neoclassical economics. Together they embrace all variations of non-Marxian economic thought, from left to right, across a relatively large period. With the exception of a few authors who would be classified as anthropologists, historians, or social scientists rather than economists, they all err with respect to the same point. The error is to naturalize the commodity social relationship. We have seen that socialist economists before Marx naturalized the labor theory of value and could not solve the enigma of the law of value. If labor was the ultimate source of value, why do laborers not have control over the whole economic output? When trying to overcome this limitation, they offered a solution based on the fundamentals of private property. 'From each according to his/her capacities, to each according to his/her contribution' is the universal principle underpinning commodity social relations of production and distribution. Equality here is only equality in the sense that everyone is a private proprietor. How does this same naturalization occur in the utility theory of value?

The utility approach makes this mistake when it takes the exercise of Robinson Crusoe to its ultimate level. It transposes the logic of quantitative relations between use values to an economy of only one individual. If total labor is used to meet all different needs and the individual is satisfied with this allocation of his/her energy, then there is a strange coincidence: the perspectives of labor and of utility generate the same set of exchange values for all use values. It is curious that both antagonistic theories of value admit a similar reasoning for explaining the movement in relative values of all useful items. We must understand that, according to the pure logic of quantitative analysis, all theories of values are able to describe accurately how exchange relations are formed. They all have reasonably good explanations for how useful goods are valued and how these valuations may change.

Nonetheless, no matter how accurately a theory of value describes the dynamics of quantitative relations of exchange, it cannot explain why it uses a certain quality parameter to measure quantities. The problem here is that, in the absence of social relations, there are no historical and institutional determinants to explain why a specific quality has been chosen and not another. It is important to remember that Marx indicated right away in the third paragraph of the opening chapter of *Capital* that the choice of the qualitative element responsible for measuring the quantity of value is a sociohistorical process:

> To discover the various uses of things is the work of history. So also is the
> establishment of socially-recognized standards of measure for the quan-
> tities of these useful objects.
>
> MARX ([1867] 2015), p. 27

If we set aside this historical and social dimension, there are no real parameters to justify why a specific standard of measure should be used and not
another. In the absence of this dimension, all theories of value become theories of *quantity of value* and all are equally valid.

Why have some authors chosen labor while others have chosen utility?
When Robinson Crusoe is our standard framework in political economy, any
theory of value whatsoever will work. It is important to note that this kind of
error is not necessarily the result of a conscious procedure, because it derives
from commodity fetishism. Both the labor theory of value and the utility theory
of value describe quantitative relations of exchange between useful items as if
these relations were entirely given by the conditions of interaction between
human and nature. In fact, there is also another aspect that influences these
relations that are related to the rules of how humans relate to other humans.
Instead of making it explicit that economic relations are the result of two different kinds of interactions (human-nature and human-human), naturalizing
theories of value considers only one dimension. They only see the process of
the economy as the interaction of human(s) with nature. Because of this, value
is always something purely physical or individually psychological. It is never
influenced by the specific historical conditions that frame how humans relate
to other humans.

So, instead of being the point of departure for investigating the history of
useful objects that became private property, value becomes a purely material
or even corporeal relation. It expresses with precision how difficult it is to produce or obtain each useful item based on a comparison between the objective measure of available productive forces and the subjective measure of how
each item meets one's utility function. Both pre-Marx socialists and the theoreticians of utility value mix the general laws of the economy with the specific
laws that refer to an economy centered on the market, as Oskar Lange showed
(Lange ([1959] 1963)).

If the market is the center of the economic system and the entire output is
transformed into commodity and money, how can we conceptualize capital
and its infinite movement of expansion as a specific kind of economic system?
The standard behavior of an agent in the market becomes the normal case for
human behavior in any period of history. He/she acts to increase the quantity
of value in his/her property. The agent struggles to augment utility, well-being,

or any other qualitative element connected to what utilitarians call pleasure. In the case of a labor theory of value, this means the continuous increase of the labor stock of the economy. The infinite search for more can be characterized as the infinite search for what is specified by any given theory of value as the source of value. Thus, Robinson Crusoe inherits all the characteristics of the automata operating the logic of capital accumulation without end.

There is an awkward convergence in that both naturalized theories of value, labor, and utility, fuse the contradictory sides of the commodity: use value and value are treated as if there could be systematic coincidence between them. It is as if the centrifugal force of capital dynamics acting to amplify the divergence between use value and value is permanently countered by a centripetal force holding them together. The logic of value expansion is artificially forced to serve the goal of meeting the needs of individual humans. So, the market economy appears as if the will of both buyers and sellers is the ultimate gravitational force holding the system together. Consumption controls demand. It is the same kind of arrangement as the law of débouchés of Jean Baptiste Say. The economy is represented as being pulled by people's needs, and not pushed by capital's impetus for infinite growth.

Most authors forget the fact that the economic system is dominated by the law of value and that its tendency is to increase value and not use value. Ideally, value expansion enables the continuation of *use value* expansion. But when both sides of the commodity (use value and value) do not grow together, tension increases. It is like a pressure cooker: a system that sustains the difference of pressure between the inside and the outside. Capitalist crisis is like an explosion, which restores the balance violently. Even when a crisis interrupts the capitalist reproduction cycle, the cycle is soon restored and value expansion proceeds further at a higher level. Theoreticians of value who think that the law of value is only an instrument to direct resources towards needs through a completely decentralized scheme forget that the very logic of the commodity leads to the opposite. The law of value in its full developed form puts value at the center and use value at the periphery. Infinite accumulation of capital is the necessary result if there are no social mechanisms that impede the systematic transformation of money into capital.

In those cases where theoreticians of value do not forget about this, they mentally create these mechanisms. They make individual decisions artificially match collective societal needs, as Mandeville and Smith did. Accordingly, abstract solutions to the mystery of social cohesion based on the principles of the market continue to spread through the 19th and 20th centuries in economic thought. Furthermore, when economists recognize that an imagined solution is not enough, they develop concrete proposals of economic policy for the regulation of capitalism. This is so in the case of John Maynard Keynes. If the impetus of value expansion is accompanied by the expansion of production of useful goods that can be sold and transformed back to money, then the circuit is not interrupted, and an equilibrated trajectory of expansion can be designed.

Having utility at the center of the system means that the economy always has the purpose of meeting defined needs. Similarly, value means how well these needs are fulfilled. The phenomena of prices indicate that the exchange relations and the consumer's actions have only one explanation: value is measured by the subjective evaluation of how the useful item accrues utility. Deviations between price and value show disparities in evaluation because everyone has individual preferences. Here, the law of value also exists, but it does not relate directly to the content of labor in each useful good. It derives from the movement of production to match the demands of all market agents, who struggle to serve the consumer-king. Because of this, the commodity becomes a synonym of 'output produced to meet a specific human need'. Social relations of private property appear as natural things. It is as if the pattern of production and distribution could only follow a blind rule that assures meeting all needs through the decentralized, homogeneous, and equal mechanism of the market. The invisible hand guarantees that everything will go fine, and all the positive aspects of the market will prevail over its negative aspects.

5   Desideratum of the Marginalist Revolution: Simple Commodity
     Production

Mainstream pro-capitalist economics is the offspring of classical political economy. The marginalist approach developed at the margins of the most famous treatises on classical political economy. It became central from the 1870s onwards. Politically, the Marginalist Revolution represents the forces against socialism, and it selected the labor theory of value to be its flag in the battle of economics. As I have argued, however, the Marginalist Revolution arrives at the same contradictory impasse as Ricardian socialists. Because of the methodological error of naturalizing their respective theories of value, both strands idealize an economic system of equal agents that are trapped in commodity fetishism.

It is important to remember that the difference between these two paths—the labor theory of value and the utility theory of value—only became clear after the definitive end of the classical era of economics. It is only after many authors abandon the old consensus of the theory of value that formed around

Adam Smith that we can clearly see two distinct alternative theories of value competing for supremacy. Before this critical point, there were various ways to reconcile the two perspectives. This fact is further evidence that the rupture between the classical and neoclassical eras is not an insignificant one. This transition constitutes both a technical and political change.

It is not so complicated to combine different theories of value in epochs of social stability. The junction of the labor theory of value with the utility theory of value is a longstanding project underlying the writings of many value theoreticians. Both objective and subjective approaches to value are valid because they express the two sides pressing the exchange relations that refer to the technical coefficients of production (how much of a use value is necessary to create another use value) as well as to individual desires (how much of a use value I am willing to give away in exchange for another use value). Values and prices refer to these two dimensions that coexist and need to have their place in any theory of value claiming to be complete and coherent. Alfred Marshall, for example, represents this kind of middle solution for the new paradigm launched in the 1870s. Marshall's scissor refers to the idea that a symmetrical solution has great potential to reconcile opposing views.

One of the first authors who openly tried to merge labor and utility during the conflict between economists and the socialist movement was the Irish political and philosophical writer William Thompson (1775–1833). Thompson was a social reformer whose main influences were the labor theory of value, utilitarianism, and the philosophy of the cooperative movement under the leadership of Robert Owen (Hunt 1981, p. 172).

Individual preferences and costs of production are also combined in Jeremy Bentham's system. Bentham reconsidered the problem of the invisible hand and admitted that, if State intervention leads to a greater level of collective utility, then it would be justified. Having utility as the central parameter for value judgements can thus bring close connections to socialist discourse. Social wellbeing is as important as the wellbeing of an individual person. Moreover, in the beginning of the 19th century, the idea that individual interests necessarily coincide with social interests is no longer accepted as it was earlier. Accordingly, the utilitarian approach could be applied not only to a particular member of society, but also to the whole social body.[16]

---

16   For a presentation of neoclassical economics and its connections to socialist ideas, see Steedman (1995) and Bockman (2011). Welfare economics, a branch of neoclassical mainstream economics, may be regarded as the developed form of this collectivist approach to the principles of utility maximization. See Pareto ([1906] 2014) and Pigou ([1920] 1932).

So utilitarianism does not reject a collectivist view. It is not a philosophy of pure individualism, but can also become a collectivist mantra. Many heterodox economists claim that utilitarianism and individualism are so strongly tied together that there could be no social considerations. If we look closer, however, we notice that there is an entire branch of mainstream neoclassical thought dedicated to the economics of social wellbeing. Accordingly, the dividing line has nothing to do with the opposition between individual and collective approaches. As I argue, the distinction that really matters is related to whether the theory of value is naturalized or not.

In accordance with this broad understanding of the utilitarian approach, Thompson attacks the prevailing structure of wealth distribution in the early 19th century. In his view, the high concentration of wealth and inequality in capitalist countries generates a negative balance of total pleasure or utility for the whole community. The pattern of distribution was a regular cause of suffering for the entire society, because huge disparities between the wealthy and the poor had negative impacts on social wellbeing. Consequently, an economic policy of distribution that aimed at a greater degree of income and wealth equality could be easily justified based on the philosophy of utilitarianism.

The parallels between the utility and the labor perspectives on value are clear here. By defending a certain kind of egalitarianism, William Thompson promotes a subtle alliance between the utility theory of value and the labor theory of value. Labor creates wealth. Wealth has the capacity to raise utility. So, both entities determine value. Labor initiates a process capable of satisfying needs through the increase of wealth. The syncretism of both theories of value avoids the contradiction between the objective and subjective sides in the science of value. Thompson's attention to the brutal shock of a wealthy society having such a high level of poverty is decisive for his defense of social reform. If the State takes from the rich and gives to the poor, the level of utility for the whole society will increase.

Nevertheless, another path towards this higher stage of social wellbeing was conceivable. Thompson also thought that a hypothetical case of perfect market competition without any State intervention would generate the desired maximum of total collective utility. This is exactly the standard argument of basic mainstream neoclassical economics. Liberty of action in an environment where no agent has market power should be capable of sustaining the ideal economy. The reality, however, is far removed from this. The exchange

Following Oskar Lange, I endorse the approach that seeks to locate the common ground between neoclassicism and socialism. For a critique on this view, see Dobb (1969).

of commodities is not a process made up of entirely free acts of cooperation, because many of these acts are objectively imposed by the economic weakness of millions of tiny unities. Thompson feels, for example, that the salary worker has only one commodity to sell, while others are proprietors of innumerous commodities of various degrees of complexity.

The asymmetrical relation behind capital and labor is easy to notice. What is the solution? Following the rules of equivalent value, Thompson finds that the society of just exchanges can only exist if workers have their own capital, i.e., their own means of production. They can then reproduce without being forced to work for a salary. They do not have to be in a state of autarky and can specialize in a particular area. Necessary items that are not self-produced can be obtained in the market, through exchange. In this situation, everyone would have the same amount of economic force, or, at least, there would be no great difference among proprietors. Free competition would then reinforce the tendency to equality, and everyone could have similar opportunities to guarantee his/her economic wellbeing. But what kind of society is this?

This society is that of simple commodity production. It is the same outcome as that produced by the naturalized labor theory of value. Each member of society represents an economic unity that operates without direct contact with other units. Afterwards, all members meet at the market with their respective outputs that are exchanged according to the individual analysis of how well they meet needs. The subjective judgement behind each transaction complements the objective conditions that each producer has experienced in his/her private unity. If homogeneity is high, no one has sufficient power to influence price levels and there is no coercion. All exchange relations contribute towards reaching maximum utility in the individual and collective spheres. Based on this reasoning, (which is not very different from the invisible hand logic of Mandeville and Adam Smith), it is possible to reach an ideal situation in which the greatest quantity of utility for all derives from the free actions of self-interested individuals. Everything is regulated by one principle alone: the law of value.

It is crucial to remember that simple commodity production is an abstract model. It is an abstraction with intriguing characteristics. It seems to be an idealized equivalent of communist equality but is founded on its opposite principle: private property. It is the last station on the journey of economic science before it reaches Marx. It is the last systemic contradiction expressing the ultimate boundary between two mutually repelling modes of production. Simple commodity production is an analytical invention derived from the logical development of the commodity. It models a society where all social relations are based on exchange relations of private property that follow the ideology of equal rights for all humans. Such a society has never existed in practice. It is true that the exchange of commodities and markets have a long history before capitalism. But private property and interest rates exist long before there is a regularity of exchange that can support output reproduction in the form of commodity. This means that there has never been a real, concrete situation in which the law of value operates as the classical economists conceive it. Simple commodity production is neither an historical stage nor a coherent logical step in explaining the formation of capitalism. It is merely a picture of the bourgeois socialist ideal based on the core elements of capital relations of production: private property and the logic of infinite value accumulation. It is the ultimate contradictory result of the antagonistic naturalized theories of value.

Simple commodity production is not the correct solution for the challenges of scientific political economy. It is an illusion that tries to justify the birth of socialism based on the essential principles of capitalism. The equality behind the circuit C-M-C (commodity-money-commodity) is unstable because of the contradiction between use value and value. The only way to avoid this is through a mechanism that ties the production of value to an equivalent production of use value. If every impulse towards value accumulation can be directed to the production of useful items that find their consumers, then there is no break in the circuit of capital, at least in theory. The private impetus to use the social force of money to accumulate abstract wealth can be controlled only by the power of imagination.

This produces a strange result: a society of equal members based on the premise, of which the member as unconscious, that each one has a role and a bond to the collective totality. Each Crusoe is an island without any objective relation to any other island. Simple commodity production is tricky, because it is the portal to the world of commodity fetishism, of naturalizing private property. Bourgeois socialism is the pinnacle of this development.

There are similarities between the simple mercantile society of the labor theory of value and of the utility theory of value. Both theories of value have market egalitarianism as a common basis. They converge on the rules defined by the law of value for organizing production and distribution. Value is the center around which everything moves in both theories. They believe value has the capacity to unify labor and utility because they picture a competitive market that would enforce the meeting of social needs.

Both roads lead to the same point, to the last stage in the development of bourgeois equality. The authors of each theory of value have their individual elements, but they all share the same characteristic of making moral judgements about the how the economy is organized. The debate about the superiority of capitalism or socialism leads to the end of (classical) political economy because the polarization between theoreticians is no longer a matter of scientific debates, but of the simply political defense of material interests.

How does this outcome relate to the problem of value? Although there is an evident political chasm between these two theories of value, it would be a mistake to adopt either one of them. The classical labor theory of value and the neoclassical theory of value are equally wrong, even though they represent opposed political forces. The attention of value theoreticians was entirely absorbed by the question of quantity. They tried to explain why values/prices had specific magnitudes. There was no deep engagement with the question of why they chose labor or utility to be the qualitative parameter for measuring value. This is their error. They want to explain how quantitative relations of exchange are formed without acknowledging that this presupposes the choice of a qualitative element. They do not admit that their choice of qualitative element arises from a political positioning in class struggle. Marx's critical argument regarding the theory of value is not based on any problem in the quantitative determination of value, even though this determination is fundamental for conceptualizing the law of value and the transition from the market to a planned economy. Marx wants to show that the choice of qualitative element that explains value creation depends on the position of the value theoretician in the class struggle.

When authors focus only on the quantitative determination of value, they cannot escape the narrow confines of classical political economy. Market and capitalism become natural systems of economic organization. They treat all the fundamentals that allow the law of value to come into existence as if they were natural institutions and not human social creations. A one-sided approach to the theory of value cannot advance towards the materialist conception of history.

The qualitative approach to value theory is an important current of Marxian value theoreticians influenced by Isaak Rubin's *Essays on Marx's Theory of Value* (Rubin [1928] 1973). Here, however, I want to draw attention to the importance of the quantitative solutions proposed by non-Marxian theories of value. Even though they are unilateral theories of value, paying attention to quantity only, nevertheless, they contribute to developing patterns of accounting that are essential for economic planning. Marxian economics in Western countries tends to underestimate this crucial point. Accounting is of great importance for the investigation of the law of value and the possibilities of controlling it.

Theoreticians of labor value and theoreticians of utility value do not explain adequately the reasons why they adopt labor or utility as their parameter for measuring value. The creation of value is a natural process in both cases. Marx's uniqueness contribution to the development of the theory of value and to the understanding of the law of value lies in the fact that he analyzes the process of choosing the qualitative element capable of generating value. The insightful explanation of the naturalization of capitalism is one of the most evident results, indicating that the entire field of non-Marxian economics needs to be under constant critique.

Marx's critique of political economy is usually presented as a project targeting the economic thought of a particular epoch. The fundamental principles of Marx's work, however, are not dependent on the variable 'time', but rather on the variable 'class'. Thus, his critique must strike classical and neoclassical economics in the same way. Mainstream economic thought is always dominated by the ideology of the ruling class, because 'the ideas of the ruling class are in every epoch the ruling ideas' (Marx and Engels [1846] 1932). Marx's political economy shows that every theory of value expresses a position in the class struggle. The utility theory of value and the (naturalized) labor theory of value are both vulgar forms of economic science. Marx's theory of value is different because it does not have the pretension of being a neutral theory based on universally valid economic principles. Because of this, there are no 'reasonable' or 'just' prices, since all of them represent the fragile contract that avoids the direct use of violence. Marx's theory of value is a theory of power.

CHAPTER 6

Marx's Path to Political Economy

As we have seen in chapters 4 and 5, the labor theory of value of utopian socialism and the utility theory of value of the Marginalist Revolution are two antagonistic but parallel approaches that describe the operation of the law of value. They describe the movement of exchange relations, each noting with their own terminology that there is a universal logic behind price formation. My argument is that all the different kinds of theories of value, by focusing only on quantity, deal with the same objective phenomenon called the law of value. Thus, every theory of value involves the mental processing of a real thing. There is no wrong theory of value: all theories of value are partially true, and each of them also expresses a concrete political position in the class struggle. Accordingly, when we are dealing with competing theories of value, standard empirical analysis cannot provide a definitive answer as to which is superior. Empirical investigation is, of course, important, but both sides can present valid data to defend their own cause.[1]

Marx's contribution to economic science is the result of a long trajectory of study about modern society and its capitalist economy. He is faced with the same rule of motion of modern society first systematized and popularized by Adam Smith: the law of value. How does Marx tackle the law of value and what

---

[1] An empirical foundation for the labor theory of value has been put forward by Petrovic (1987), Shaikh (1998), Cockshott and Cottrell (1997) and others. I support these approaches to value theory, but I believe they focus too much on defending Marx based on illuminist reasoning. Due to the subjectivist tendency of marginalist mainstream economics, Cockshott (2019), p. 69, for example argues that the utility theory of value has no empirical basis and should be completely ignored. I do not share this view. For me, it is not a matter of ignoring neoclassical mainstream economics, but of making sense of it. This is a secure way to promote class education among economists who continue to be trained in the mainstream paradigm. For a review of the literature on empirical evidence against the neoclassical utility theory, see Karacuka and Zaman (2012). In my interpretation, a theory of value cannot be proven valid by empirical testing. The lack of empirical justification for the neoclassical utility theory of value will not change the status quo of economic thought, precisely because the ideology of the capitalist class does not care about the scientific status of a theory that suits its interests well. Marx's insight was that there is no such thing as a pure or true theory of value that can be validated through empirical testing only. All theories of value are expressions of a concrete position in the social and political struggle around the economic output. For an empirical defense of the utility theory of value from the perspective of mainstream economics see Praag (1991), who considers both dimensions of utility: ordinal and cardinal. For a historical account of the problems of measurement in utility theory see Moscati (2018).

is his final judgement about it in *Capital*? Marx studies the law of value under a much broader framework than previous economists had (and than many still have). He uses all his knowledge of philosophy, history, and political science to understand what this phenomenon is that appears as a natural law to the eyes of economists.

There are two main insights that distinguish Marx's view from that of all other economists who have dealt with the law of value. First, the law of value is not limited to the minor circuit of simple commodity reproduction and is not in contradiction with the trajectory of value expansion. Second, the content of value is a matter of political decision. This second element is related to the quality of value and is totally original because no other economist treats the quality side of value as Marx does.

Mainstream economics usually has a partial view of the totality of what the law of value is because it lacks a deeper methodological framework to deal with the complicated relations between natural and social phenomena. It is impossible to unveil the mysteries of the law of value without materialist dialectics. Quantity and quality as opposing and complementary poles reflect a contradiction between value and price. Value and price, in turn, reflect their connection to production and distribution, respectively. But production and distribution cannot be separated, as if they were dimensions of the physical world of use values. They are organized within a social and historical system that must be taken into consideration.

Marx provides the basis on which to demonstrate that every theory of value is valid for determining the quantitative relations of exchange. This leads to a complex conclusion: it means that the essential differences between theories of value are related to aspects of power involved in the struggle to control wealth. The theory of value is the abstract core of political economy where class struggle expresses itself most sharply. The way in which an economist formulates his/her theory of value is decisive in sustaining political force in favor of or against the prevailing conditions of production and distribution.

Classical political economy is a body of knowledge that integrates various analyses about wealth management. Marx called attention to the fact that the development of this branch of investigation was closely related to the dispute between narratives justifying specific patterns of how wealth was produced and distributed.

When we simplify these conflicts, we arrive at the most basic form of opposition between the theories of value: one that defends the current state of economic organization and another that argues in favor of a different structure for production and distribution. The first one symbolizes the theory of value of the status quo, the second one represents the theory of value of new political forces that defy the prevailing conditions in the economy. The entire history of economic thought is a sequence of changes in the theory of value. This record is like an archive for the changing structure of the economy and how certain social classes managed to impose their own theory of value on the whole society. All theories of value are expressions of only a part of society because they always indicate the normative direction of production and distribution according to the material interests of a social class. The plurality of theories of value means that there are different groups in conflict. There can be no definitive and unique theory of value while class society exists.

Marx's contribution to economic science is closely related to this aspect. Class struggle is a reality that has an impact on the development of any intellectual exercise. Consequently, it interferes in science as a whole and in the science of wealth management in particular. *Critique of Political Economy* is the subtitle of his main work, *Capital*. This is the result of his systematic studies about how philosophers have conceived of social and individual wealth since the emergence of capitalism. To his advantage, Marx has complete command of the latest developments and highest achievements in philosophy, and an accurate and broad view of the historical events in the pioneer capitalist countries.

How can we summarize Marx's positive contribution to economic science? In sum, he argues that capitalism is a mode of production that exists because specific historical conditions have arisen. First, labor power must have been commodified. Then, it must be captured by the infinite movement of capital through the creation en masse of a population that can only survive by selling its labor power. Once this movement reaches a certain point, it expands across the globe. So, capitalism is a form of economic organization with the imperative to absorb and convert every human society into one global economic system.

Mainstream economists, differently, think of capitalism as the natural or ideal form of economic organization. Most of them do not perceive any difference between the concepts of 'economy' and 'market', because they do not recognize that the economic system under investigation is a specific institutional setting of social relations that developed as part of a historical process. There are many forms of social organization that can perform economic reproduction. In fact, most of the history of the human economy does not rest on the operation of a law of value. Markets are ancient institutions indeed, but they have become the center of whole system only recently. Marx explains that the social relationship called commodity develops historically and that only in capitalism does it becomes the organizing core of the economy. Thus, it is impossible for the production of commodities to be viewed as the norm for the human economy.

Classical economists thought that the modern system was the most appropriate for human nature. Of course, this merely indicates that their economic thinking expresses the interests of the social class at the top of this society. English political economy is not only the most advanced stage of economic science in the 19th century, but also the field of knowledge that represents the powers of the ruling club of industrial capitalists over the world economy. It comes as no surprise that capitalism, or modern society, appears as a very promising economic structure for everybody. Capitalism is presented not only as the best economic system, but sometimes as the unique mode of production in accordance with human nature. There is no alternative to it. Naturalization is the final argument to defend the status quo.

Accordingly, commodity, money and capital are naturalized in the theoretical systems of political economy outside the Marxian framework. As we have seen, even the economic thought of non-Marxian socialists is infected by naturalization. In this case, naturalization is not resorted to in order to defend the status quo of capitalism but rather to argue against exploitation. It is idealist reasoning to argue that the correct functioning of the law of value will lead to an equal society where there will be no distinction between capitalists and wage workers. As is the case with reactionary vulgar economics, market society also emerges in utopian socialism as the only alternative possible for humankind.

Marx's directed his efforts to showing that the methodology behind naturalization is not correct. Markets and capitalism are transient forms of economic organization that once came into being, and that can be overcome if the working class masters the fundamentals of political economy. The commodity and capital are specific social forms of the output. They require specific historical conditions to exist, like private property. This is the main line of argument in the manuscript *A Contribution to the Critique of Political Economy*, written between 1858 and 1859. A few years later, in *Capital*, Marx states with greater confidence that the most important historical event that allows capitalism to rise as a full-blown mode of production is the systematic separation of workers from the means of production. He explains that this is the only way by which a mass of dispossessed laborers is constantly recreated as wage proletarians, which is the basis upon which capital can expand itself indefinitely.

The notion of mode of production has a central role in Marx's system. It explains how the organization of the economy varies according to the social relations of production that change over time. These changes, in turn, are closely related to the development of productive forces. Different kinds of economies can emerge depending on the knowledge applied to modify nature and how humans relate to each other.

The exact pattern of transformation from one mode of production into another is a controversial topic. It relates to what Marx and Engels referred to as the materialist conception of history (materialistische Geschichtsauffassung),[2] to Marx's theory of history and the ultimate causes of the contradictions between the social relations of production and the productive forces. These contradictions are easier to see during times of social revolution because there emerges a battle of ideas in the superstructure of society. But Marx's purpose in *Capital* is not to reveal the universal rules framing the modification of modes of production in history. His intent is to deliver a scientific account of what capitalism is. It is only collaterally that he also launches a theory that explains the general development of economic systems of all human civilizations. So, the study of capitalism offers lessons on how class societies are structured in history, and this is certainly useful for the struggle of working people against exploitation of any sort.

Based on the correct understanding of the rules governing the transformation of one mode of production into another, it would be possible to consciously build the social relations of production. This is a first step towards eliminating the exploitation of humans by humans so that non-primitive communism can be achieved. Also, such step is fundamental for avoiding that separation between natural and social sciences which fortify conservatism. It is common, yet highly controversial, to make an analogy between Marx's theory of the development of civilization and Darwin's theory of the evolution of life forms. Engels announced in his speech on Marx's death that 'just as Darwin discovered the law of development of organic nature, so Marx discovered the law of development of human history' (Engels [1883]). Today, the fundamentals of biology are used by humans to change nature at its core through gene editing. But science can also change society. Through the ages the ruling classes have smartly used accumulated knowledge to structure various types of societies based on human exploitation and oppression. Why should the working class, which is scientifically trained through the development of capitalism, not employ science to shape society as well? In line with this, Marx was not only an observer but a real scientist whose discoveries were always targeted on change and constructing non-primitive communism.

---

2   The expression historical materialism (historischer Materialismus) was not used by Marx and Engels. It is a shorter term that established itself in the Marxist literature during the 20th century. The polemics around the theory of history in Marx and Engels cannot be dealt with here. There are significant divergences among the followers of Marx on this topic.

The point here is not to enter into a discussion about patterns of evolution and if modes of production could be lined up sequentially. Neither is here the place to investigate the complexities of Engels's late work regarding the fusion of natural and social sciences. Our task is to explain that the concept of mode of production is a distinguishing characteristic of Marx as an economist and that his scientific leitmotif is the goal of concrete change in socio-political reality. Therefore, it is necessary to remember Marx's approach to the field of political economy. By doing so, we will be able to see more clearly how he analyses the notion of the law of value and how the understanding of this law should help the transition from capitalism to socialism and to communism. The law of value is the law of motion of capitalism and, as he stated in the preface to the first German edition of *Capital*, 'it is the ultimate aim of this work, to lay bare the economic law of motion of modern society' so that we 'can shorten and lessen the birth-pangs' of its future development (Marx [1867] 2015).

My approach to presenting Marx's *Critique of Political Economy* has a twofold focus. First, I aim to show that rupture and continuity exist in the transition from 18th and 19th century classical political economy to Marx's political economy. Second, I will show that a similar dialectical relation of break and connection exists between 20th and 21st century Marxian political economy and non-Marxian economics. We do not need to treat Marxian and non-Marxian worlds as parallel universes, as if there was no point of contact between them. Although this separation is important in some contexts, it may contribute to increasing the distance between Marxism and mainstream economics. The greater this distance, the smaller is the influence of the working class over what is understood as official economic science. This is why it is so important to establish a solid framework for how to relate Marx's work to mainstream economics.

Marx's *Critique of Political Economy* was explicitly directed at the economic thought of the 18th and 19th centuries. I argue that the structure of this critique targets equally well the economic thought of the 20th and 21st centuries. This is because both past and present economics naturalize capitalist social relations of production. Marx's theory will always remain up to date because of this. Marx's system remains today as the frontier of economic science. To unveil the historical specificities behind capitalism is the greatest achievement in the science of value.

Before entering the world of political economy, Marx began his formal studies in law at the end of the 1830s, but he dedicated most of his attention to discussions in philosophy. At that time, great social and political transformations in Europe brought a widespread and urgent search for answers to the new questions they raised. The socialist movement was becoming more and more organized. New views of society emerged daily. What would be the role of the working class?

In philosophy, the dominant Hegelian synthesis was already undergoing a strong critique. A new generation of minds was ready to revolutionize the way in which theory and practice were conceived. Young thinkers wanted to apply centuries of accumulated knowledge to the solution of social problems. But the movement for social change was still under the influence of idealism. The pledge for equality and justice was too abstract. This movement wanted to end privileges, but only a few had the courage to take action in reality ... and even fewer understood that direct action requires massive organization. The revolutionary process needed a theory.

The consolidation of the bourgeois revolution indicates that a new epoch had been initiated, the epoch of the proletarian revolution. In this context, many thinkers were not satisfied with Hegel's system. Marx was involved with these circles and noticed the importance of a matter that previously had been not adequately considered. He felt the importance of understanding the laws of the material reproduction of society in order to comprehend the ideological conflicts between two contradictory worlds—first, the shock to the feudal world of the bourgeois world; second, the shock to the bourgeois world of the world of the wage working class. In short, he noticed the importance of understanding how the economy works and how its functioning changes through time.

The first occasion on which Marx felt obliged to investigate what he called material or economic interests was in a report to the newspaper *Rheinische Zeitung* in 1842 and 1843 about the alleged theft of wood by the peasantry in Germany. Also, as a journalist and commentator on international relations, he had to give his opinion on the controversy about free trade and protective tariffs. At the same time, Marx was also pressured to analyze the situation in France, where social revolution was a subject of intense debate. However, before making any judgement about socialism and communism, Marx preferred to refrain from public debate to make a more detailed study (Marx [1859b] 1977). This study would lead him to political economy and, finally, to writing *Capital*.

First, he revised Hegel's philosophy of right. His notes were archived in two works: *A Contribution to the Critique of Hegel's Philosophy of Right* and *On the Jewish Question*. We find in the first of these writings his initial steps, in miniature, towards rupture with the established philosophy. In it, he tries to understand the process through which people become citizens, that is, bourgeois agents with separate kinds of subordination: religion and civil. In the second work, we have a specific analysis of this process regarding the Jewish people, for whom the separation between these two spheres of dominance is a unique case, because of the lack of its nation state.

According to *A Contribution to the Critique of Hegel's Philosophy of Right*, the analysis of religion as a product of human creativity was the point of departure for the ideological world of the bourgeoisie. This reasoning was fundamental to the break with feudalist tradition. The connection between knowledge and freedom from oppression is key. There began a journey to dismantle all instruments of ideological control and exploitation, and the first thing to get rid of was the oppressive character of religion. Next, in a further stage of the bourgeois revolution, religion was replaced by philosophy as the standard guide to truth. Philosophy, in turn, assumed the role of unmasking the real misery of the people. Philosophy became an instrument for attacking religion because it showed that religion was a human invention to offer solace in a world where humans were dominated by other humans. Religion is the expression of how people suffer and how intensely people want to react against these conditions of exploitation. It resembles 'the sigh of the oppressed creature, the heart of a heartless world, and the soul of soulless conditions. It is the *opium* of the people' (Marx [1844a] 2009). Philosophy changes the focus from heaven to earth and forces thinkers to deal with matters of our earthly reality, such as law and politics. The root of human suffering is not to be found in the powers of a deity, but in the structure of society, which created this deity in the first place.

Thus, the problems of society do not originate from God, but from the relations between real persons that are members of what we call society. Marx's critique of Hegel is not an abstract counterposition against his philosophical thinking, but a critical reading of how one passes from the critique of religion to the critique of society, and finally to the critique of a specific form of society, namely capitalism. We have here the first outlines of two of the three pillars of Marx's entire thought: dialectical materialist philosophy and the political movement of socialism. The main conclusion is that the socialist movement must conquer the intellectual world if it wants to succeed. In the case of the German people, the creation of a nation free from the *ancien régime* coincides with the emancipation of the human being from the bourgeois state itself. The dual revolution in France and England—that is, the profound political and the industrial changes that constitute the consolidation of the capitalist regime, as Eric Hobsbawm ([1977] 2014) argues—proceeds to a new level in Germany.

Marx is aware of the peculiarities of the German case at the end of the *ancien régime*. The capitalist class triumphed in previous countries that led the revolution. Now, the working class, as consolidated wage workers, is the new force capable of pushing it forward. This is the only class that has a true interest in changing things. Germany is going through two transformations: first, from feudal to capitalist institutions and, in turn, from capitalist to socialist institutions. Germany is relatively late regarding the consolidation of the bourgeois regime, but it is at the forefront of the revolution of the workers. The bourgeois revolution and the socialist revolution are like sequential steps on a ladder. As soon as one is completed, the next one comes and the sequential social transformations in favor of the working class advance. This explains why Germany becomes the next hot spot in the revolutionary process after England and France.

We observe a great mismatch between the old superstructure and the new base of the capitalist economy in the birth of the late bourgeois state. The main questions of the epoch acquire a different flavor in Germany. Here, human emancipation no longer appears as the transformation of the individual from a servant into a wage worker. It is no longer possible to solve the issue by transforming all previous economic agents into the same category of civilian. The capitalist nation state is already limiting the revolutionary process. The revolution has become a global process and the world capitalist class must stop it. It is no longer just a matter of national formation. The revolution is no longer a question of a particular people with a particular culture and history; it is now about the emancipation of the entirety of humanity on the planet.

The particular political condition of the Jewish people illustrates how the national question becomes an international one. In his essay *On the Jewish Question*, Marx ([1843] 2009) explains how the separation of politics from religion contributed to the notion of the individual as a civil member of the nation state. He then asks: what does political emancipation mean for the Jewish people? Because of the historical conditions leading to the absence of a Jewish nation state, its political emancipation has distinct dimensions in comparison to that of other nations. The political emancipation of the Jews means the emancipation of all humanity. As Marx wrote: 'In the final analysis, the *emancipation of the Jews* is the emancipation of mankind from *Judaism*' (Marx [1843] 2009).[3]

Marx describes how, historically, certain groups accumulated money and from an early date assumed a special role in the relationship with other national groups. They do not belong to any country with spatial boundaries, just like capital itself. They integrate into any nation because their superior ruler is not a specific nation state, but capital in general. The groups are dispersed around the globe and constitute an international clique. Because of

---

3 Marx's work *On the Jewish Question*, particularly the part discussed here, has been the topic of a controversial debate. It is not within the scope of this work to analyze this in detail. For a presentation of the debate around the 'Jewish Question' within Marxism, see Traverso (2019).

this, when the working Jewish people get rid of their relations of exploitation, they do not acquire a particular national citizenship, but one which coincides with the notion of world citizen. They do not have a national state of which they can become citizens. As the oppressor is capital in general, this emancipation implies the freedom from capital itself and thus entering the flow of the international communist movement and denying capitalism. The emancipation of mankind from Judaism, obviously, does not refer to people as a race, or as a group of persons that practice a certain culture and religion. It refers to the emancipation of humans from a specific economic order ruled by, as in every class society, real people, as human as everyone else.

The relationship between global and national is always a concern for Marx. His reflection on the problem of nations is a decisive step in Marx's journey towards political economy. It also shows that Marx was far ahead of all German economists who did not accept the ideas of English liberal economists. We must remember that there is a paradox in Adam Smith's synthesis of mercantilism and physiocracy. On the one hand, political economy is thought of as the science of wealth accumulation by nations; on the other, it is also the science of improving the conditions of life for all humans. Nationalism and globalism are two sides of the same discipline called the science of wealth. In Germany, political economy cannot assume the cosmopolitan shape it does in Britain, because there can be only one nation ruling the market economy. Imperialist competition organizes all national economies in a rigid hierarchy, where only the one on the top can announce, of course with hypocrisy, the universality of *laissez-faire*. This is why the discipline of *Volkswirtschaftlehre* (principles of national economy) recovers various aspects of the mercantilist nationalist advancement towards domination of the world market and rejects the logic of liberalism (which is merely a different name for the same imperialist economic policy used by the leading capitalist nation).

The concept of society in English political economy embraces the whole human population across the globe, while the concept of society in German political economy, as in that of any other competitor struggling to achieve the highest ranks of the capitalist imperialist pyramid, refers only to a specific group of humans that constitute a nation with territorial, cultural and economic borders. Accordingly, while British political economy opens the path to internationalism as a principle for organizing the world economy in theory, German political economy recovers the mercantilist schemes of protectionist tariffs. Friedrich List's ([1841] 1909) *The National System of Political Economy* is the most significant example of this type of economic thinking. The issue of liberalism versus protectionism was of great importance in the late 19th century, as it is again now since the rise of neoliberalism.

How should the contradiction between these two sides—laissez-faire liberalism and interventionism—be solved? It seemed impossible to determine which was right, because each side managed the theories of wealth accumulation reasonably well. Luckily, there appeared an ingenious paper entitled *Umrisse zu einer Kritik der Nationalökonomie* in the *Deutsch–Französische Jahrbücher* (*German–French Annals*), in the same edition in which Marx's *On the Jewish Question* was published, in 1844. Its author was Friedrich Engels, a German industrial proprietor and intellectual.

The importance of Engel's *Umrisse* for Marx's intellectual trajectory is enormous. Many topics are addressed, such as private property, competition, and the theory of value. At that time, free trade and protective tariffs were intensely debated. There were powerful economic interests behind each sector and the increasing complexity of international trade led to fierce conflicts regarding the import and export conditions for both goods and capital. Engel's text was crucial for helping Marx to take a first step into these complicated matters. The explanation for the conflict between liberals and protectionists was that both sides were only expressing imperialist pressure for the expansion of their respective national capital. So, neither side was correct. Free trade and protectionism are two sides of the same coin. The theory of political economy in the 19th century could not solve the problem and a new theory had to be developed: a theory that would overcome imperialist disputes and turn the science of the wealth of nations into the science of the wealth of the people.

The first drafts that archive Marx's reading of the classics of political economy are called *Economic and Philosophic Manuscripts* from 1844 (Marx [1844b] 2009). There is not a one-to-one correspondence between the various concepts presented in the *Manuscripts* and the final text of *Capital* but we can already notice important critical remarks about the limits of economic thought in the 19th century. The *Manuscripts* are a continuation of Marx's studies about the relationship between the science of economics (political economy, Nationalökonomie), the State, Law, moral and bourgeois culture. Furthermore, Marx calls attention to Feuerbach's courage in challenging the paradigm around Hegel on the grounds that it helps both the critique of economic thought and also the critique of society in general.

The *Manuscripts* are divided into three parts. The first part deals with three central categories that refer to the main kinds of income in modern economies: salary, capital profit and land rent. This part concludes that labor appears in the writings of political economy only as an activity performed in exchange for a sum of money, that is, labor appears only as wage labor. Labor in general, i.e. a human action to transform nature in any mode of production, is treated as equivalent to labor in a specific context. Wage labor eclipses other forms and economists forget that various kinds of labor organization have existed throughout history. The dynamics of labor dominated by capital is conceived of as an ahistorical, quasi-eternal feature. As a result, the worker never appears in political economy as a free human being who employs his/her force to change nature according to his/her needs. The worker is here only a carrier of labor power that performs labor in the abstract: it is practically irrelevant what kind of concrete labor is needed. The human body, as far as concerns the social task of a worker, is only one tool beside many others in the production process.

In the second part of the *Manuscripts*, Marx attempts a first systematization of the phenomenon of alienation or estrangement.[4] When the production process occurs in the social setting of a society centered around capital, the product of labor becomes an alien entity. The entity created by workers dominates them. This event is strictly tied to the foundations of private property, which is a natural feature in the eyes of political economists. The fact that the direct producer (the worker) confronts the result of his/her labor as an external thing that has power seems a banal occasion, something normal and trivial. Political economy treats the wage worker as if labor had always been dominated by the capitalist process. For this reason, it cannot explain the production process in any other terms than as a process of value expansion. Even when it eventually thinks of a fisher or a hunter on an isolated island, there emerges a Robinson Crusoe who always acts rationally to increase output as an abstract aggregate.

It is important to keep in mind that Marx associates the worker (as a human individual) with the commodity itself (as an object controlled by the logic of capital) in the *Manuscripts* from 1844. This is remarkably close to a general critique typical among radical humanist bourgeois economists who were aware of the declining living standards of the masses in the glorious days of the Industrial Revolution. Of course, Marx is just beginning to develop his own theory and at this stage we do not have a clear distinction between labor and labor power. Consequently, it is not yet possible to solve the paradox of value creation without violating the rules of the exchange of equivalents. The law of value and permanent capital formation cannot yet go together in a coherent way.

Marx asks in precise terms about human development in the context of modernity. If the population is paid so that it can come back to work the next day, what is the purpose of living if not laboring? In class societies, living to work is the fate of the working class. Political economy, even in its most

---

4   For an explanation on the difference between alienation, estrangement and reification, see Ross (2020).

progressive form, does not question the roots of the process through which humans become slaves of the institutions they create themselves, such as religion, private property, money, capital, etc.

Marx's theory of exploitation is unique when we compare it to the superficial clash between positions for and against capitalism. On one side, the defenders of capital do not even recognize that the prevailing social structures oppress the workers. On the other side, some socialist thinkers interpret these structures as being deliberately created by the exploiters. Radical reformers do not understand that the division of society into classes, and the specific form of this division in capitalist societies, are the result of the alienation process, and that the conditions allowing for the exploitation of humans by humans are given by the exploited themselves.

Both defenders and critics of modern society tend to explain the inequalities of power without grasping that capital is a social phenomenon derived from estrangement, which forces everyone to put money into the system in order to exploit everyone else. Capitalist society is not only the reign of the equal right to exploit others, but also the reign of the equal right to be exploited by others. Marx's perspective is different from other socialist ideas. For him, the goal is not a matter of creating equal conditions for everyone to become a proprietor, but rather of complete liberation from the chains of private property. An equal distribution of property can only show that everybody is chained to the impersonal force of money and capital, which exploits every single agent in the same way through the mechanism of alienation. This is one of Marx's singular insights (and it becomes clearer in the later debate with Proudhon).

In the third part of the *Manuscripts*, Marx relates the general concepts of economics to private property. He makes initial notes on a social system of non-capitalist production and distribution. We find traces of his thinking about communism, which is a social architecture with various instantiations throughout history. Marx began to understand that there could be a movement towards recreating this kind of architecture on a global scale. The capitalist mode of production would play a fundamental role in this. Communal systems of production and distribution that were once the standard of primitive human societies could be restored on a planetary scale. Communism has always been a powerful idea in the history of human thinking. Economic science could contribute to turning it from a utopian dream into reality, if it could reveal how global common ownership can be implemented. Based on the dialectical materialist philosophy that overturns Hegel, Marx initiates a new protocol to act and to think about the socialist and communist movement.

It is important to notice that Marx's philosophical instrument is not yet ready in the 1840s. He begins with a simple direct negation of Hegel's idealism, but this is not a completely worked out theory. The *Manuscripts* are equipped with a solid materialist discourse and an aggressive subjective positioning against the dominant ideas of the world of the 19th century. This is not enough to lay out a new path for the socialist movement. At the time, Feuerbach was still the reference point for the counter position to Hegelian idealism. It was already possible to comprehend that there was a systematic appropriation of political economy by the wage working class. However, comprehension is not equal to transformation. Understanding the problem does not necessarily produce action to solve the problem. Comprehension means contemplation, and at most, reclamation, claim, vindication. 19th century philosophers thought that the society in which they lived was in accordance with human nature, that the members of this society could not alter its shape, and so all one could do was to complain. That was about to change.

If one could show that the bourgeois individual is not the human individual, but the social form of the human agent in a specific area at a specific time, then it should be possible to show that any institutional social setting can be created through an organization of the people. Once we perceive the social and historical conditions of private property, we will be able to see the differences between the human being in general and the bourgeois citizen. Marx's plan at this stage of his investigation was to systematically analyze all the conceptual categories of political economy, such as money, commodity, and capital in order to show that they are social forms of general economic categories. There are universal rules of the economy and more specifically, social norms of economic organization that refer to a concrete social setting in time and space. This distinction is crucial for helping the communist movement to construct a new economic system in which the capitalist class no longer controls the state.[5]

As mentioned, the existence of private property emerges as the negation of a primitive era in which humans did not relate economically to each other as private owners of useful items. Primitive communism is a broad term to indicate this stage prior to the ascension of class societies and capitalism. There were no rules of exchange based on money. Economic relations were not entirely regulated by the law of value, because the meetings of distinct communes were occasional, framed by a myriad of cultural and religious norms, specific to each location and time. In anthropology, these relations are one type of what is called a gift economy. These are relations established between

---

5   As indicated earlier, Oskar Lange was one of Marx's followers who explored this distinction further in his work.

different communes with the aim of articulating and negotiating possible modes of co-existence via, for example, relationships of hostility, friendship, and assistance. Peace and war are possible outcomes.[6]

The socialist movement that was born with the bourgeois revolution appears as the negation of this negation, inasmuch as private property embodies in concentrated form all the contradictions of the debates on equality. But without an entirely new system of political economy, the socialist movement will never recognize that the wage working class is the only agent interested in taking this next step towards non-primitive communism. Political economy will not discover that the wage working class is the only one capable of revolutionary leadership. As a result, at this stage, in the first half of the 1840s, the critique of modern society is still haunted by a normative position of the most radical humanism that repudiates money and all its perverse derivations based on cultural values such as love and trust. This is not the unique position of what is to become the Marxist critique of capitalism.

The next steps in the construction of scientific socialism and the political economy of the working class are marked by two essays that constitute the intellectual marriage of Marx and Engels. Between 1844 and 1846 they co-wrote *The Holy Family* (Marx and Engels [1845] 1956) and *The German Ideology* (Marx and Engels [1846] 1932). These writings mark a decisive transition. They symbolize the rupture with the debates around Hegel's system because they escape from the dialectical contradiction between spirit and matter. Hegelian influenced philosophers tried to defend either one of these two sides, but the choice of one of these two alternatives implies the immediate recreation of the opposite option. How could one overcome this and take philosophy to the next level?

A summary of Marx's reaction to Hegelian philosophy may be helpful at this point, especially because the triad Hegel-Feuerbach-Marx is not very well understood among progressive intellectuals and the left in general, including many radical economists. One of Marx's most famous attempts to explain his method of inquiry appears in the afterword to the second German edition of book 1 of *Capital*, in 1873 (Marx [1873] 1985). He argues that his philosophical approach represents a new way to systematically study capitalism. It starts with the most singular and abstract determinations of value expansion behind the logic of interest (Zinsen) and advances towards the analysis of capitalism

---

6   On the relationship between political economy and the economic thinking in anthropology, see Mauss ([1925] 1966) and Graeber (2011). The social rules of stateless and classless societies are extremely complex and diverse. We are only indicating here that, in contrast to capitalism, these rules are not centered at the law of value.

at the end of the 19th century. Marx talks about his method as the direct antithesis of Hegelian dialectic. It is as if Hegel departed from idealism and Marx from materialism. In this sense, the system was inverted.

However, there is an extremely important remark that expels once and for all every accusation of economicism or determinism against Marx's economic theory. When we think of Hegel's dialectics as something standing on its head, we cannot forget that Marx has already performed a triangular synthesis of the dialectical contradiction between spirit and matter. As he notes in the afterword: 'The mystifying side of Hegelian dialectic I criticized nearly thirty years ago, at a time when it was still the fashion.' (Marx [1873] 1985). Marx is explaining that his correction of Hegel is not a replacement of idealism by materialism. The correction has to do with the way we think and act over reality. Hegel described precisely how dialectics could be used to apprehend the contradictions of reality. Marx showed that dialectics can deliver more than that: in addition to correctly understanding how the world works, we can also shape the universe, which is what really matters. Marx does not make a symmetrical error of moving from idealism to materialism. Such a change forms the philosophical position of Feuerbach inasmuch as it directly negates Hegel's system with the defense of vulgar materialism. Economic determinism that emerges from the attempt to simply oppose Hegel with the most superficial notion of materialism is of course a dead end. This is Feuerbach's limitation, not Marx's. Because Feuerbach was only a courageous thinker to defy mighty Hegel, he will almost never be remembered in the long history of human Philosophy. Feuerbach wanted to overthrow Hegel by inverting the dominant pole in the contradiction between spirit (ideal) and matter (reality). But the problem is not how to replace idealism by materialism in order to *know* reality, but rather to organize the relationship between theory and praxis in order to *change* reality.

Marx's materialism is not a rock without soul. There is a simple way to show that his material basis is much more complex than the superficial notion that there is no place for subjective creativity. We must emphasize the adjective 'dialectical'. *Dialectical* materialism does not deny the idea or reject the ideal as a creation of the forces of spirit. The confusion between vulgar and dialectical materialism is common because of the context of the scientific revolution of modernity. The accusation of determinism is an old attack that reinforces dogmatic approaches that convert Marx's method into a system full of laws and commandments. The expression 'orthodox Marxism' shows that scholastic discussion developed around Marx's intellectual legacy. We should not go into detail about this, because the debate about Marxism(s) would take us too far away from our aim. Here, we must only know that Marx's system does not waste time with the struggle of matter versus spirit. It focuses on directing all accumulated knowledge towards realizing the goals of the working class and dialectics should also function with the same goals in mind.

Hegel ([1833] 1979) explains in his lectures on the history of philosophy that the dialectical method has long held a central position in the discovery of contradictory phenomena that stimulate mental activity and debate. This method is the result of many centuries of human reflection about the observed world. According to Hegel, it is the most developed method for comprehending the nature of reality, that is, the best philosophical instrument of inquiry had already been built. If there was nothing left to construct in terms of the tools of observation and study, it seemed that philosophy had come to its conclusion. Hegel's absolute Idea stood as the final stage in the long journey of philosophy. Where to go now? The increasing importance of materialism in the context of illuminism and its critique of religion was not enough to surpass that paradigm in philosophy, but it was a necessary step. Rudimentary materialism first countered idealism through Feuerbach ([1839] 1972), 'the only one who has a *serious, critical* attitude to the Hegelian dialectic and who has made genuine discoveries in this field. He is in fact the true conqueror of the old philosophy' (Marx [1844b] 2009).

At first sight, Feuerbach seems to be a weak philosopher, because he embraces materialism and abandons Hegel too quickly. Feuerbach is indeed highly praised by Marx and Engels, not because of the materialist perspective he represents, which is incomplete, but because he courageously defied the standard thinking around Hegel's system. The problem with Feuerbach's critique is that it intends to surpass Hegel without taking the contradiction to a higher level.

Many years after this important moment in the development of what would become Marxism (or dialectical materialism, philosophy of praxis, etc.), Engels ([1886] 1975), explained the limits of Feuerbach's critique by remembering the context of the German philosophical debates of the 1840s. When Feuerbach launched his attack, there was a frenzy among thinkers. Everybody thought Hegel was over. But this feeling of 'eureka!' was short-lived. Why? Marx and Engels realized that turning Hegel upside down does not constitute completely overcoming his system, because to pass from idealism to materialism is merely to change one side of the unity for the opposite side. It is the same system with inverted signs. To surpass Hegel completely, one last maneuver is necessary.

There is no reason to stop at a stage where we can correctly understand and interpret reality. There is no justification for remaining satisfied with simply discovering the truth. *We can use this knowledge to change the world in the direction we want to.* This is one way to appreciate Marx's 11th thesis on Feuerbach,

Marx and Engels

Hegel   Feuerbach

FIGURE 2   Marx and Engel's philosophy of praxis

a powerful phrase written in 1845: 'Philosophers have hitherto only *interpreted* the world in various ways; the point is to *change* it.' (Marx [1845] 1978).

Figure 2 above illustrates the relationship between the three philosophical systems of Hegel, Feuerbach, and Marx and Engels. Feuerbach is in direct opposition to Hegel and represents a mirror of his system. It is an opposition on the same level since idealism is only replaced by its contrary, materialism. This kind of critique generates vulgar materialism and all its derivatives that suppress all forces of subjective creativity. Marx and Engels recognized Feuerbach's brave posture and soon jumped to a higher baseline. The synthesis between thesis and antithesis symbolized respectively by Hegel and Feuerbach is overcome and embraced by the two antagonistic positions in a new philosophical system, where the end goal is not to find the final explanation for how the world works, but to shape it according to our own wishes.

It is important to highlight the fact that Marx and Engels do not simply discard the old system. They integrate the entirety of it into a new system. This is a fundamental characteristic of Marx's philosophy, because it indicates that every form of knowledge produced outside of the system that will later be called 'Marxism' can and, in a certain way, must be integrated into Marx's world. After proper critique and translation, every idea alien to Marx's system can be made to function in accordance with the interests of the working class. Thus, Hegel finds himself within Marx's system, as well as every bourgeois economist and pre-Marxian socialist. The overcoming of past systems does not entail the discarding of any element of previous knowledge. It only edits the anterior content to fit into the new system. As a result, any production of knowledge, even the strongest capital apologetic, can be conquered and put to work according to the analyst's own position in class struggle.

The relationship between Marx and Hegel is complex and we should not go into too much detail,[7] but there are at least two points that are worth

---

7   For a presentation of the connection between Marx and Hegel inspired by Lenin, see Anderson (1995). For a collection of essays on the relationship between Hegel's logic and Marx's *Capital*, see Moseley and Smith (2014).

mentioning. First, it is important to note Marx's real purpose in praising Hegel so much in the afterword to the German second edition of *Capital* (Marx [1873] 1985). It became popular and fashionable to debunk Hegel in the 1840s. After the great old German philosopher was surpassed by a new generation of thinkers, many treated Hegel with disdain and arrogance. Marx wanted to make it explicit that an entirely new mode of philosophy was only possible because of previous works, among which Hegel's oeuvre was crucial. Being one of the most eminent intellectuals of his generation, if not the greatest,[8] Marx paid homage to the mighty thinker Hegel in order to show that it is not acceptable to disdain the giants upon whose shoulders we stand today. This is the reason why he makes a comparison between Hegel's method and his own and praises his role in the construction of *Capital*.

This is the background to Marx's statement that Hegel's dialectics 'is standing on its head'. In the same manner, we need to understand the simple description in which Marx argues that his 'dialectic method is not only different from the Hegelian but is its direct opposite' (Marx [1873] 1985). Marx wants to indicate that Hegel is a thinker of the highest rank, but that his time is over. Hegel is not inferior due to his intellectual limitations, as the arrogant new generation might think, it is simply that the historical context in which he lived is gone.

Second, Marx ([1873] 1985) is concerned with showing his method as an instrument for the inquiry (*Forschung*) and presentation (*Darstellung*) of any object. The afterword to the second German edition of *Capital* is a lecture on a scientific methodology that sets aside the subjective position of the scientist. *Capital* is a work of science that has one single object of investigation: the capitalist mode of production. Regardless of the position or the political interest that the reader might have, the book is intended to be the most accurate source for everyone who wants to understand what capitalism is and how it functions. As we have seen, there is no need to engage with the complete account of Marx's philosophy of praxis if we only want to understand our socio-economic reality. An understanding of Hegel upside down and a superficial notion of Feuerbach's achievements is enough to perceive the central discoveries in *Capital*. Of course, a passive reading of *Capital* is not enough when we consider

---

8 In 1886, Engels assessed Marx's participation in the philosophical debates of the 1840s in the essay *Ludwig Feuerbach and the End of Classical German Philosophy*. When comparing his own and others' contributions to the only tendency 'which has borne real fruit' after the dissolution of the Hegelian school, Engels wrote: 'Marx stood higher, saw further, and took a wider and quicker view than all the rest of us. Marx was a genius; we others were at best talented.' (Engels [1886] 1975).

Marx's entire thinking and political practice, because such an assimilation of Marx's teachings is a negation of the 11th thesis itself.[9]

Marx and Engels' break with old German philosophy marks an essential step in the history of the socialist movement. By combining this advancement with the concrete political happenings in France and the economic thinking in British political economy, there emerges a coherent proposal to treat society scientifically. It is not only nature that can be changed and modified according to the wishes of humans. Social relations can also be put under the conscious control of humans.

The manuscript *The German Ideology*, which contains almost all of Marx and Engels' reflections on the paradigms of philosophy in the first half of the 19th century, could not be published at the time due to political and technical difficulties. But that did not matter to the authors. As Marx ([1859b] 1977) explained in the *Preface to a Contribution to the Critique of Political Economy*, it was abandoned 'to the gnawing criticism of the mice', since he and Engels were happy to have organized and fully apprehended their own ideas. The socialist movement already had some engagement with the ideas of political economy and materialist philosophy but with various shortcomings. Now it would acquire strong support to master the science of wealth and value. Marx was about to equip the movement with a proper political economy, that is, a political economy in full accordance with the goals of the working class.

9   For a proposed reading of *Capital*, emphasizing the practical and political aspect of Marx's theory and which is critical to the way economists usually assimilate Marx's *Capital*, see Cleaver ([1979] 2000).

CHAPTER 7

The Law of Value in Marx's Critique of Political Economy

1   Marx's Theory of the Commodity

While the law of value is an objective phenomenon, theories of value are the different ways in which economists try to conceptualize this phenomenon.[1] There are as many theories of value as theoretical economists: every value theoretician constructs his own abstract apparatus for both describing and researching the law of value. With the help of this instrument, the economist may also defend bending the law of value towards specific material interests. Any analysis of capitalism must inevitably be based on an analysis of the law of value. Since all modern economic thinking is conditioned by capitalist relations, all modern thinking involves translating the reality of the law of value into the specific language of certain schools of economic thought. Although many theories of value do not even mention the expression 'law of value', they are dealing with it nonetheless because the essentials of capital are the same for every ideological manifestation in economics.[2]

It is crucial to explain that an economist's adoption of a specific theory of value is closely related to his/her political position. As previously argued, the choice of the qualitative element to measure the quantity of abstract wealth is not a technical problem, but a social and political one. Mainstream economists

---

1   Although it is correct to make the distinction that the law of value is not the labor theory of value, as Dooley (2005) also argues, a similar distinction applies to any kind of theory of value because a theory of value is not the law of value. I am drawing attention to the fact that the law of value is the real phenomenon of the quantitative arrangement of relations of exchange. All theoretical constructions aimed at making sense of this phenomenon lead to specific theories of value. Thus, both the labor theory of value and the utility theory of value derive from the observation that there is a universal logic behind the valuation of useful things.

2   The concept of the law of value is therefore an absolute necessity. The analyst cannot set it aside, as if he had another option. The only way to avoid the law of value is to investigate a mode of production that is entirely free from the logic of private property. But even in that case, for some authors, the logic of the law of value as an allocator of labor still holds. For an analytical perspective on the operation of the law of value in non-capitalist economies, see Bryceson (1983). For an analysis of the significance of the law of value as an inevitable concept for any analyst of the capitalist economy, see Sekine (1980) and Gontijo (2009).

are often not aware of the political forces of class struggle influencing their intellectual activities. So, the most important task of educators in the field of economics is to highlight how they are manipulated by these forces. In this context, I present a pluralistic argument to explain why Marx chose labor, and why this choice was inevitable given the circumstances of class struggle in the 19th century.

The conclusion of the first phase of Marx's thinking caused a significant change in the socialist movement. Socialism was based on an idea of equality between all humans. However, the limited achievements of the French Revolution showed that the end of exploitation could only be the result of an organized project of the working class. Moreover, only a complete reorganization of the economy could open the path to the structural changes that the bourgeois revolution could not implement. Socialist authors and leaders did not fully understand how an economy worked. Marx's decisive contribution was to master the science of wealth and translate it into an economics of the working class. The history of economic thought showed that every class society produced an economic theory to provide an ideological justification for the status quo of economic organization. Accordingly, British political economy was a body of knowledge about wealth dominated by the industrial capitalist ruling class. The future of economic science lay in a political economy that could translate all previous philosophical accounts about wealth into the reality and wishes of the working class.

Accordingly, the central axis of the second phase of Marx's thinking is targeted at mastering political economy. It culminates in *Capital*, a broad treatise about capitalism, and indeed one that remained open for further development.[3] Marx's critique is not limited to denouncing the economists who defend capitalism (as most standard introductory accounts of Marxian economics argue). He also attacks the authors who ideologically defend socialism but who lack knowledge about the functioning of either the capitalist mode of production or of any economic system whatsoever. In this sense, *Capital* is a true scientific work in the field of economics. It is not a pamphlet, but a dense study whose main thesis systematically dismantles both vulgar strands of economic thinking in the 19th century (reactionary and progressive).

---

3 I do not consider *Capital* to be an unfinished work. It is finished in the sense that the core elements are meticulously developed and presented in book 1, *The Process of Production of Capital*, published by Marx in 1867. I regard Engels's edition and publication of books 2 and 3 of *Capital* as fine works of continuation. They expand the theoretical foundations presented by Marx and indicate that the oeuvre is open for development in many directions.

This dual focus for the theory of value pervades the oeuvre *Capital: Critique of Political Economy*. On one hand, he shows that the true spirit of inquiry behind the political economy of the times of Adam Smith and David Ricardo has turned into a club of vulgar economists who seek only to ideologically defend the capitalist system. On the other hand, Marx also criticizes the defenders of socialism because they have clung to the naturalized version of labor theory of value like blind believers. We can find this duality throughout its thousands of pages and in the preparatory manuscripts, but it is more evident in the beginning, particularly in chapter 1, *Die Ware* (The Commodity). Marx develops this duality with methodological and analytical rigor, employing his powerful philosophical approach that departed from Hegel.

Marx's position requires a delicate maneuver. On one side, he cannot endorse a theory of value that does not represent the economic interests of wage workers. So, he must develop a certain sort of *labor* theory value. On the other side, he must show that the Ricardian socialist system naturalizes the notion that labor creates value in any social institutional setting, which is a grave error. Subject to these constraints, Marx needs to elaborate a theory of value in a specific way that must match the political position of the working class and, at the same time, explain that there is no natural theory of value. The labor theory of value is not the absolutely true theory of value, because the criteria of value creation are defined in class struggle. This is a crucial difference between Marx's and non-Marxian approaches to the theory of value. Thus, to investigate Marx's theory of value, instead of taking our starting point from labor, we should begin with the basic unity of the capitalist system. More accurately, we should say that Marx's theory of value is a corollary of his theory of the commodity.

Let us take a look at the two fundamental questions behind any theory of value.[4] First, we need to ask about the quantity of abstract wealth that each useful item embodies. This is the traditional investigation of classical and neoclassical economics. The focus is on the size of values/prices. Second, we need to ask about the qualitative element used as a standard to measure the quantities of values/prices. To the question of what these magnitudes are measuring, the answer is natural, for both classical and neoclassical economics: labor and utility, respectively.

---

4   The following presentation derives from my previous work, Camarinha Lopes (2014), especially pages 716–722. For an analysis of Ricardian socialists and their relation to the distinction between scientific and utopian socialism, see King (1983). Ronald Meek ([1956] 1973, p. 306) presents these two questions in a similar way, but he does not make a clear distinction between quantity and quality in the problem of value.

Marx's unique contribution lies in this second question because he investigates the context in which certain things are defined as social parameters for measuring the quantities of the various useful items that constitute the economy. Although Marx's uniqueness as an economist is focused on the question of the quality of value, he also contributed significantly to the quantitative side of value by developing a protocol to transform values into production prices.

In short, we can express these questions as follows:

(i)   why do commodities have these specific prices/values as pure quantities, i.e., what is the magnitude of the prices/values of commodities?

(ii) why is labor/utility[5] the standard to measure the magnitude of values/ prices?

A complete theory of value must answer these two questions. The process of unifying the contradiction quantity and quality is mandatory in dialectics. Let us take this double perspective to investigate the relationship between different theories of value. As argued, we can reduce all possible kinds of theories of value to only two large groups: the labor theory of value and the utility theory of value. Dialectically speaking, these represent the thesis and antithesis that scientific political economy needs to synthesize and thus overcome, as Marx did with Hegel and Feuerbach.

Figure 3 shows that there are two kinds of relationship between the classical labor theory of value and the neoclassical theory of value. There is an analytical congruency on the side of quantity and there is a political incongruency on the side of quality. If we consider that 'value theory' is the totality under analysis, we split this entity into two opposing sides, quantity, and quality and thus we reach the two previous questions (i) and (ii).

On one side, value theory explains why commodities have certain values/ prices. It explains the magnitude of these indexes. On the side of quantity, value theory justifies why there is a specific balance equation between different commodities or baskets of goods. Why is one useful item more valuable than another? The answer to this question varies according to each theory of value. For the labor theory of value, the reason is that one item needs more

---

5   Labor and utility are not the only two options to serve as the basis for a theory of value. Any other thing would work, because any qualitative concept necessarily serves as a standard to measure quantity. 'Time', for example, is another typical option in the history of the theory of value that can be derived from comparing utility of consumption in two distinct points in time. 'Energy', which can be derived from a physiological approach to the labor theory of value, has also been mentioned by some value theoreticians coming from the debate on ecology (Roegen (1971), Judson (1989)). Our focus here is only on the dichotomy between labor and utility because I am considering that any theory of value can be classified into one of these two options. A broader treatment should be done elsewhere.

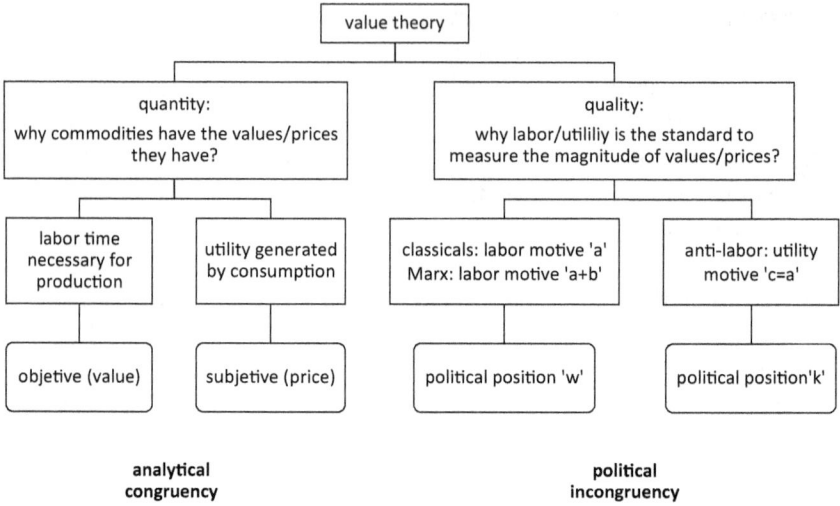

```
                        ┌──────────────────┐
                        │   value theory   │
                        └──────────────────┘
```

quantity: why commodities have the values/prices they have?	quality: why labor/utililiy is the standard to measure the magnitude of values/prices?

labor time necessary for production	utility generated by consumption	classicals: labor motive 'a' Marx: labor motive 'a+b'	anti-labor: utility motive 'c=a'

objetive (value)	subjetive (price)	political position 'w'	political position'k'

**analytical   political
congruency   incongruency**

'a': labor, in the sense of physics, is the only way humans can modify the natural environment in which they live [unconscious positioning at the side of the working class]

'b': labor power is the only commodity that wage workers own. If the value theoretician struggles at the side of workers, then this must analytically be chosen as the unique commodity with the capacity to create value [conscious positioning at the side of the working class]

'c': useful things, when consumed or used, generate positive effects for the wellbeing of the economic agent

'w': qualitative element responsible for value creation leads to a working-class friendly theory of value

'k': qualitative element responsible for value creation leads to a capitalist-class friendly theory of value

FIGURE 3   Analytical congruency and political incongruency in value theory

labor to be produced than the other. Quantity of labor is what explains quantities of abstract wealth. For the utility theory of value, however, the reason is that one item or one basket of items generates more utility than the other item or basket of items. The magnitude of abstract wealth is given by the quantity of what economists call utility, an abstract entity that resembles the notion of unspecified labor. In the same way as abstract labor does not indicate if it refers to 'tillage, cattle tending, spinning, weaving and making clothes', utility does not specify 'the nature of such wants, whether, for instance, they spring from the stomach or from fancy' (Marx [1867] 2015), p. 27.

The difference between the two is that, while abstract labor possesses a clear objective dimension due to its physiological aspect (labor as expenditure of muscle, brains, etc.), utility moves towards subjectivity. Accordingly, there emerges a curious contradiction between these two perspectives, which can be classified as a *contradiction of analytical congruency*. This means that, despite the contradiction, both sides complement each other in the sense that they both contribute to the explanation of values/prices as pure quantitative relations. In the literature of Marxian political economy, the labor theory of value focuses on the concept of *value* and the utility theory of value focuses on the concept of *price*. The dichotomy between value and price from a purely quantitative perspective is not a grave one. There is a connection between value and price. When we think only of the quantitative connection between these two sides, we see that we are dealing with the transformation problem of value indexes of production into empirical prices at the market. Logically, there is a reciprocal and complementary relationship here. This identity is also supported by the naturalizing characteristics of both theories of value, as I have argued previously.

Returning to the totality of value theory, (at the top of Figure 3), on the side of quality, value theory must explain why a specific quality was chosen to serve as the standard to measure quantities. It is not a matter of analyzing the size of values or prices but of deciphering the meaning of these magnitudes, i.e., what do value and prices measure? They both measure an idealized thing, which can be called wealth. But the source of this wealth can be located in different mechanisms. The labor theory of value argues that the content of wealth is labor, since without labor nothing would be produced. So, wealth is derived from labor. The utility theory of value, on the other hand, argues that the content of wealth is the satisfaction provided by the use of that wealth.

When economists choose labor or utility as the qualitative parameter, it is not a matter of picking the most suitable one to fulfill the analytical task of transforming value into prices, nor is it a matter of inferring from empirical analysis which one, labor or utility, is closer to the truth. When the analyst chooses a specific qualitative parameter to be the source of value, he/she is (consciously or unconsciously) preparing the discursive framework for defending the right of appropriation of the social output based on the rules of market exchange.

Classical economists choose labor based on a purely objectivist and physiological reasoning. The motive for their choice is that labor, in the scientific physics sense, is the only way humans can modify the natural surroundings in which they live ('a' in figure 3).[6] This is a rigorous concept derived from the scientific study of the human-nature relation and it leads to a politically progressive position when a huge part of the population become salary workers. Thus, the naturalizing labor theory of value of classical economists leads to a defense of distribution that favors labor (a position that Utopian socialism would take further).

Marx has a somewhat different explanation for choosing labor. In fact, he adds one more layer to the original theory of the classical economists ('a + b' in figure 3). Marx's theory of value and the labor theory of value of the classical economists (and utopian socialists) are not mutually exclusive. They are not disjoint events. Using mathematical language, the labor theory of value of classical economists is a subset of the set 'Marx's theory of value'. Marx's theory of value is a superset of classical's theory of value.[7]

Marx agrees that it is possible to derive a 'natural' labor theory of value as classical economists do, but he calls attention to the fact that this alone is not sufficient for a complete value theory. Why? Because 'the establishment of socially-recognized standards of measure for the quantities of these useful objects' is also the work of history (Marx [1867] 2015, p. 27). It is indeed possible to derive an abstract concept behind the equal content in each use value. Explanation 'a' is all right if we are playing Robinson Crusoe. However, another additional reason must be brought. Otherwise, value theory will not be contextualized in history and in class struggle.

---

6   In physics, work is the process of energy transfer to the motion of an object via application of a force. Where does this force come from? It comes from the energy within the living organism. But, even before that, it comes from points of accumulated energy in the non-living world. Notice that this definition of work does not distinguish between work performed by humans and other living entities. It does not even distinguish between the living and non-living worlds. In this perspective, the human working population is identical to cattle. So, why does work performed by humans create value, but work performed by animals (and machines!) does not? It is impossible to justify this distinction when labor is apprehended in the physiological sense.

7   Similarly, Wright (2019), inspired by the works of Pasinetti, shows that a suitable generalized labor theory of value spans both natural and institutional stages of analysis. I maintain that Marx's theory of value is a suitable generalized labor theory of value precisely because he was aware of the division between a natural/physiological and a social/historical/institutional stage of analysis. In my interpretation, this division lies behind Pasinetti's (2009) separation theorem. If we apply Pasinetti's separation theorem to figure 3, we would see that motive 'a' for defending a labor theory of value resembles the 'pre-institutional', 'natural' stage of investigation, while motive 'b' for defending the labor theory of value resembles the 'institutional stage'.

This additional motive for electing labor as the source of value is represented by letter 'b' in figure 3. What is Marx's additional explanation for choosing labor? Marx argues that motive 'a' is insufficient for presenting a full theory of value. Perspective 'a' considers labor only as the source of use values, that is, as concrete labor. This entails the correct description that complex use values require more concrete labor to be produced. This relation between necessary labor and the difficulty of obtaining or producing a larger amount of a use value is precisely what allows the universalization of the 'Robinson Crusoe' exercise. No matter how accurate perspective 'a' is for describing the quantitative relations of equivalence between all use values, *it does not explain why the labor theory of value became a socially accepted idea only with the formation of modern society*. This is the question answered by Marx's additional explanation.

Why did labor become the standard measure for the quantity of useful things? In short, more and more people could only be part of the emerging capitalist society if they obtained money through selling their labor power. The idea that wealth and value depend on labor (which was not entirely new) spread to the point of becoming a social consensus. The ideals of bourgeois equality and its democratic ideology contributed to turning the labor theory of value into the mainstream theory of value in political economy. It is a specific socio-historical context that allows the labor theory of value to rise to the position of the main value theory in economic science. When political economists realized that their theory of value was perfectly suited to the interests of the working class, it was already too late. They had to come up with another qualitative element as the source of value. This is the story behind the Marginalist Revolution.

Marx's additional explanation ('b' in figure 3) is important in two main ways. First, it shows that Marx accepts explanation 'a' given certain conditions. For counting quantities of value/price, the concept of the naturalized labor theory of value of classical economists is perfectly serviceable. Second, it indicates that the qualitative component of value theory must be contextualized in the historical reality of class struggle. Behind every choice of the qualitative component there is an analyst's political position. Marx maintains his discursive framework on the side of labor not because there is a neutral, empirical proof that labor is the source of value, but because *it is both empirically robust and, more importantly, allied in its political content with the working class*.[8]

---

8 Empirical consistency is indeed an important factor in explaining why Marx chooses labor to fulfill the task of being the substance of value, but it is definitely not the only one, as is implied in the work of Paul Cockshott (1997) and Anwar Shaikh (1998). Likewise, logical reasoning is of course necessary to sustain a theory of value, but in no way can Marx's theory of

Value theoreticians using the utility theory of value have a different explanation for choosing utility ('c' in figure 3). As I have presented previously, they argue that useful things, when consumed or used, generate positive outcomes for the economic agent. It should be noted that the motives of both classical economists and neoclassical economists are identical in the sense that they pretend to derive their theories of value from an abstract 'Robinson Crusoe' world ('c = a'). Both perspectives 'c' and 'a' choose the qualitative element responsible for creating value based purely on the human-nature relation. Neither of them consider the historical and political dimension that influences the superstructure of economic science.

Accordingly, with respect to quality, we come to different political positions, which I call 'w' (for work) and 'k' (for capital). Political position 'w' means that value theory is used to defend labor as the sole source of value. Political position 'k' in contrast means that value theory is used to defend utility as the sole source of value. They represent the political incongruency between the labor and the utility theories of value. The purpose of figure 3 is to draw my argument that there is both analytical congruency and political incongruency between two non-Marxian theories of value: the naturalized labor theory of value of

---

value rest on logical reasoning alone. It was a scandal in the debate on the transformation problem when a 'peanut theory of value' was logically derived from Sraffa's model (see Gintis and Bowles (1981), Roemer (1982), Samuelson (1982), Ganssmann (1983), Laibman (1992), Lee (1993) and Lee (1998)). The positive point that emerged from the controversy is that it showed, once again, that the defense of any theory of value is related to an active engagement in class struggle, whether the value theoretician is aware of it or not. Kurz (2018) presents a fine summary of the problem of value theory and the law of value. I agree with Kurz when he states that Marx's insistence on labor as the common third of any two commodities is a weak move *today*. Similarly, I endorse Steve Keen's demonstration that "the entire dispute between Marxians and Sraffians can itself be judged a chimera, since Marx's theory of value in fact provides the philosophical foundation for an absolute theory of value, consonant with Sraffian analysis (...)" (Keen (1993), p. 119). As I argued recently when commenting the debate between Moseley (2021) and Hahnel (2021) (Camarinha Lopes (2021a)), followers of Sraffa and Marx must cooperate. Sraffa was right when he asked with genuine curiosity why Marx chose labor to be the qualitative element that generates the quantity of value. As I am arguing, to understand Marx's choice we need to contextualize his struggle at the side of socialists in general against capitalist economic thinking. Moreover, at that time, it was not controversial to employ a labor theory of value, since this was the mainstream value theory in the 19th century. Even so, Marx showed in detail that he was not employing Adam Smith's and Ricardo's theory without problematizing the assertion that 'labor creates value'. It is perfectly fine to defend a classical, purely physiological, and empirical labor theory of value when we are dealing only with the quantitative dimension of value. On the other hand, in my approach, it is equally fine to defend a neoclassical, purely psychological, and inductive utility theory of value when explaining only the formation of prices.

classical political economy and the standard utility of value of neoclassical economics. Marx criticizes both theories of value equally when he shows that there is no 'natural' value theory, but in terms of their political difference, Marx is a radical supporter of the labor theory of value against the utility theory of value. This is not because of a 'technical superiority' of the labor theory of value over the utility theory of value (Lange (1935)), but because the labor theory of value is the ideological form of economics in the interests of the working class while the utility theory of value is the ideological form of economics in the interests of exploiters.

Before considering the law of value in Marx's *Critique of Political Economy*, we need first to focus attention on Marx's theory of the commodity. As I have mentioned, it is more accurate to speak of Marx's theory of the commodity than it is to speak of his theory of value. Methodologically, we must remember that everything derives from Marx's concept of the commodity; it is the basic unity of capitalism. All features of capitalism derive from this simplest form. Value, price, money, property, interests, capital, etc. are all related to this entity. According to Marx, 'The wealth of those societies in which the capitalist mode of production prevails, presents itself as an immense accumulation of commodities, its unit being a single commodity. Our investigation must therefore begin with the analysis of a commodity.' (Marx [1867] 2015, p. 27).

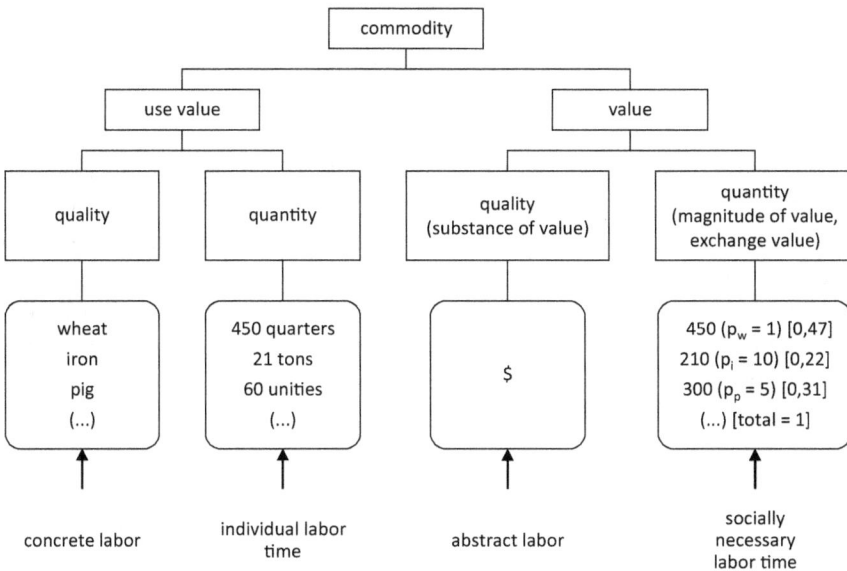

FIGURE 4   Marx's theory of the commodity[a]
a This figure was first presented by me in Portuguese in an article published in the journal *Economia & Sociedade*. See Camarinha Lopes (2014).

Marx's first step is to break the unity of this thing called commodity in two. This is the first division. On one side, the commodity is use value, on the other it is value; these are the two halves of the commodity. Whereas use value is the dimension of natural analysis, where we investigate how acting entities relate to external things, value is the dimension of social analysis. In accordance with the materialist foundations of Marx's philosophy, the social dimension depends on the natural dimension. There cannot be social relations without a material basis upon which the social agents exist.

In a second division, Marx unfolds both use value and value into the contradictory entities quantity and quality. So, we need to explain for both sides what does it mean. Note that, with this second division, we no longer have only two systems in dialectical complementarity (use value and value), but rather four systems (quality and quantity of use value; quality and quantity of value). The commodity not only represents the union of two contradictory worlds, it also represents the unity of four vectors.

The analysis of use value is straightforward, as Marx argues. Every concrete use value has a qualitative and quantitative dimension: 'Every useful thing, as iron, paper, etc., may be looked at from the two points of view of quality and quantity.' (Marx [1867] 2015, p. 27). No use value can be determined without these two dimensions. For example, 'wheat', is not a complete use value. We know that 'wheat' is useful for feeding, but how many people or animals can 'wheat' supply? We need to specify the quantity of the item. 'Wheat' alone is only a general description of qualitative character for a use value. Without specifying the quantity, use value remains an abstract notion. Every concrete use value has both quality and quantity.

Let us use Sraffa's model of three commodities as a basis of our example (Sraffa (1960)). His description provides us with: 450 quarters of wheat. This is a completely defined use value, where quality = wheat and quantity = 450 quarters. Likewise, we can say 21 tons of iron and 60 (unities of) pigs. Each commodity, as use value, has its proper unit of account. Wheat is usually measured in mass (although it could easily be measured in volume), iron is measured in mass and pigs are counted with natural numbers.[9]

---

9   The unit quarter may refer to length, weight, or volume. The quarter (meaning "one-fourth") is used as the name of several distinct units based on ¼ sizes of some base unit. It was used in England as the standard for the quantity of grains in tons. Sraffa's model indicates that uses 450 quarters = ¼ tons of wheat. I will maintain the unit 'quarter' as a measure of mass, although it would be more symmetrical to employ here a unit for volume because then we would have three different dimensions for counting: wheat (volume), iron (mass) and pigs (natural numbers).

Each one of these things—wheat, iron, and pigs—requires a specific form of interaction between humans and the environment. Production of wheat requires preparation of the soil, iron requires mining, and pigs require taming and care. All these tasks, among many others, are aided by the forces of nature. Without rain and sun, wheat will not grow. Without proper geological formation, iron is not accessible. Without the natural rules of life, encoded in the DNA, pigs cannot grow and reproduce. Each single qualitative dimension of use value is accompanied by a specific kind of labor performed by humans. This is concrete labor.

Concrete labor alone is insufficient for determining a complete use value. Concrete labor must also have a quantitative dimension. How many hours of field work are necessary to raise 450 quarters of wheat? The answer to this question ascribes a quantity to the concrete labor that generates wheat. In this way, we can calculate individual labor time, as figure 4 illustrates. The same reasoning applies to the other items (iron and pigs). Concrete labor and individual labor time are concepts related to the side of use value.

The analysis of value is a little more complicated. Figure 4 illustrates this analysis by employing the same dialectical logic of breaking the unity into quantity and quality. Just as use value has a qualitative and a quantitative dimension, so does value. Marx uses the expression 'substance of value' to refer to the quality of value and the expression 'magnitude of value' and 'exchange value' to refer to the quantity of value.[10]

Marx enters the world of value through the gate of exchange value. After presenting the uncomplicated notion that use values 'constitute the substance of all wealth, whatever may be the social form of that wealth', he indicates that in 'the form of society we are about to consider', use values 'are, in addition, the material depositories of exchange value.' (Marx ([1867] 2015), p. 27) Marx arrives at exchange value by putting different use values in quantitative relations of equality. In Sraffa's model (on which our example was based), the

---

10   Notice that the full title of chapter 1, section 1 of *Capital* chapter 1 is: 'The two factors of a commodity: use-value and value (the *substance of value* and the *magnitude of value*)'. In German: "Die zwei Faktoren der Ware: Gebrauchswert und Wert (*Wertsubstanz, Wertgröße*)" (emphasis mine). The difference between the concepts of 'value' and 'exchange value' is tricky and there is much confusion in the literature. Marx employs the expression 'Tauschwert' [exchange value] to indicate that he is talking about the quantitative side of 'Wert', although sometimes he writes only 'Wert' (instead of the more precise 'Tauschwert') to refer to the purely quantitative dimension of value.

equation is 10 quarters of wheat = 1 ton of iron = 2 pigs. These are 'the exchange-values which ensure replacement all around' (Sraffa (1960)).

Marx explains that these equations of quantitative equivalence are only possible if there is a common quality behind these different items. The mathematical expression of equality, the sign '=', means that the compared entities share something of the same magnitude. They have the same quantities of the same thing, i.e., they have the same quantity (magnitude) of value (substance). Mathematically, the system of equations that reveal the exchange-values between all the items in our Sraffian example is:

$$240p_w + 12p_i + 18p_p = 450p_w$$

$$90p_w + 6p_i + 12p_p = 21p_i$$

$$120p_w + 3p_i + 30p_p = 60p_p$$

Where p_w represents the quantity of $\$^{11}$ (substance of value) in one quarter of wheat, p_i represents the quantity of $ in one ton of iron, and p_p represents the quantity of $ in one pig. Setting as numeraire $p_w = 1$, we arrive at $p_i = 10$ and $p_p = 5$. On the side of quantity of value, we can read the specific amount of the substance of value in each expression of the total concrete wealth of this society (450 quarters of wheat, 21 tons of iron and 60 pigs). 450 quarters of wheat are labelled '$ 450', 21 tons of iron are labelled '$ 210' and 60 pigs are labelled '$ 300'. Figure 5 illustrates the total wealth of this 'extremely simple society which produces just enough to maintain itself' (Sraffa (1960)).

What exactly does '$' mean (see figure 5)? We know it is the substance of value, 'something common to them all, of which thing they represent a greater or less quantity' (Marx [1867] 2015, 28). According to Marx:

> This common 'something' cannot be either a geometrical, a chemical, or any other natural property of commodities. Such properties claim our attention only in so far as they affect the utility of those commodities, make them use values. But the exchange of commodities is evidently an act characterised by a total abstraction from use value. (...).

---

11   The choice of the symbol '$' is arbitrary. Any reference to currency would work, such as €, US$, ¥, £, R$, etc.

> If then we leave out of consideration the use value of commodities, they have only one common property left, that of being products of labour.
>
> MARX [1867] 2015, p. 28

The term 'labor' is not precise enough here. The kind of labor Marx means here is different from the labor that generates use values. It is human labor in the abstract, 'the same unsubstantial reality' and 'a mere congelation of homogeneous human labor' (Marx [1867] 2015, p. 28). (Figure 4 indicates abstract labor beneath the box labeled '$'.)

We count abstract labor in time, just as we count concrete labor. The quantity of value, however, refers to the socially necessary labor time. Individual labor time does not coincide with the average required by the whole society, because the means employed in production vary among all producers of the same item. Some individuals use powerful equipment, while others use simple tools.

In figure 4 (to the right of '$'), we can see the proportion of the total abstract wealth at the disposal of this society and how it is distributed in concrete forms of wealth. The quantity of value of 450 quarters of wheat is 450. This means that 47%, (in brackets [] in figure 4, [0,47]) of the total wealth of this society has the concrete form of 450 quarters of wheat. In the same manner, iron and pigs have their share in the total abstract output (usually represented by letter 'Y' in macroeconomic textbooks).

FIGURE 5   The wealth as commodities[a]
a   Sraffa's model is often criticized because it seems like all material was being mixed spontaneously, as if there were no activation of the production process by someone. The active element of the economy is also a part of the transformed material. In this drawing, the choice for pigs as the activator of the process, instead of wheat and iron, derives both from the materialist hierarchy that goes from the non-living world up to human beings and from a reference to Orwell's *Animal Farm* (Orwell ([1945] 2009).

Thus far, this presentation is merely an introduction to the complexities of Marx's theory of the commodity. The concept of labor is also broken down into many categories so that Marx can explain the socio-historical determinant. As I have argued, Marx is demystifying the idea that labor generates value in any mode of production, because he must explain that commodity production is not universal. It is a specific system of the economy that arises only when certain institutions are present. At the same time, he maintains the centrality of labor as the active element that triggers the entire process of production.

The notion that commodity production is eternal or universal is a dangerous one because it leads to the idea that the law of value works like a force of nature in a way that suits human needs. This idea culminates in the vision that capital accumulation and human satisfaction go hand in hand. This match is not real, but derives from the schemes of reproduction that are forced to repeat themselves as self-restoring systems. It is true that there is a certain kind of self-adjustment in the process, but in societies centered on commodity production, such as capitalism, these adjustments occur only through crisis. Unregulated capitalism reproduces at the expense of life and nature and puts the system itself in danger. The law of value requires planning to function at maximum power: capitalist economic planning.

Furthermore, to conceive commodity production as a natural, spontaneous form of economy leads to the Robinson Crusoe paradox. Note that all logical reasoning to calculate the amount of effort that Robinson Crusoe must expend forms a coherent explanation of the quantitative relations of equivalence between all use values. The determinants leading to prices, as pure quantitative relations deriving from the relation between a human and the exterior world of use values, are present in every mode of production. Therefore, the operation of the law of value can be hypothesized in non-capitalist and even non-market social environments. This is also the reason why Robinson Crusoe's paradox supports both the naturalized labor theory of value and the utility theory of value. As Marx explains,

> All the relations between Robinson and the objects that form this wealth of his own creation, are here so simple and clear as to be intelligible without exertion, even to Mr. Sedley Taylor. *And yet those relations contain all that is essential to the determination of value.*
>
> MARX [1867] 2015, p. 50, emphasis mine

The pattern of distribution behind Sraffa's models—and all exercises of drawing the schemes of reproduction that go back to the *Tableau Économique* of Quesnay—is subordinated to a specific logic. The output is distributed so as to restore the initial conditions to reinitiate the reproduction cycle, whether it be at a fixed level (such as in simple commodity reproduction) or at an expanded scale (expanded reproduction). I call this logic 'the logic of equilibrated restoration of the system'. This enables a model of (expanded) simple commodity production (as previously presented in chapters 4 and 5). This is the logic behind the concept of the law of value in classical political economy.[12]

Marx builds upon this notion, but he also indicates that there is an important contradiction at play here. The law of value is not only a force holding the system together, but also a force pushing apart. If we want to further investigate the law of value as the dialectical contradiction of the organization and disarray of the capitalist economy, we need to make a crucial differentiation between the law of value as a real phenomenon and the theories of value that economists develop when they investigate this phenomenon. This distinction is fundamental in order to understand both the contradictory dynamics of capitalism as a self-reproducing system and the difference between the law of value and a theory of value.

Let us look at this contradictory movement and difference in detail. Marx was trying to make sense of the rise of the socialist movement. He had concluded that it was necessary to know how the 'laws of the economy' worked and initiated the most extensive critical analysis of the literature in political economy. He noticed that capitalism—or modern society, as he called it in the preface to the German first edition of *Capital*—was a specific form of economic organization with a singular 'economic law of motion'. The economists have tackled that law and produced various theories. The important distinction here is that the law is not the theory. The law of motion and structure of the economy under investigation is an objective phenomenon. It is a given entity upon which the economist must work scientifically in order to fully comprehend the phenomenon (and influence it). In physics, gravity is a phenomenon that exists objectively and there are various mental constructs to make sense of it. Accordingly, we have different theories to explain and to help humans master the exterior phenomenon. In political economy, the law of value must

---

12   For further details on the relationship between the law of value and the physiocratic tradition, see our presentation on the political economy of input-output economics (Camarinha Lopes and Neder 2017). In the subjectivist tradition of neoclassical economics, the same logic applies but with a different meaning: *Homo economicus*'s subjective evaluation leads to a permanent adjustment of how he modifies the exterior world, so that the technical coefficients of production coincide with his utility preferences.

be treated like this objective thing and every systematization of it is expressed in a certain theory of value.

Marx shows how each author in the field of political economy theorized the concrete fact that useful items are exchanged (or valued) according to one unique logic. Of course, this logic was not as clear as it became in the 19th century, because the market was not always the center of the economic system. But as it increased in importance and the formation of the wage working class occurred due to the violent process of dispossession, the law of value became the most important phenomenon through which to understand not just the modern economy, but all aspects of modern society. It also became the decisive concept with which to analyze how capitalism can emerge from market relations. Political economy is the stage in the history of economic thought when the law of value is the common object of research. All authors develop their own theories in order to comprehend one and the same phenomenon. So, we have only one law of value, but many different theories of value. And since all of them are connected in some way to the objective phenomenon called the law of value (some strongly, others less so), all theories of value may contain truths and useful guidance to better understand and to control it.

Our main conclusion here is that it is not helpful to try to delineate precisely what Marx's theory of value is. This misses the essential contribution he made and may lead to a classification of Marx's theory into a minor episode in the history of the science of value. For example, too often Marx is placed in the same school as Ricardo, and similarly, there is an idea that Marx's opposition to Bentham's utilitarianism and neoclassical economics is merely a complaint against their defense of the capitalist status quo. Both approaches miss the fact that Marx has a solid critique of both classical and neoclassical political economy. Instead of trying to find Marx's theory of value, we should continue to focus on Marx's theory of the commodity. His entire system derives from the uniqueness of the commodity. It is impossible to have an accurate account of Marx's approach to the theory of value without considering fully his theory of the commodity.

Similarly, the law of value in Marx is not just a result of his view on value, which is a subsequent category to the commodity. The law of value in Marx must work in strict accordance with his theory of the commodity. The concept of the law of value in Marx, as was the case in classical political economy, is a central axis of his economic theory of capitalism. I propose to analyze three important aspects in order to appreciate Marx's perspective on the law of value: the law of value as unity between value and price, the law of value as lack of control over economic reproduction and the law of value as an objective phenomenon.[13]

2   The Law of Value as Unity of Value and Price

The capitalist mode of production has unique characteristics. One of them is that its entire economic structure follows only one pattern of individual behavior. Other modes of production involve various cultural elements that variously affect the way people relate to each other. In capitalism, ideally, every agent behaves as the standard proprietor of commodities (C). Since every commodity incorporates a sum of money, every agent carries a sum of money (M). Money can be used as a means to obtain use value, however, in capitalism, the normal case is that all money is used as a means to obtain value, that is, all money is used to obtain more money. This creates a unique way of using economic resources, because there is only one unambiguous goal: to increase the quantity of abstract wealth. This pattern of economic movement ranges from the macro system to the micro agents. All economic activity accomplishes the flow of money increase that is expressed in the general formula of capital: M—C—M' (Money—Commodity—More Money).

Because this scheme is universal in capitalism, it seems natural, as if every economic decision must always match the protocol of wealth augmentation. It implies that abstract wealth is a notion inherent in every kind of mode of production, but not all societies have a clear concept for abstract wealth, even though they are interested in knowing how much labor time the production of each useful item costs. The transformation of every conceivable use value into a commodity is the first step towards homogenizing and universalizing

---

13   This threefold examination of the law of value in Marx is a summary of aspects and does not intend to develop a definition for the law of value based on Marx. The expression 'law of value' appears dispersed within the three books of *Capital*. It appears more frequently in books 1 and 3, and only once in book 2. It is used to describe the dynamics of quantitative equality between different commodities, to explain the contradictions between an overall equal rate of profit and Ricardo's 'doctrine of value', to indicate how international trade is also ruled by the law of value, etc. The expression 'law of value' is concentrated in Engels's introductory and final commentaries to *Capital* Books 2 and 3. There may be important divergences between Marx and Engels here, because the law of value does not have a closed, fixed definition in Marx, but is an open concept requiring further specifications. See Marx ([1867] 2015) [*Capital* Book 1], Marx ([1885] 1956) [*Capital* Book 2], Marx ([1894] 2010) [*Capital* Book 3]. For a conceptualization of the law of value focusing on the dynamics of labor allocation within the economy, see Borges Neto (2004).

the protocol of capitalist activity. At the point when the means of production have become concentrated in the control of a ruling entity and out of the reach of most agents, we have the appropriate conditions for revolutionizing production according to capitalist logic. This second step is the historical process, involving great violence, that created the wage working class and the capitalist class.

Of course, this is a simplification of class struggle into that between only two classes, but we must remember that the protocol of action is the same for every agent in the system. In reality, wage workers do not perform the movement M—C—M' simply because the sum of money they control is insufficient. It is a quantitative barrier that explains the qualitative difference between labor and capital. As soon as the wage worker manages to feed him/herself and guarantee the renewal of his/her labor power, he/she is free to execute the circuit of money expansion with whatever money remains. In this sense, all agents are indeed equal inasmuch as they all are proprietors of commodities. The systemic inequality derives from rules that do not allow for the resetting of the game of capital accumulation. Many inherit only one type of commodity, their own labor power, while few inherit other kinds of commodities (apart from their own labor power that is not put to use) that form the means of production.

This general pattern of the economic use of resources creates the impression that the social relations observed in modern society derive from natural phenomena, i.e., that capitalism is the standard form of organizing production and distribution. It is as if humankind could not change it. This is what we call the naturalization of the social relations of capital, and this is the error made by both strands of non-Marxian political economy.

The utopian socialists argue that the solution to the paradox of inequality between value and price can be found when labor is paid fairly. They naturalize the labor theory of value and disregard the fact that labor does not create value if certain historical institutions are absent. Equivalence between individual and social necessary labor is artificially imposed, as if the market could be corrected in the light of our perception of its failures.

On the other hand, the Marginalist Revolution's utility theory of value also treats value as a natural phenomenon. It is also normal to perform the circuit of infinite value expansion here. Robinson Crusoe becomes a *Homo economicus* who is never satisfied since there is always room to increase his utility level. Both strands are in error, but from opposing perspectives. While non-Marxian socialist economics starts from value, mainstream neoclassical economics consider first prices as they appear in the market. This separation between value and price should never have occurred in the first place and is one of the strongest signs that the scientific approach to the problem had reached an impasse.

One of Marx's goals in writing *Capital* is to find a solid connection between value and price. The incongruence between them is one of the main reasons for developing a theory that explains how the law of value works. Failure to determine how values and price relate means that there is no theory capable of correctly understanding how this law operates. Therefore, initially, we must interpret the law of value as the unification of value and price. The connection between value and price was fundamental in Adam Smith's assessment of the law of value. According to Marx, this was one of his greatest achievements and it should be promoted in the political economy of the future.

Marx knows that the separation between the value and price systems creates a dichotomy. When the focus is only on the quantitative side, there emerges an analytical problem of how these two systems relate to each other. There is a connection between value and price that is fundamental for a correct comprehension of the law of value. Without this linkage, the law of value disappears as the central entity organizing the resource allocation in a market economy. To avoid this, Marx must overcome the limits reached in political economy, many of which were identified by the most eminent author in French socialism, Pierre-Joseph Proudhon. Proudhon shows that the principles of equality in modern society contradict the reality of exploitation. In *The Poverty of Philosophy*, Marx ([1847] 1955) does not deal only with the pledge for the full payment of labor, but also with the way Proudhon analyzes political economy.

In chapter 1 of *The Poverty of Philosophy*, Marx explains that Proudhon develops a good account of the contradiction between the two sides of value (use value and value, the latter still identified as exchange value). After making some points on the determinants of the quantity of value, Proudhon concludes that two major aspects play the most decisive role: costs of production and individual wants. Even though the meeting of individual wishes is relevant, the basis for the quantitative determination of value is expenditure at production, mainly labor. This is Proudhon's scientific discovery that Marx discusses in the first chapter of *The Poverty of Philosophy*.

The scientific discovery is the fact that labor constitutes a quality to measure the quantity of value. Marx recognizes here that the pattern of proportionality in exchanges creates the conditions for the establishment of a labor theory of value. However, this pattern does not avoid a systematic disparity between value and price. There remains a gap between the effort input in production and the results obtained after selling the output at the market. Finding the explanation for this difference between value and price is one of the central axes of the Smithian political economy and Marx wants to pursue this fundamental insight further. This form of explanation is fundamental for avoiding the separation between the objective and subjective evaluative influences over the exchange relations of commodities. Thus, the law of value works as a unity of the two systems, as a movement with logic that shows how well the input costs meet the demand for concrete, useful outputs.

The second and last chapter of *The Poverty of Philosophy* presents a profound methodological critique of Proudhon's economic thinking. Marx argues that Proudhon is trapped inside an ancient contemplative model of philosophy that does not engage with changing reality. Even though Proudhon comprehends with precision the contradictions of political economy, he cannot escape them. He cannot proceed to a superior overarching synthesis because he does not integrate the concrete elements of the living changes in society and the economy. The rules of private property are about to collapse and yet he wants to maintain the relations of exchange based on the law of value.

Political economy is moving toward the description of an economy where private property is no longer sacred. At the same time, economists insist on following the rules of commodity exchange. Marx explains here that the class struggle leaves its footprints in economic theory. The greater the presence of political conflict, the deeper the hole into which economists sink in contradiction. Divergence among various schools of economic thought emerge, signaling that the principles of economic science are under dispute by different classes.

In short, Marx indicates that Adam Smith and David Ricardo first showed how wealth is produced in modern society. Then, 'romantic' economists repeat the classical ideas and disdain the growing number of impoverished masses in the midst of a marvelous explosion of material wealth in capitalism. In a third moment, there arises a 'humanitarian school' where economists begin to feel sympathy for the poor and exploited. They start to grasp the contradictions between wealth and poverty, between the theory and praxis of political economy. Finally, a 'philanthropic school' appears. Here, economists want to transform everyone into a bourgeois proprietor. The radical pledge for equality means that it is not enough if some have only their own labor power as property; the distribution of the means of production is also necessary. However, this still does not overcome the limits of proprietarian political economy, because the total domination of capital over labor is obscured, in the vision of a society of independent and identical producers of commodities, where no one can directly exploit the other.

Marx explains that economists act like representatives of the capitalist class because they insist on the sociability of equal exchange. Communists, by contrast, act as theoreticians of the wage working class. The advancement of the productive forces demands full global cooperation, which is only possible by overturning the capitalist state. The national economy only becomes a capitalist nation state so as to parasitize other people through imperialism. International organization of the world's working class is thus essential, as well as economic planning on a global scale.

Economic planning is the practical result of the solution to the systematic divergence between values and prices. Since the deviation between values and prices is an expression of the operation of the law of value, economic planning is a conscious action to organize labor to meet human needs. The point is that economic planning should not be used to make values converge to those prices that arise in a market society. These prices are biased by the general alienation process that sustains the whole system. Economic planning should be used to reconfigure production according to a logic other than M—C—M'. Production must not be controlled by the invisible force of capital, but it must be consciously organized to meet the needs of humans. In this sense, the unity of value and price brought about by the law of value represents the lack of control over economic reproduction. Production and distribution are structured unconsciously by a society in which capital commands everything and each member becomes an automaton fulfilling the necessities of infinite value expansion.

The law of value as unity of value and price means that these two sides are connected to each other. There cannot be a theory of value separated from a theory of price, simply because value and price are one dialectical unity when we consider the totality of a market economy. Thus, the process of separating value and price that occurred in the development of economic science must be reversed.

3   The Law of Value as Lack of Control over Economic Reproduction

In contrast to the historical analysis of the *Manifesto of the Communist Party* of 1848, the utopian imagining of communist models of society had become a trend in the 19th century.[14] Johan Karl Rodbertus (1805–1875), a German economist and socialist author who defended a labor theory of value, conceptualized one such model. He called attention to the fact that a completely planned economic system, where value and price converge, does not mean the end

---

14   The *Manifesto of the Communist Party* from 1848 initiates the analysis of historical events for the orientation of the communist movement based on Marx and Engel's theory. After this work, there appeared *The Class Struggles in France,* from 1848 to 1850, *The Eighteenth*

of exploitation. This is important because most socialist authors think that exploitation is the result of the difference between value and price. According to Marx's theory of value, the distinction between value and price only promotes the distribution of a previously created mass of value, which has been extracted by the exploitative process of production. Thus, exploitation does not depend on whether value and price coincide quantitatively.

In the preface to the first German edition of *The Poverty of Philosophy*, Engels ([1885b] 1955) draws on Rodbertus to reinforce the idea that economic planning does not automatically entail the political control of the working class. Although there was a rumor that Marx had plagiarized Rodbertus, Engels recognizes that Rodbertus had at least one important and novel idea. Engels explains that this important idea is also associated with an erroneous interpretation of the labor theory of value. According to Rodbertus, Ricardo's labor theory of value would lead directly to communism, because the principle of full payment of labor would be the realization of what the theory proclaims: labor alone is responsible for creating value.

Engels ([1885b] 1955) explains that even though it seems logical, the defense of the principle of full payment for labor is a formally false solution, because it is based on a moral argument. The contradiction between theory and reality expresses a sentiment of injustice, but Marx does not build his theory of value on this basis. Although it is extremely important to repudiate interest rates, profits, and all kinds of non-labor income, this is not enough to break with the logic of bourgeois economic relations. Communism is based on a qualitatively different logic, not on the perfection of the standard bourgeois ideal of equality. It is not the correction of 'deficiencies' found in economic reality that contrast with the beautiful ideals that destroyed the Anción Regime.

Rodbertus's treatment of the problem of value leads to a paradoxical result, as Proudhon had so clearly illustrated. Rodbertus does not break with the conventions of proprietarianism and thinks that the law of value must govern any kind of economy, even the socialist, post-capitalist ones. The organizing core of capitalism becomes the standard around which a full planned economy should revolve. It is an acute contradiction. On one side, there is the effort to overcome the relations of exchange between equals, on the other side, there is

---

Brumaire of Louis Bonaparte from 1852 and *The Civil War in France* from 1871, among other articles on political and economic matters in different countries. Then, Marx's attention returned to Germany in the *Critique of the Gotha Program* from 1875. None of these works aim at designing a perfectly functioning communist society. They analyze the concrete changes by indicating how the ideological clashes amount to transformations in the social relations of productions.

the reinforcement of the law of value. This is the pinnacle of the errors made by the pre-Marxian socialists who so bravely took control of political economy in the 1830s and 1840s, such as John Gray in England, Rodbertus in Germany, and Proudhon in France.

Engels calls this line of Ricardian socialists 'Arbeitsgeld-Utopisten' (labor-voucher utopians) because they wanted to implement a system in which vouchers (also called certificates) would represent labor time in hours directly. According to them, money does not function to represent labor time accurately and so it must be replaced by something else that ensures just treatment and remuneration for workers. This type of system has the notorious feature of coincidence of value and price, as if this could guarantee that the worker received one hundred percent of what he/she has produced. They claimed that exploitation would cease and none of them saw the possible result of having both the coincidence of all values and prices and the permanence of exploitation. This is because they believed that exploitation is something that is only possible through the quantitative divergence between value and price. They did not realize that the creation and distribution of value is a two-dimensional totality—generation and the distribution of what has been generated—that is not responsible for direct exploitation.

The pattern of production and distribution created by the market is at the center of the issue under discussion. Divergence between value and price is relevant for determining the distribution, but the process of production is not affected by this difference. Engels recognizes the problem of economic calculation in the absence of the market and points out an important advancement in Rodbertus that differentiates him at this point from other utopian socialists. According to Engels, Rodbertus explained along general lines how a perfectly centralized planned economy would function. It would be an economy in which production is organized to meet all demands of each member of society without using the usual mechanisms of blind market coordination. Instead of first producing and then checking what has been absorbed by money in order to make adjustments in the next round of production, the production would be directed to a previously known schedule of necessities. A perfect match would mean no divergence between value and price. Rodbertus does not expound the details of how such an economy could be built, but presents it as the antithesis of the market.

Engels argues that the description of this antithesis is naive, even though it is correct from the point of view of traditional philosophy. Utopians treat real problems in an abstract manner in order to sketch a solution, but do not set out the concrete means to achieve this result. Nonetheless, Rodbertus has a distinctive idea in comparison to other socialists (from Gray to Proudhon). The standard economic reasoning of the socialist movement at the time was that if labor was paid fully, then exploitation would be eliminated because exploitation was the result of labor being paid less than it should. Accordingly, if it were paid justly, its value and price would coincide, and no exploitation would be possible. In reaction against this, Rodbertus points out that wage labor and its exploitation still go on when value and price coincide. According to Engels, this is a really new and important insight for understanding that the transition to a planned economy does not necessarily mean the end of capitalism.

In this preface, Engels ([1885b] 1955) indicates that we cannot immediately identify a centrally organized economy (in opposition to the decentralized market system) with communism. Economic planning does not guarantee the end of exploitation and the capitalist state. An economic system based on the dialectical opposition to the market is a planned organization where the agents still do not control the economy, which is now directed by a superior entity. It is only a mirror image of the market economy. Alienation, which was dispersed in the decentralized commodity society, is now structured around a coherent whole under the command of the central planning board.

Let us take a closer look into this curious parallel, because it will help us understand the phenomenon of economic planning under capitalism. Rodbertus's insight shows that the total output of an economy must be distributed among different functions, so that reproduction can continue. In a market system, the flow of all use value of the output matrix back into each slot of the input matrix follows the money: purchasing power is what determines how the economy repeats its reproduction cycle. In a planned system, however, the reproduction does not derive from the dispersed logic of private property. Decision-making about how society will use the total output is decentralized and there is no sacred liberty for the individual capitalist. The bourgeois agent cannot freely decide what to buy, as both sale and purchase are merged into the plan. Theoretically, this eliminates the tension between money and commodity, as well as the contradiction between use value and value.

From the standpoint of the system overall, however, the dynamics of capital can still exist. In total, all members of society have the rights over all social output, but the isolated individual does not have the right to his/her individual share of the total production. This is the economic situation in the absence of private property. But it does not signify that workers control the law of value because a fully planned economic system can still follow the alienating logic of the expansion of abstract wealth. Collectivist systems of states that operate the movement M—C—M' (money—commodity—more money) show that exploitation continues. In this dystopian scene, the workers do not control the destiny of the use values, which move according to the necessities of capital expansion.

Engels notices that planning does not correspond to the final aim of the communist movement. Rodbertus's conjecture illustrates that the state remains the only controlling entity that decides, in a 'top-down' fashion, about the use of economic resources. All agents (capitalist and worker) participate as powerless parts of a huge machine. The state and capital are so symbiotically related that there is no room for political divergence among sectors of society. One could even say that classes have vanished, and the entire population per-form the various tasks in an egalitarian program. The only drawback is that this program is of capitalist nature. There is no emancipation and no end of exploitation. Production of the means of production in order to increase the production of the means of production is an inexorable cycle, which shows that there must be a conscious plan to escape the infinite logic of the develop-ment of productive forces. Otherwise, the law of value dominates everything and everyone.

Real 20th century economies in various countries demonstrate the experi-ence of planning with similar characteristics to this situation. This indicates that economic activity along these lines is not necessarily tied to a defined political direction. Transition to non-liberal capitalism can embrace many forms of polit-ical architecture. Planning alone does not offer a secure path towards socialism and communism because the real phenomena of alienation and exploitation can find various ways to persist even outside the chaotic order of free markets. This means that the control over the law of value does not constitute per se the control by direct producers over the economy. Entities alien to the working class may master the law of value and eradicate the typical fluctuations of capitalism, thus maintaining its exploitative features in a stable way. If the production of value and use value are aligned, the contradictions of the commodity are safely contained, and the expansion of capital may continue indefinitely. This is the political problem behind planning. It is not possible to overcome the law of value without addressing the question of who is in command.[15]

Economic planning is one of the least visible aspects of Marx's political economy. Oligopoly capitalism only became a decisive structure with the national efforts of World War I. However, the elements of planning were

---

15   For the difference between centralist socialism and democratic socialism, see Prado
     (2014). The concept of state capitalism is also useful here. My concept of economic plan-
     ning of a capitalist nature is similar to the concept of state capitalism, or state monopoly
     capitalism, but it focuses on the abstract dimension of value theory instead of looking
     at the concrete historical events of the world economy after World War I, the Russian
     Revolution and the Great Depression of 1929. I do not employ the concept of state

already detectable in the 19th century, for example, the model of labor-vouchers proposed by the 'Arbeitsgeld-utopisten' (labor-vouchers utopians), the increasing separation between property and administration, and the spread and growth of joint-stock companies.

Economic planning, the transition to communism and the limits of bourgeois socialist theory are dealt with by Marx ([1865] 1969) in a letter to J. B. Schweitzer in 1865, a few days after Proudhon's death. Marx explains here his critique of Proudhon, giving us an excellent summary of his views at that time. For Marx, Proudhon made a great contribution with his book *What is property?* because it struck hard against the legal principles of capitalist society. In his subsequent works, however, Proudhon was not able to correctly expound the contradictions of the world of commodities and so he was not able to find an exit path from the system. For this reason, Marx's description ranks Proudhon, the man of science, beneath both the economists and the socialists. Comparing France with Germany, Marx writes that Proudhon relates to Saint-Simon and Fourier as Feuerbach relates to Hegel. In other words, Proudhon tries courageously to overcome the limits faced by other socialists by pointing the finger at private property as the main institution responsible for the disgraces of modern society. But his system, like that of any other socialist, is dominated by bourgeois political economy. The principles of production and distribution are the same: equal rights for commodities of equal values and equal quality to measure different quantities. Everything becomes a matter of how much an individual proprietor possesses. Although Proudhon took this ambiguity to its ultimate logical frontier, he could not find a way to break with the logic of the social relation called commodity.

Proudhon's last attempts to reconcile the institution of private property with the rising force of the communal use of resources are embodied in his proposals for 'gratuitous credit' and the 'bank of the people'. These institutions are designed to promote equality through a reform of the monetary system. Money would then function as it always should and exploitation would cease. Money would no longer be a veil obscuring the relationship between value and price, but a social certificate guaranteeing harmony between labor and the law of value.

Marx's answers to the various schemes of labor vouchers are in the manuscript *Zur Kritik der Politischen Ökonomie* from 1859. Here, he investigates the

---

capitalism from a historical perspective to criticize real capitalist or socialist economies such as those of the United States and Western countries, the Soviet Union, China, etc. For an overview on the concept of state capitalism, see Pannekoek (1936), Mandel (1951), Binns (1986) and Howard and King (2001).

complicated relation between commodity and money.[16] Marx argues that the socialists' main mistake is to praise the commodity as the highest principle of communism. This only shows a general ignorance about what the commodity really is. Even staunch socialists do not understand the nexus of dependency between commodity and money. The commodity is not an external thing, it is not a use value, rather it is a social relationship of production and distribution.

Marx's critical engagement with the proposals of labor vouchers derives from his complex conception of commodity. He is particularly worried about not endorsing a solution that is rooted in the same vital source of bourgeois society. He wants to show that communism cannot be based on an abstract matching between use value and value. If it were only a matter of fitting the value vector into the use value matrix, a perfectly equilibrated market could solve the problem. This is precisely the formal solution that emerged in the socialist economic calculation debate in the 1930s. This kind of answer, however, does not touch the essentials of what distinguishes a communist economy from a capitalist economy.

We need to be careful at this point about the line that separates Marx and Engels from all previous traditions of socialism. I believe it is increasingly important to have an open attitude towards revising our view of this divide, because Marxism hegemonized the socialist movement only in the 20th century. The 19th and 21st centuries demand an alternative approach in which dialog, mutual understanding and support between Marxist and non-Marxists socialists are possible. There must be an open and free interaction so that we can deal scientifically with the experiences of and thoughts on labor vouchers. The fact that Marx and Engels rejected the schemes of labor vouchers does not mean that these schemes are simply wrong or always condemned to failure. If they are tied to a program of full transition and detached from the ideology of mere compensation for individual effort, it is worth engaging with them.[17]

What was Marx's argument for dismissing the labor vouchers? Chapter 2 of *Zur Kritik* gives us a first clue by pointing to the limits of socialism when it is trapped in the carousel of money and simple circulation. John Gray was one of the authors who first worked out the relation between the necessary labor time

---

16   Marx wrote the manuscript *Zur Kritik der Politischen Ökonomie* after reading Bastiat and Carey and taking notes in the *Grundrisse* (Marx ([1857–1858] 2011). For an extensive commentary on the relationship between commodity and money in Marx's preparation to write *Capital* during the years 1857–1858, see Rosdolsky ([1968] 2020).

17   For a careful analysis of the case of labor-vouchers based on Marx's theory and its relation to the socialist economic calculation debate, see Cottrell and Cockshott (1993a) and their book *Towards a New Socialism* (Cockshott and Cottrell (1993b)), where they consider all theoretical and historical development of the 20th century. My assessment of

for the production of use values and the quantity of value of these same use values measured in money (Marx [1859a] 1971, pp. 66–67). He emphasizes that money is both a register of hours of labor and of quantity of value. Gray imagines that a national bank could transform 'normal money' into another kind of money, a 'special money' that could not be used to exploit other humans. The idea was simple: if every voucher corresponded exactly to the duration of labor performed by the owner of the voucher, then all national net income would be appropriated by those who labor. Non-laborers would not be entitled to *labor* vouchers.

Marx explains the problems behind this apparently simple solution by indicating that the replacement of money by vouchers does not lead necessarily to an end of exploitation. This is because the basis of capitalist exploitation is not the result of a quantitative difference between value and price. It does not rest on a supposedly unequal or unjust exchange, but on the real phenomenon of alienation. As long as the production process follows the infinite circuit of capital accumulation M—C—M' (money—commodity—more money), exploitation is present, even in the ideal case of perfect coincidence between all values and all prices. One of Marx's main aims in Capital is precisely to explain how, even with total coincidence between value and price, exploitation still exists.

Marx emphasizes that Gray's solution leads to an incorrect apprehension of socio-economic reality. In Gray's scheme, the output no longer exists in the social form of commodity because individual labor and social labor always coincide. There is no room for divergence between the individual expenditure of labor and the social demand for it. The concrete problem, however, is that to create such a convergence, there must be a plan that can anticipate the individual efforts required to meet society's needs. The market does not act as an adjustment tool, but this correction needs to take place anyway. If the whole social output perfectly meets all individual needs, it means that the previously employed labor in total has been perfectly used, and no single second of individual labor time has been wasted. Proudhon's school thinks that the market, and consequently the commodity, can undergo a reform that guarantees this kind of equilibrium. Marx argues that, even in the improbable case in which this equilibrium is consistently achieved, the problems remain because such an economy is still dominated by capital.

Let us briefly focus on the dialectical contradiction of quantity and quality. This is necessary in order to dig deeper into Marx's theory of value. Since the

---

the question presented in this book is intended to expose the fundamentals of the issue focusing on Marx's work only.

quantitative aspect of value attracts almost all the attention of economists, across the political spectrum, we need to say something about the quality of value. Marx deals with both quantity and quality in his theory of value. He chooses the quality labor to fulfill the task of measuring quantity but, differently from other labor value theoreticians, Marx does not believe that labor has natural properties that generate value. Labor as an entity that generates value is an ideological concept that has emerged together with capitalism. There is nothing natural about labor as the qualitative element of value in the same manner as there is nothing natural about time or utility as the quantitative element of value.

The qualitative element of value always involves a choice and this choice is not a neutral procedure but reflects a political position towards the autonomous movement of the law of value. Marx's adherence to the labor theory of value is not a simple repetition of the argument of classical economists or of socialist economists before him. In addition to a degree of continuity, which is real and sometimes may be useful (for example, regarding empirical tests of the labor theory of value), there is an additional justification for Marx selection of labor to fulfill the role of the qualitative element of value.

According to his presentation of the theory of commodity in chapter 1 of *Capital*, any use value that fulfills certain conditions in the reproduction of the economy can theoretically function as the common element to measure the quantity of value. The selection of this element is a social and historical process. This is so because all of them are equally valid from the standpoint of the relations between humans and nature. With the rise of capitalism and the increasing importance of a working class that survives through the sale of its labor power, the idea spread that equal exchanges resemble the exchange of equal quantities of labor. Accordingly, the notion that labor is the main or only source of value (and wealth) gained popularity. In past societies, labor had already been recognized as a fundamental factor in production costs, and there were various thinkers who anticipated the labor theory of value of classical political economy. But it was only after the majority of the population gained access to use values through money obtained by labor that the association between labor and value became so strong. In this sense, the labor theory of value is the proper theory of value for the wage working class and it was born with the development of Adam Smith's system.

Marx takes this new idea and emphasizes that there has always been a dispute around the theory of value. Class struggle shows itself in economic thought most blatantly in value theory since it concerns the element responsible for creating value. Thus, it is also a means to justify access to the social output. Marx is a labor value theoretician in two senses: as a technical defender of value as a result of the physiological effort to generate concrete wealth (similar to classical economists) and as a political defender of value as the social consensus that laborers are responsible for creating everything that sustains the whole society.

The next step is to relate the dialectical duality of quantity and quality of value to the law of value. The law of value, differently from the theory of value, normally refers only to the quantitative aspect. It is assumed as obvious that one is talking about the allocation of labor and not of other economic factors. The qualitative aspect of value comes into play whenever one wants to distinguish Marx's socialism from utopian socialism, and it is crucial to problematize it. But it is necessary to maintain attention on the quantitative problem of value because it contains all the issues of economic planning and of control over the law of value. Focus on the qualitative aspect correctly reveals the necessity of overcoming wage labor, but it does not contribute to the development of a concrete framework for the conscious organization of production and distribution, which needs an objective system of accounting.

Quantity and quality must remain equally present in our analysis. Any abstract solution to the problem of the transformation of values into prices merely illustrates a theoretical matching of supply and demand through the market. The coincidence of the value and price systems eliminates the transfer of value between individual capitalists, but it does not eliminate the total exploitation process that stems from alienation.

Socialist authors thought that the difference between value and price (that is, the difference between produced quantity and appropriated quantity) was the source of surplus value, as if the workers could overcome exploitation when their labor power was paid its 'true' value and not its 'fake' price. Marx's approach in book 1 of *Capital* is one in which there is absolute coincidence between the value and price systems, so that he can show how surplus value originates through the concrete process of matter being transformed by labor within the institutions of commodity relations of production. As Rodbertus correctly anticipated and Engels acknowledged, the identity between the value and price systems does not imply the end of exploitation. As a result, if economic planning is understood in a narrow sense of eliminating the discrepancies or imbalances between market supply and demand, this is far from a socialist political concept. Accordingly, planning per se is not bound to any political direction. Its operation does not mean either the end of capitalism nor the beginning of communism. It only shows that a systematic coincidence between value and price at both micro and macro levels is possible without affecting the essential features of capitalist exploitation.

Modern economic planning is a byproduct of 20th century capitalism. The historical development of capitalism itself leads to an increasingly stronger symbiosis between capital and the state. Social control over economic reproduction becomes a pressing matter in class struggle. The battle is not market versus planning but capitalist planning versus socialist planning, and depends on who is in command of the economic policy. In fact, economics has always been essentially political. Accordingly, there is a new challenge. If the working class is not politically and technically prepared to take control over economic planning, the system will continue to be controlled by its own logic of capital.

The traditional view in political economy was that market relations were irreconcilable with planning directives. The truth is that this kind of opposition (market versus plan) makes no sense as soon as we realize that there exists a special kind of capital reproduction that does not depend on the spontaneous and multiple actions of independent individuals. Since Adam Smith, the belief in the possibility of a real open system of free individuals that leads to a coherent and positive social outcome has spread. In fact, this notion only indicates that most members in society do not participate in the relevant decisions that affect the whole system.

In Marx, the law of value must describe the way in which the anarchy of the market culminates in a coherent self-reproducing system. It must explain how the value system transforms itself into the price system. This system is not an organization of labor (and of every other economic resource) allocation aimed at meeting specific, concrete human needs, but has only one goal. The law of value rearranges the input and output matrices according to the general impetus of infinite capital accumulation. The movement M—C—M' (money—commodity—more money) is the guiding principle for the economic organization of capital. Capitalism is not a chaotic and dispersed system like the idealized market of simple commodity production. It is a very narrowly structured economy that expands itself as quickly as possible. The law of value is the expression of this organization. It is a special case of economic planning, in which the dispersed rationality once described by Adam Smith is put under the political control of the infinite accumulation of abstract wealth. Capitalist economic planning allows a relatively stable expansion of value. It does not eliminate exploitation, alienation, and the social form of the commodity for the output. But it does eliminate the uncertainties typical of the anarchic roots of the market that explode in crises. The remaining uncertainties are only those related to natural phenomena, for example, weather conditions that may harm production.

We see that the law of value and the control of economic reproduction are closely related. If working people do not control the law of value, it evolves from a horizontal frame of power relations into a vertical, hierarchical system of social relations of production, which is known as capitalism. When the law of value is in operation, it indicates that people are not controlling the economic reproduction of the systems in which they live. Does this mean that there is no control whatsoever? No, because the capital movement has direction and it forces an organization or planned system to sustain the infinity of M—C—M' (money—commodity—more money).

4   The Law of Value as an Objective Phenomenon

After seeing that the law of value is a unity of value and price and an expression of people's lack of control over economic reproduction, it is time to understand better the difference between the law of value and the theory of value. These are two different things that appear to be only one.

First, we have the law of value as an objective phenomenon. It is something real that organizes production and distribution according to the diktats of private property. It is a concrete force that allocate resources according to the logic of value. It was first studied by moral philosophers and classical political economists, and Adam Smith popularized a specific version of it with the result that the law of value became practically a synonym for the labor theory of value. But this is not correct. The law of value is not the same as the labor theory of value.

Second, we have the mental process through which the analyst captures the law of value. Here we talk about theories of value, a variety of ideas trying to understand and analyze an external, objective phenomenon. All theories of value are attempts to apprehend the law of value. Even though the tradition of neoclassical political economy abandoned the expression 'law of value', they studied the same conditions and regularities, because the foundations of the economy under investigation are the same. Private property establishes certain social relations between the members of society that are described by the pattern of market transitions.

This distinction is important to show that the law of value is a concrete element that exists independently from the form it assumes in any economic theory. Although Marx did not explicitly mention this division, his approach indicates that theories of value diverge mainly due to their political implications, and not the extent to which they do (or do not) capture the movement of the law of value. Like the theories of prices, all theories of value describe with varying degrees of accuracy what the law of value does.

In this sense, the law of value and the theory of value are two different entities. The first one refers to the object under investigation by all economists. The second one refers to the shape of the theory after the analyst has studied the real phenomenon of exchange relations. It is important to notice that, even when the economist is not aware of the institutional specificities that sustain private property, the economist at least describes how individuals relate to each other and to economic goods. Thus, every theory of value represents a different view about the workings of the law of value, and each one of them reveals the preferences and concerns of the analyst.

Marx's theory of value is unique in the sense that it is the only one that problematizes the quality of value. It is the only one which wants to explain the fundamentals behind the choice of the element that generates value. It is the best one to explain that, in the end, the controversy about value theory is a matter of politics. Value and price do not derive only from the quantitative relationships between different items that after combination are transformed into new objects. They are not simply technical coefficients of production. Both value and price, in their permanent mutual adjustment, represent social conflict around those coefficients.

The controversy about value theory is typically represented as the question of how well a theory of value describes or predicts the movement of prices as pure quantitative relations of exchange. But the issue cannot be settled on these terms, because competing theories of value will register reasonably good indicators for this criterion.

Marx's preference for a labor theory of value is not based primarily on the fact that it works better to describe the movement of prices. In fact, Marx does not advocate for a labor theory of value against other theories of value. What he does is to explain that all theories of value—including the labor theory of value of Adam Smith, David Ricardo, and the socialists—must not naturalize the element that is regarded as the creator of value. If there is no natural basis for choosing an element to explain the origin of value, why choose labor? Put simply, the choice of labor reflects the standpoint of those who possess only one kind commodity: labor power. A labor theory of value can also work well to describe the movement of prices, but this is not the main reason why one should defend it. The main reason is one of a political nature.

The political conflict around theories of value is complex. The two theories of value that we reviewed in chapters 4 and 5 (the labor theory of value of utopian socialists and the utility theory of value of the Marginalist Revolution) do not immediately resemble the opposition between labor and capital. Certainly, class struggle indicates that the utility theory of value is closer to the political forces of capital while the labor theory of value is closer to the political views of working people. But as soon as we enter the complexities of value theory in general, this clash is not so straightforward. Once we recognize that the law of value is a real phenomenon, all theories of value gain a certain status that undermines this simple dichotomy. In the proposed reading, the utility theory of value is just another way to apprehend the law of value. It is equally valid as the labor theory of value of non-Marxian socialists. Neither theory of value questions the possibility of bending the law of value according to specific goals, nor interrogates why value measures a specific quality, such as labor or utility. They both naturalize the qualitative aspect and are not able to analyze their own position in class struggle.

Now it is time to ask a question that is crucial for understanding Marx's perspective on the law of value and on his own theory of value. If all theories of value are valid in some sense, why did Marx defend with ferocity a labor theory of value? We must bear in mind the duality of the *Critique of Political Economy*. It targets both reactionary authors and progressive ones. Marx's theory of value has two achievements: first, it maintains the connection between value and price to relate final market prices to labor time and, second, it denaturalizes the notion that labor creates value in any social institutional setting. These two aspects relate to the quantitative and qualitative sides of value. Accordingly, it is important to perceive correctly the relationship between Marx's labor theory of value and the labor theory of value of other economists. The proposed reading suggests that the embodied labor theory of value (physiological expenditure of muscles and brain) and the social labor theory of value (abstract labor as the common entity) can coexist in mutual support.

The choice of labor as the element responsible for value is part of a social process to vindicate labor's right to the total output of production. Of course, it is possible to establish a labor theory of value based on the principle of human labor as the sole way to interact with nature. But this perspective is limited because it does not distinguish the two sides of the commodity, the basic unit of the whole capitalist system. When there is no clear division between the world of use value and the world of value, there can be no adequate treatment of the concept of labor. By following the standard theory of value of his time, Marx expanded its development by unfolding labor into two subcategories: concrete labor and abstract labor. His intention was to indicate that labor performed in society is both a relation of the kind human-nature and a relation of the kind human-human (Figure 6). Laboring is a social process to change nature and a triangular relation.

Marx never failed to highlight that the development of the labor theory of value derives from the increasing importance of the wage working class in the economy. But, when the direct conflict between the two new modern classes

Human   Human

Nature

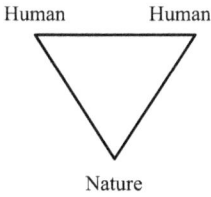

FIGURE 6   Human social laboring

became evident, this theory began to be marginalized. Economists rapidly found another element to serve as the source of value, namely utility. The decisive component for founding a theory of value is not merely technical, but also, and mainly, of political character. The labor theory of value would be better called a 'laborers' theory of value'. This would indicate the contradiction in the theory: it claims the right for the workers to the full products of labor based on an ahistorical argument that labor is the natural source of value.

Since the qualitative element of value is decided in the process of class struggle, why not accept this choice at the side of workers and, at the same time, show that this choice has very little to do with a natural phenomenon?[18] My argument points in this direction. When Marx first encountered the labor theory of value in the literature of political economy, he rejected it because of its grounding in claims to be natural.[19] In short, the argument was the following: since labor is needed to produce economic goods, and economic goods have value, labor is claimed to be the true creator of value. Because of this,

---

18   Choosing the labor theory of value without criticizing its natural justification is progressive, but vulgar economics. I have argued that vulgar economics can also be of politically progressive character, which is a novelty for the Marxist literature on value theory.

19   'Marx's refusal of the labor theory of value' is the catchy title of a recent provocative paper by Harvey (2018), who wants to call attention to the fact that Marx does not use the same theory as Ricardo. Among others (for example, Roberts (2020)), Cockshott (2018) responded, explaining that empirical studies proved Ricardo and Marx to be right when it comes to explaining prices by the necessary labor time to produce the commodities under investigation. As a matter of fact, according to Gorender (1985) and Mandel (1968), Marx and Engels did not accept the classical labor theory of value before writing *The German Ideology* in 1845–1846. In chapter 3 of his book, *The Formation of the Economic Thought of Karl Marx*, Mandel (1968) explains that they embraced the theory for two reasons. First, the political reason was to demark a position in the clash between socialist authors who defended the labor theory of value and capital allied economists who were abandoning it. Second, there was also a technical reason related to a better study of and solution to the contradictions between value and price. According to my research, Marx's

labor would create value in any socioeconomic context whatsoever and the specificity of commodity relations and capitalism would be entirely lost.

Instead of rejecting this natural version of the labor theory of value as a whole, I believe Marx saw himself as obliged to give a new meaning to the labor theory of value. The increasing influence of socialism over the English literature on political economy made the idea that labor creates value too important to be abandoned. The labor theory of value had become one of the most important elements in the economics of the working class. Marx could not simply reject it. He had to devise a proper argument and unfold the concept of labor into concrete labor and abstract labor, according to the duality originating in the commodity. By doing this, he was endorsing labor as the political component to explain the origin of wealth and also explaining that value is not simply the technical result of the interaction between human and nature, but a transformation of nature in a social environment.

This maneuver was necessary because it was not possible to simply discard the prevailing theory of value of the 19th century. Political economy, the mainstream economics of the time, held that labor was the main source of value. Marx had to transfer all the ambiguities of this idea to his system and worked arduously to explain the specificities of his own labor theory of value. Even though the standard, classical argument in defense of labor was limited (for example, it could not question the wage system per se but only the magnitude of wages), it was a very strong and unifying component of the political economy of workers. Thus, it seems to me that Marx formulated a strategy of argumentation in favor of the labor theory of value that, on one side, denaturalizes it and, on the other side, allows it to continue serving as ideological support for the day-to-day struggle of the working class and socialist intellectuals in general.

This duality in Marx's theory of value should not confuse us nor should it be seen as a weakness in Marx's system. There are elements of continuity as well as rupture between Marx and other labor value theoreticians. There is a continuity aspect in quantitative accounts of value, and rupture in the qualitative analysis of value. The approach that sees rupture focuses on quality and tends to overlook quantity. Continuist readings, by contrast, tend to put Marx side by side with Adam Smith and David Ricardo and focus on quantity. We already know by now that no theory of value can be complete if only one side

---

positive engagement with the classical, traditional labor theory of value began with his reaction to Proudhon (Marx [1847] 1955).

of the dialectical unity quantity-quality is involved. Our task is to understand the complementary functioning of each side.

I want to draw attention here to the importance of the quantitative aspect for the law of value and its relation to the transition to a planned economy. Once we see the relevance of the quantitative connection between value and price, we see that the socialist economic calculation becomes a necessary step in the development of both the theory of value and the law of value. The debate about economic calculation recovers an important question that almost disappears when our focus is only directed on how Marx surpassed classical political economy and all derivative petty bourgeois socialist thinking.

The ground-breaking discovery of the specific historical circumstances that allow capitalism to emerge as a full mode of production diverts the attention of many from the fact that Marx himself was very concerned with understanding the purely quantitative dynamics of exchange relations, i.e., the movement of prices as indexes of quantities. Among Marxists, Marxist *economists* are more prone to keeping the problem in view, because economic science deals mainly with questions of quantitative order. If we look at all three books of *Capital* through the lenses of a standard economist, we will see that the fundamental issue they address is the problem of the equalization of the profit rates across all sectors, and how this equal rate converges to the general interest rate of the economy. In other words, in the eyes of a neoclassical mainstream economist, Marx's *Critique of Political Economy* is almost equivalent to the construction of a solution to the transformation problem of values into production prices. Of course, this is a limited perspective. But this is how economists trained under the hegemony of Paul Anthony Samuelson begin to engage with Marx.

From perspective, we can say that, after chapter 1 on commodity, *Capital* deals mostly with the quantitative problem of transforming values into prices. So, the understanding of these dynamics is fundamental if we want to change them according to the political aims of the working class. It is not only a matter of describing how the law of value operates, but also how we can alter and control it. Labor allocation is always an issue for any society. It is so obvious that it makes little sense to explain in detail why the content of value quantities is made of labor. In this sense, the explanation of the law of value as a mechanism of resource allocation is mostly given by the quantitative approach.

Marx's ([1875] 1970) *Critique of the Gotha Programme* is known to be a text that rejects the imagined utopias of communist societies. For Marx, communism is a real movement that is building the new mode of production here and now. It is not an intellectual creation to be implemented later in the future. But it is not enough for Marx to merely observe the birth of the new socioeconomic system; there must also be conscious intervention. In the process of transition, the new will be born out of the old and, instead of merely describing the final outcome (as utopian socialists do) it is necessary to undertake a theoretical systematization of all revolutionary experiences in order to discover how to arrive at this final situation.

Marx criticizes the Gotha program, the party platform adopted in 1875 by the political groups that would jointly become the Social Democratic Party of Germany (SPD), because it claims to implement a 'just distribution' based on morality. Moreover, the moral standard for rightness of distribution coincides with the bourgeois norm. Each member of society receives a share of the social output that is equivalent to his/her individual contribution to its creation. Marx recognizes that this is an advance considering the huge disparity between wealth and poverty, but considers that it does not go far enough. The pattern of distribution is not detached from the organization of production. Thus, an entirely new economic order is needed to achieve the ideals of the working class.

Revolution is a process. In a first step, the principle of equivalence of exchange should be established. The quantity of labor which the individual offers to the collective gives him/her the right to obtain the same amount of labor in the form of produced goods. In a second stage, when spiritual and material abundance is achieved, society should finally be able to realize the dream of communal economic reproduction in which each member puts his/her individual capacities at the full disposal of the entire collective and each one takes from the collective what he/she needs. This principle is radically distinct from that of equal exchange. Equality is not applying the same standard to everyone. Equality as a real social achievement is the inclusion of every single individual in respecting the individualities of all. For this, we need new social relations of production capable of surpassing the limits of private property and capitalism.

How is the accounting system going to work in an economy of this kind? Is there an accounting system at all? These questions resemble the challenge popularized by Ludwig von Mises in 1920. In his paper *Economic Calculation in the Socialist Commonwealth* he argued that the principles of common ownership would lead the economy to decay. According to Mises, since there is no private ownership of economic goods, there are also no prices and consequently, no reliable information as the basis for how to allocate economic resources rationally. Lack of rationality is what he considered to be a striking feature of the communist economy.

This kind of problem is similar to that involved in changing from a market system (invisible hand) to a system of planning. As noted, utopian socialists tried to conceive a planned economy based on the same foundations as the market. They argued for a system of labor vouchers, through which workers would receive the real value of their contribution. Labor vouchers would replace money. Real existing money was viewed as a kind of 'fake voucher' because it allowed exploitation and income from capital, such as rent, profit, and interest. The possibility of abandoning the principle of equal exchange could then be attempted later, but this was not in sight for most utopian socialists.

But the transition from market to planning is not quite the same thing as the transition from capitalism to socialism or communism. The controversy about the socialist economic calculation does not clearly distinguish these two different kinds of change. What we have in history is a process of increasing control over economic reproduction with various political directions. Transition to planning is a real process already in motion, rather than a hypothetical challenge. The challenge is how to control the plan, instead of being controlled by it.

In the context of the real socialist revolutions, the problem of an alternative accounting system emerged alongside the rise of national economic planning. Many theoretical reflections and studies have traced this historical development and related debates. The zigzag in the Soviet Union between War Communism and the implementation of five-year plans was one of the most intense experiences of the contradictions of this transition. The New Economic Policy (NEP) was based on a delicate alliance of central planning and decentralized economic decisions by agents who act according to the law of value. In Cuba in the 1960s, this debate also appeared when the revolutionary government wanted to establish a new pattern of national economic accounting that did not follow the dynamics of mercantile allocation. Since the end of the 20th century, China has adopted a project that combines market and plan and that also has its roots in the problem of finding an alternative accounting system that can lead society to communism.

On the side of reformed capitalism in the West, after the transformations of the Great Crash of 1929 and of the Second World War, planning assumed a pragmatic form. The overall aim here is to enable capital reproduction and meet some demands of the working class in order to alleviate revolutionary pressure. Employment and industrialization are two aspects that capitalism pursued through planning. Every capitalist country of the 20th century had some sort of economic control to reconcile the logic of capital accumulation and the pressures of the working class. This balance was broken after the rise of the neoliberal era.

The controversies about the transition from liberalism to planning are not based on the validity of any theory of value. The real dispute here is about the possibility of manipulating the law of value to achieve pre-determined social and political outcomes. In the 19th century, economic science thought that the quantitative relations of exchange could not be consciously altered. Liberalism and laissez-faire were strong paradigms. Since the great crisis of 1929, however, all political systems have purposefully altered the results of markets. Coordination became so broad that political economy can no longer be thought of as a science of observation of markets, but truly a science of management of the economy.

The profundities of the quality of value do not need to come into discussion when we examine the law of value as a purely quantitative phenomenon. The quantitative problem of value is important because it allows an examination of the calculation problem in any social setting. In this sense, there is a clear continuity between classical political economy and Marx. It is true that focus on quantity is dangerous because we lose the qualitative analysis that shows the historical specificities of capitalism. But Marx inherits the theory of value from both classical economists and socialists, and struggles to find a solution to the transformation of values into prices as a purely quantitative problem. The law of value cannot be either understood or controlled without a coherent framework which explains how quantitative relations of equivalence between different use values are formed.

Marx's strategy for presenting his labor theory of value is challenging. It is not limited to a quantitative or a qualitative analysis since both sides must come into the same single system. According to the reading presented here, Marx's theory of value proves that there is no natural basis for choosing any quality to be the source and measure of quantity of value. At the same time, it shows that, for whatever quality is chosen, the general lines that explain the formation of empirical prices are the same. Thus, although there are many theories of value, there is only one law of value. The law of value is the real object of investigation of economic science. The great division is between those theoreticians who think humans cannot control it and those who intend to master it to overcome the general alienation that sustains it.

CHAPTER 8

The Law of Value under the Rule of Capitalist Economic Planning

1   Capitalist Economic Planning

The idea that capitalism and economic planning are antagonistic concepts is incorrect. Control over the law of value does not lead to a predetermined political system. If we accept Marx's concept of the law of value, then we must recognize that there is a specific form of capitalism that demands our attention. We may describe it as the most developed form of the capitalist mode of production and the most difficult to debunk. It does not rest on free proprietors buying and selling at free and competitive markets, nor does it reflect the harmonious scenarios of the neoclassical economics textbooks. It refers to the reality of highly concentrated capitalist sectors associated with the state. It conceptualizes the final stage of capitalist organization as an infinite entity that has mastered humanity just as humanity has mastered nature. I call this kind of economic architecture 'capitalist economic planning'.

This notion is not new. As a contribution to the debate about state capitalism, in this chapter I develop a more abstract notion of a fully planned capitalism to show that economic planning and capitalism are not contradictory entities. My approach to conceptualizing capitalist economic planning is to derive the logic of such a system from the fundamentals of Marx's initial exposition in *Capital*. The traditional approach relies on historical evidence to indicate that all real economies, no matter how they are classified (capitalist, socialist, regulated, democratic, authoritarian etc.), are some sort of planned economy.

Marx's theory of capitalist crisis points to an endless movement of capital reproduction in which wealth creation and destruction alternate. The process through which money becomes more money is an infinite circuit, as the notation M—C—M' indicates. The question is: can this process avoid the crisis points and achieve a less turbulent trajectory—one in which it becomes clear that an environmentally sustainable and socially just capitalism is a dystopia? The answer is yes, at least in theory.

After identifying that the ultimate explanation for capitalist crisis lies in the separation of use value and value inside the commodity, Marx concluded that capitalism does not come to an end due to external circumstances. The only thing that puts a limit to capital is capital itself. What does this mean? It means that capital expansion has no objective constraints. There is no materialist barrier against capital. The amount of destruction and suffering it causes to life on the planet does not limit its continued expansion. Nothing can stop capitalism except the massive and organized action of the working class to overcome alienation.

Control over this system is crucial. Economic planning was once thought of as the opposite to capitalism, but nothing is further from the truth. Economic planning to fulfill the goal of infinite value expansion is a real process created during the 20th century. History proves that the true dynamics of the law of value (a self-enlarging amount of abstract wealth based on the social relationship of the commodity) are viable under a regime of economic planning. Theory also indicates that this connection is not so strange as it may seem.

The striking feature here is that an overall planned economic system does not lead to the end of alienation if the goal of that planning is to expand value forever. Real capitalism throughout the world after World War II is a coordinated economic system to sustain the growth of abstract wealth and restrain the working classes from accomplishing the socialist revolution. Even though laissez-faire capitalism and classical liberalism no longer prevail, capitalism continues to exist in a framework of economic planning. This argument has been put forward many times by analysts who focus on concrete historical studies.[1] But theory also shows that capital and its law of motion, the law of value, can operate the economic reproduction in a setting that political economists call planning.

The idealized competitive market, with several competing proprietors, is not necessary to sustain capitalism. Capitalist economic planning is a system in which the capitalist mode of production does not depend on the anarchical roots of free markets. It is a stage where competition has culminated in a full association of individual capitals with the state. The aim is to continuously expand the quantity of value. It is a control of the material economic reproduction that allows the maximum growth of abstract wealth without great crashes or social turmoil. Capitalism, at least in theory, is flexible enough to absorb planning both at the national and at the global levels.

The material basis of any economic system is the input and output matrices of use values. Each component of this aggregated stuff has its own characteristics. This is the concrete wealth of any society. This material basis can be formatted so as to allow the infinite expansion of abstract wealth.

---

1   One recent analysis is provided by Phillips and Rozworski who conclude accurately that 'planning works, just not yet for us' (Phillips and Rozworski (2019), p. 179).

Accordingly, the capitalist logic of expansion and the law of value itself do not contradict a fully planned economic system. The ultimate reason for the existence of capital is the endless expansion of money. In this sense, it has a precise aim. If the input and output matrices of use values are consciously organized to meet this goal, then we can no longer speak of the economic system as rooted in the freedom of the private proprietor of economic resources. This liberty of choice gives way to overall planning to achieve the maximum augment of total social capital. The capitalist as an individual who decides no longer exists in this final stage of capitalism. All individual arrangements are subordinated to the broader structure that guarantees the correct allocation of all resources according to the logic of M—C—M' for all the economy.

Let us formalize this reasoning. The concept of state capitalism, and similar forms of a regulated capitalist economy, is well developed in works of applied or descriptive political economy. My goal here is not to repeat this kind of analysis but rather to present an initial scheme to show how the basics of Marx's theory of value relate to the abstract concept of capitalist economic planning.

Economic reproduction can be expressed as the successive transformation of a matrix that is made of the various use values of the economy. The input matrix becomes the output matrix that is the starting point for the next cycle of production. Marx's schemes of reproduction in book 2 of *Capital* are one kind of formalization of this process (which goes back to Quesnay's *Tableau Économique*). We draw the economy as a circular flow of materials that are both transformed and distributed through space and time. Production is the moment when these materials (use values) have their inner properties modified. Distribution is the moment when these materials (use values) do not undergo changes in their internal bodies, but only move from one place to another.[2]

---

2   The following is derived from a previous presentation of the matrices from Quesnay to Sraffa (Camarinha Lopes e Neder (2017). For Marx's defense of the positive legacy of the physiocratic school, see Marx ([1862–1863] 1968) [*Theories of Surplus Value*] and Marx ([1885] 1956) [*Capital* book 2]. This model is limited and should not be read as a definitive description of the presented concept of capitalist economic planning. There are many elements left out of the model because we remove relevant differences between sectors. These differences are responsible for the different periods of capital turnover of each sector and derive from the disparities of the relation between constant and variable capital in each sector. The purpose here is not to present a complete model, but to indicate to the reader that the exercise of drawing schemes of reproduction shows that stable economic reproduction, even in the case of capitalist reproduction, is possible.

Based on Sraffa's (1960) notation, we begin with a simple model that shows how use values enter as inputs and come out as outputs to restart the reproduction cycle.

$$280 \text{ qr. wheat} + 12 \text{ t. iron} \rightarrow 400 \text{ qr. wheat}$$

$$120 \text{ qr. wheat} + 8 \text{ t. iron} \rightarrow 20 \text{ t. iron}$$

These two lines represent an economy that has only two use values: wheat and iron. These are both concrete, useful items that make up the whole economic system. Given technology and laws of nature, it is possible to combine these use values in a proportion that produces the same use values, wheat and iron, in quantities just enough to maintain the economic system. Each line of the scheme represents an economic sector. The first line is the production sector of wheat. The second line represents the sector producing iron. The sector producing wheat uses 280 quarters (qr.—a measure for mass) of wheat and 12 tons (t.—a measure for mass) of iron to produce 400 quarters of wheat. The sector producing iron uses 120 quarters of wheat and 8 tons of iron to produce 20 tons of iron. Each sector uses both wheat and iron as input in the indicated quantities.

The system can be expanded when we add another use value, pigs. In this case, given technology and the laws of matter transformation framed by nature, we can write the following scheme:

$$240 \text{ qr. wheat} + 12 \text{ t. iron} + 18 \text{ pigs} \rightarrow 450 \text{ qr. wheat}$$

$$90 \text{ qr. wheat} + 6 \text{ t. iron} + 12 \text{ pigs} \rightarrow 21 \text{ t. iron}$$

$$120 \text{ qr. wheat} + 3 \text{ t. iron} + 30 \text{ pigs} \rightarrow 60 \text{ pigs}$$

Now our economy has three different use values, wheat, iron, and pigs. A third sector, in the third line, uses 120 quarters of wheat, 3 tons of iron and 30 pigs to produce 60 pigs. Again, this is a subsistence economy since all output is just enough to restart the cycle. 450 quarters of wheat is the output of the first sector and it is distributed among all sectors in the following way: 240 quarters of wheat go to the first sector, 90 quarters of wheat go to the second sector and 120 quarters of wheat go to the third sector. The same applies to the total amount of iron and pigs.

We can expand this model indefinitely by adding more and more sectors that are responsible for the production of a single use value. The model for a subsistence economy, that is, for a system with k products, can be expressed as follows:

$$A_a + B_a + \ldots + K_a \rightarrow A$$

$$A_b + B_b + \ldots + K_b \rightarrow B$$

$$\ldots$$

$$A_k + B_k + \ldots + K_k \rightarrow K$$

Each use value is represented by a letter. The sector producing the use value 'a' uses the quantities $A_a, B_a, \ldots K_a$ of the use values $a, b, \ldots, k$; the sector producing the use value 'b' uses the quantities $A_b, B_b, \ldots K_b$ of the use values $a, b, \ldots, k$; etc. We call 'A' the existing quantity of use value 'a' after the production process, 'B' the existing quantity of use value 'b' after the production process, etc. and 'A_a' the quantity of use value 'a' used in the sector producing the use value 'a', 'A_b' the quantity of use value 'a' used in the sector producing the use value 'b', etc.

A capital letter indicates a fully determined use value, both qualitatively and quantitatively, whereas a lower case letter indicates qualitatively of which use value we are talking about. For example, 'pig', as a qualitatively useful item would be written as 'c'. 60 pigs, as in the case above, would be written as 'C'. We no longer need to specify the concrete quantities of each use value. We only need to know that the system is made of fully determined use values, both qualitatively and quantitatively.

Let us rearrange this same system in matrix form. This is useful to show that we are dealing with a reproduction process and not with a production process that ceases after one cycle. There is a continuous transformation of the input matrix into the output matrix.

$$
\begin{bmatrix}
A_a & B_a & \cdots & K_a \\
A_b & B_b & \cdots & K_b \\
\vdots & \vdots & \vdots & \vdots \\
A_k & B_k & \cdots & K_k
\end{bmatrix}
\rightarrow
\begin{bmatrix}
A \\ B \\ \vdots \\ K
\end{bmatrix}
\rightarrow
\begin{bmatrix}
A_a & B_a & \cdots & K_a \\
A_b & B_b & \cdots & K_b \\
\vdots & \vdots & \vdots & \vdots \\
A_k & B_k & \cdots & K_k
\end{bmatrix}
\rightarrow
\begin{bmatrix}
A \\ B \\ \vdots \\ K
\end{bmatrix}
\rightarrow \ldots
$$

Or:

$$q \rightarrow Q \rightarrow q \rightarrow Q \rightarrow \ldots$$

So, after a first round of production, distribution takes place. The total amount of wheat and iron must go in the correct proportions back to the beginning of the production process, if the process is to be repeated continuously. The total amount of use value 'a', indicated by 'A' is distributed among all sectors according to their needs of use value 'a', as indicated by A_a, A_b, A_c ... A_k. The representation above indicates that the input matrix 'q' is a combination of all use values A_a, A_b, A_c ... A_k, B_a, B_b, B_c ... B_k (...) K_k that leads to the output matrix 'Q' made of the total quantities of each use value of the economy, A, B, C ... K. The sign '→' means that there has been a transformation from one matrix into the other. If it is a change from q to Q, it refers to the changes that use values undergo in the production process. If it is a change from Q to q, it refers to the spatial allocation of use values that do not undergo any inner transformation. Their bodies travel through sectors without changing their internal physical/chemical/biological properties, as distribution should be conceived when we set aside the rights of property.

Our economy is now a self-reproducing system that restores itself infinitely. But we should ask: why do outputs A, B, C ... K go back to the input matrix in these perfect proportions? What is the logic behind this distribution pattern? The idea behind this way of conceiving the economy is the circular flow that guarantees the continued existence of the system through time. Here, we assume that we want to restore the production process q → Q forever. This exercise resembles the physiocratic notion of natural systems that have self-restoring properties. Harmony and natural equilibrium were inspiring elements for various areas of science, from physics to mechanics and biology. In political economy, the logic of the equilibrated restoration of the system appears originally with Quesnay and his *Tableau Économique*. Material and social arrangements are continuously restored, so that the production process can start over. Everything must repeat itself as it occurred in the past, like a law of nature (as an apple always falls to the ground when dropped according to the law of gravity). In the case of economics, the restoration of all conditions to reinitiate the production process is guaranteed by the expression 'law of value'. It is possible to see here that the abstract foundation of the law of value is the repetition of the process, according to what has happened in the past. This is a feature of systems capable of maintaining themselves. They can correct small errors and come back to the trajectory that guarantees the continuity of the system. The law of value acts like a feedback loop, so that the adjustments may enable the ongoing reinitialization of the circuit.[3]

Thus far, our model is dynamic, but it represents a static economy in the sense that it has the same size. The economy is neither growing nor shrinking. The total quantities of all use values remain the same across time. For all sectors, the sum of the inputs of a specific use value is equal the total output of

---

3 Further formalization requires mentioning the relationship between the economy and cybernetics. For an introduction to the topic, see Lange (1970).

that use value: $A = A_a + A_b + A_c + ... + A_k$, $B = B_a + B_b + B_c + ... + B_k$, etc. Moreover, it is implicit that the methods of production do not change. In other words, the technical coefficients of production are the same through time. This means that productivity is also the same through time. Since this does not represent the reality of a capitalist economy, we need to specify if material reproduction is viable in an infinite trajectory of growth.

Let us assume that the combination of A_a, B_a, C_a ... K_a in the production process leads to an output of A', a higher quantity of use value 'a' than A ($A' > A$), and that the same applies to all other sectors. Our model now becomes:

$$\begin{bmatrix} A_a & B_a & \cdots & K_a \\ A_b & B_b & \cdots & K_b \\ \vdots & \vdots & \vdots & \vdots \\ A_k & B_k & \cdots & K_k \end{bmatrix} \rightarrow \begin{bmatrix} A' \\ B' \\ \vdots \\ K' \end{bmatrix} \rightarrow \begin{bmatrix} A'_a & B'_a & \cdots & K'_a \\ A'_b & B'_b & \cdots & K'_b \\ \vdots & \vdots & \vdots & \vdots \\ A'_k & B'_k & \cdots & K'_k \end{bmatrix} \rightarrow \begin{bmatrix} A'' \\ B'' \\ \vdots \\ K'' \end{bmatrix} \rightarrow \ldots$$

This is an economic system of expanded reproduction. All balance equations are maintained. The proportions between all use values are the same. If we repeat the cycle, we have a continuous increase where A' is more than enough to replace all inputs A_a, B_a, C_a ... K_a. So, we now have a surplus because $A' > A_a + A_b + A_c + ... + A_k$ as well as $B' > B_a + B_b + B_c + ... + B_k$, etc. The disproportionalities typical of surplus production are controlled here, as if it were possible to increase each sector by exactly the same amount as every other sector. It should be noted that real capitalist reproduction achieves this balance only through crisis.

This model represents an idea of a physically expanding system that does not break. No interruption takes place because we assume there is always a possibility to use all the surplus output in the next round of production. The dimensions of both use value and value go hand in hand. Crisis is eliminated through an abstraction that can be rigorously modelled. What we have, then, is a system that matches the logic of value expansion by increasing the use value structure indefinitely.

One of Marx's first warnings in *Capital* is that, for the basic unity of the capitalist mode of production, the commodity, it does not matter if a thing is objectively useful (such as food) or subjectively useful (such as music/culture). This is important because the limit to capital is not given by any use value structure. In other words, capital can modify the use value structure so as to permit its infinite expansion. Marx wanted to show the economic reproduction of use values under the rule of capital. Capital's infinite expanding movement requires a well-designed architecture for the dynamics of input and output matrices and so economic planning is mandatory at higher stages of capitalist development.

The anarchic and spontaneous actions of individuals do not allow such an architecture and always lead to crisis. A fully planned economy does not mean the end of capitalism. Capital accumulation can go forever once the sequence of use values is renewed in an organized fashion. Every new cycle is then able to absorb a greater amount of value in the form of concrete things that will all be used in predetermined ways. It does not mean that these things are useful per se. They are useful for the unstoppable accumulation process. So, utility in this context is subordinated to the logic of value expansion. Destruction and wars are useful outcomes for allowing capital growth, no matter how useless they are for improving human life on Earth.

Crisis is just an expression for the most acute contradiction of the commodity, the contradiction between use value and value. If use values are manipulated in such a way that this tension does not explode, then capitalist reproduction can continue without a break in the circuit. The contradiction between use value and value ignites a crisis only if the sequence of input and output matrices do not lead to the material renewal necessary to sustain value growth. Theoretically, such a system can be described, and capital reproduction may be thought of as a perpetual scheme in which the laboring population and the natural resources are used with caution. Of course, they are used with caution regarding capital, in the sense that capitalist reproduction does not destroy the material basis upon which human life exists. It is a regulated scheme where the material conditions for the further existence of social relations sustaining private property are guaranteed. Life is necessary, but *quality* of life is irrelevant. Exploitation becomes rational from the standpoint of capital and planning becomes a fundamental and indispensable tool for the capitalist class.

John Maynard Keynes recognized this fact and worked to influence economic thought in the 20th century. Economic planning is necessary to sustain all capitalist contradictions. He understood that a capitalist economy does not have as its purpose the meeting of human needs, even though it creates magnificent possibilities for satisfying previously nonexistent desires, albeit in an extremely uneven way. This is shocking for the current paradigm of economic science. Neoclassical economics believes that the economy is shaped to satisfy the needs of every single *Homo economicus*. Economics is the science responsible for investigating how humans interact among themselves to survive materially, but it must know which concrete historical society it is dealing with. This is the reason why the law of value and the paradigm of liberalism were completely modified in the discourse of political economy.

If liberalism was replaced by economic planning, what has replaced the law of value? Our approach suggests that the law of value is not only a spontaneous mechanism emerging from the dispersed structure of a competitive market. As Keynes, and many others, argued during the economic debates in the 20th century, the beginning of planning does not mean the end of capitalism. How is this possible? The answer is clear when we conceptualize the economic planning of a capitalist nature. Capitalist crises can be avoided through an adequate administration of the reproduction system. The most disturbing aspect of this fact is that the control of the economic reproduction system must not be in the hands of the working class. Only capitalist agency may be in command and guarantee the continuous expansion of the use value structure.

It is hard to admit that capitalism can theoretically exist forever. Two main arguments against this idea should be remembered here. First, many argue that the economic system cannot grow without damaging the environment. According to this view, the biophysical horizon would set a limit on capital. Material reproduction on planet Earth cannot sustain the logic of infinite value expansion. This thesis of engaged environmentalists is important, but we need to understand that it misses Marx's main thesis. Marx never indicated that capitalism would find a barrier in external elements, such as territory, water, or any other concrete resource upon which life on the planet is sustained. It is true that pollution and the destruction of nature are normal characteristics of the capitalist economy, but the notion that capitalism will destroy human life on Earth due to biological disequilibrium is not accurate. The critique of capitalism cannot depend on matters outside the founding core of alienation, which creates commodity social relations. The 19th century already knew that the natural process is modified though human intervention. The Industrial Revolution took that intervention to the highest level, but even so Marx did not suggest that capital can be blocked by the limited resources of the natural world. The expansion of value does not have to exhaust the world of use values to the point of extinguishing the human species. If natural resources are used within specific parameters, economic reproduction can feed capital's hunger for more value without destroying the material basis of life on Earth.[4]

Second, it is a common idea that world peace is impossible in real capitalism. This is so because there are various states forming their own national economic system. Capitalist nation-states are always accumulating tension between themselves because world dominance is mandatory for the logic of

---

4   Hahnel (2017), p. 65–77 argues that as long as throughput efficiency grows as fast as labor productivity, capitalism can reproduce in any given biome indefinitely. I endorse this thesis against what Hahnel calls the 'ecological Marxists school', which includes David Harvey, James O'Connor, Joel Kovel, John Bellamy Foster, Paul Burkett, and Jason Moore. See also Hahnel (2015).

capital. Hypothetically, we can see that if a capitalist economic system became the only world state, then it would eliminate territorial war between distinct political authorities. All conflicts would be reduced to the one and the same class struggle. The classical analysis of Adam Smith and David Ricardo had this utopian characteristic whereby capitalism was conceived as one and the same system for the whole of humanity. In sum: if we remove national frontiers, capitalism could still exist on a planetary scale.[5]

The issue here is not about the end of capitalism on the grounds of the impossibility of material reproduction under its domain. The point is that the law of value can be consciously controlled to sustain capitalist relations of production. A fully planned system aiming at the continuous expansion of value reveals that the law of value can be tamed without being abolished. Despite having a very peculiar system of markets, in which many things are decided by the broader plan, we still have commodity relations. Thus, controlling the law of value is not enough for turning capitalism into socialism and communism. If the controlling entity is the capitalist class, there could emerge an intriguing scenario: basic problems such as material poverty, distribution and war could be alleviated in order to disband the revolutionary forces of the working class, but at the same time, the phenomenon of alienation would remain as strong as ever.

Obviously, this situation of world peace and developmentalism under the logic of value expansion is stable only as far as working people do not participate in the decisions of production and distribution. If the working class acquires consciousness, tension will grow, and capitalist economic planning may be challenged. The law of value under the rule of capital is a delicate combination of property rights and social demands that resembles Keynes' rational approach to capitalism. It is a contradictory outcome, where culture and political education are the final trenches of class struggle. Overcoming this dystopian system requires a new level of organization. The challenge grows because the stronger capitalist economic planning becomes, the better the material and physiological needs of the masses can be met. The potential to turn humanity into happy but ignorant cattle, as in Aldous Huxley's *Brave New World* (Huxley [1932] 1998), is huge.

---

5 The concept of Super-imperialism or Ultra-imperialism from Kautsky (1914) is an example of the idea I am describing here. Theoretically, capitalism can exist in a context of peace between different people/nations. Despite their different histories and traditions, they would become a unique human mass under the rule of the same state-capital. Of course, reality is different from theory. Bukharin ([1917] 2001), also considering Hilferding's work *Finazkapital*, reminds us that Kautsky's exercise may lead to utopian reformism.

Fortunately, this same dystopian system presents the objective tools that can transform it into a good thing. When this capitalist planned economic policy guarantees income and the meeting of material needs for an increasing number of humans, there arises the possibility of political education. More time becomes available to people. Instead of wasting it with empty entertainment and dopamine generating activities, people could use it to educate themselves. This does not mean that this change is simple, because reactionary forces will strive to impede this positive use of non-labor time. In any case, the struggle becomes centered in education. The battle for socialism and communism is more than a battle for hearts, it is also a battle for minds.

2   The Aim of Capital

The law of value is not restricted to the paradigm of liberalism and uncoordinated actions and can exist in an environment of full control. There is no strict opposition between the law of value and economic planning. Economic planning may lead to various kinds of political systems (communism, capitalism, fascism etc.). There is no direct correspondence between economic planning and any set of social relations. Accordingly, depending on the kind of planning, the law of value can even be reinforced, instead of being suppressed or eliminated. When we talk about planning, we need to specify two things: the aim and the means employed to reach that aim. The most important feature to characterize the type of planning we are dealing with is the aim, because everything else is built around it.

What is the aim of capital? Its aim is to expand itself endlessly at the highest rate possible. This definition implies that there are barriers to capital accumulation. If there were no barriers, the rate of growth would not be a matter to be determined. Likewise, capital would not have a finite size at any point in time. But economic science understands that capital has a certain magnitude at each period. The barriers to capital accumulation are related to the concrete structure of production, which cannot break the laws of nature. As previously shown, the input and output matrices are to be organized in such a way that capital may expand as much as technically possible. The technicality is a matter of the in- and outflow of use values.

Capitalist economic planning ensures that these two things go hand in hand. On one side, the concrete structure of production is modified to permit a stable increase of abstract wealth, on the other side, capital's hunger for more is fed in a steady trajectory of growth that avoids crisis and ruptures that may disturb the prevailing social relations. Capitalist economic planning is a kind of planning where the aim is not chosen by politics, but it is imposed by the self-defining *raison d'être* of capital.

Any planned economic system has a political institution responsible for its control. In fact, as historians know, the notion of a capitalist system based on absolute freedom of all agents is an idea that is very distant from reality. Every class society has a planned economic system of one kind or another. Capitalism is unique in the sense that there would be no one in command if the means of production were evenly distributed. The concentration of property creates a small group with enormous decision-making power regarding the economic resources of society. This is why there should be no surprise in identifying real existing capitalism with an imperfectly planned system.

The model presented above refers to a perfect capitalist planned system in the sense that it allows the infinite movement of capital accumulation without distorting the technical conditions of balance in the input-output matrices of use values. Once the logic of M—C—M' is at the peak of this pyramid, all arrangements of use value obey the same rule. Even if we do not have a 'free' market where individual decisions to adjust supply and demand take place, we still have the same foundations of private property, commodity, money, and capital. Capital relations of production continue to exist even though the process is completely controlled. The law of value has not been abolished, nor has it been tamed in the sense suggested by the debate on the transition to socialism. It is working on a higher scale because all individual agents are integrated into one single capitalist unity.

Economic planning of the kind M—C—M' is subordinated to the permanent circuit of value expansion. This is the final purpose of economic coordination in capitalism. It restricts the liberties of individual capitalists since they must all use their properties according to the broader goal of controlled growth. Here, the state does not allow private proprietors to do as they please. Individual proprietors must obey the ruling scheme, or they become expropriated.

The effects of capitalist relations of production are not a mystery. Among others, there is an inversion of the relations of means and ends. So, humans (as well as nature) become a means to achieve the aim of infinite capital accumulation. It is also known that capitalist control over the law of value, or capitalist economic planning, does not intend to create better conditions of life for the working class or for the human species. Material improvements are a collateral effect that reinforces the phenomenon of alienation and enlarges the potential for exploitation.

What is not regularly recognized is that every economic policy within the bounds of capitalism is a form of interference to reinforce the law of value.

Distorting the free price mechanism is not something that necessarily goes against the law of value. If the price structure is adjusted through political intervention to sustain the balanced trajectory of growth, then the law of value is being reinforced. Therefore, it is not a matter of whether the law of value is acting freely or being manipulated. It is always manipulated by some party. Thus, any discussion about control over the law of value must consider how economic planning relates to class struggle.

The allocation of resources to sustain a specific cycle of economic reproduction is not the element that allows us to differentiate modes of production. All modes of production must obey the same laws of matter transformation in their production processes. The distinguishing element lies in the way the resources are allocated considering the various material interests of social classes. Accordingly, we cannot talk about how to control the law of value without first indicating who wants to control it. Political action to bend the law of value according to specific economic interests is the standard practice for defending material interests in a market environment. Clashes between classes prior to the development of market society were different because the division of classes was based on qualitative barriers. Capitalism turns the basis of this distinction from a qualitative to a quantitative parameter. In the idealized form of capitalism, all classes try to defend their material interests based on the same rules of the game. If we take the simplification of two classes, as is the case for a pure capitalist system, the difference is that a conscious capitalist class wants to control the law of value to permit continuous expansion of abstract wealth, while the working class wants to control it to avoid exploitation of human by human.

If we start from the foundations of political economy from the 18th century, we see that the economic reproduction of society depends entirely on the individual choices of each member of society. The economic problem is magically solved by the invisible hand, and the separation between economics and politics seems correct. This path, however, leads to a negation of action over the law of value, based on a reasoning of the following kind: since the law of gravity pulls everything down, there is no use in building a machine to fly.

Liberalism drives economic science to self-negation. At the same time, the problem of alienation also disappears, because here every single individual is fully aware of his/her interests and has the means to pursue these interests. It is as if the law of value was the result of a conscious decision by individuals looking to their own private interests. In fact, the law of value does not create a beautiful and harmonious paradise, but results in a mass alienation process that sustains the exploitation of wage working people. It is only in the realm of abstract political economy that the law of value presents itself as something positive.

The possibility of controlling the law of value within capitalism shows that the challenge of transition from capitalism to socialism and communism is not only a matter of economic organization, but also a matter of cultural change in which the members of society participate in the decisions of how to use resources. Therefore, to achieve this transition it is not enough to put the law of value under control. It is also necessary to specify to what end it is being controlled. By clarifying this, it will be possible to explain that economic planning may serve either to consolidate or surpass capital relations of production. Economic planning, just like everything else, is at dispute in class struggle.

Final Remarks

Political economy has an abstract core: the theory of value. As is well known, theorization about value is strongly influenced by the material interests of social classes. Therefore, there are various competing schools of political economy and each one of them creates a specific theory of value.

It is common to talk about 'the' theory of value, as if there existed only one theory. I have argued in this book that the unifying element in economic science is not the theory of value but what classical political economists called the law of value. There is not only one theory of value; there are various theories of value and each one represents a defined position in class struggle. Despite being different theories, they all meet in the same arena of the struggle for material interests. Thus, to some degree, all theories of value are furnished with the same concrete objective elements of economic reality. I explain that the totality of these concrete aspects, when they refer to the capitalist economy, can be synthesized by the concept of the law of value. It is a monotheist vision of the different currents of economic theory. More precisely, it is a materialist monotheist vision because, despite different ideologies, all theories of value grow from the same real base where the law of value exists.

My approach to the core of political economy, that is, to value theory, is also a proposal concerning the relation between Marxian and non-Marxian political economy. The essence of my proposal is to locate Marx's *Critique of Political Economy* within a broad context. The purpose is to prepare a non-dogmatic presentation of Marx and Marxism to an historically determined audience: students and professional economists who are trained in a neoliberal, neoclassical environment and who are looking for alternatives.

Moreover, progressive economists that already have a well-formed position against capitalism should also listen to the message. In my view, institutionalism and the historical methodological approaches of heterodox economics are important, but they are too weak regarding abstract theorization. A more direct connection between (apparently) extremely contradictory systems (such as the neoclassical and the utopian socialist theories of value) should work to indicate that Marx's political economy is not 'free style economics', as many disdainfully refer to the world of heterodox economics. Marx's political economy is the most rigorous system in economic science to date, embracing both theory and history.[1]

---

1   For a brief presentation of how Marx easily surpasses the paradigms of the Methodenstreit (battle of methods in economics) between German and Austrian economists, see Dobb

In sum, the typical economist trained since the end of World War II in the West is not furnished with the fundamental analytical tools to engage readily with the profound philosophy and praxis of Marx. For this reason, we must communicate with this agent in an organised manner.

With respect to value theory, I suggest that before presenting Marx's theory of value, we need to contextualize what non-Marxian political economy is in a specific way. We need to show that non-Marxian economics naturalize value and commodity relations. This is essential for the subsequent steps towards the materialist concept of history and all its implications for economic science. Let us consider this idea once more by revisiting the main arguments developed in the book.

In chapters 1 and 2, I argued that there is a reason for classifying Adam Smith as the great initiator of the 'science of value'. His synthesis of mercantilist and physiocratic doctrines generated the first systemic treatment of the foundations that leads a nation to wealth. But Smith's work is contradictory. He is an enthusiast of the new world of markets as well as a serious scholar. Thus, even though his work well suits an infant capitalist imperialist superpower, we should learn crucial lessons from him. His analysis of markets is not a superficial description, but a complex study that grows from his previous treatise, *Theory of Moral Sentiments*. In *Wealth of Nations*, he investigates value by organizing ethical considerations and factual observations. I have indicated that Smith's solution to the water-diamond paradox is not simply a defense of the labor theory of value, but an explanation for the difference between use value (which he calls value-in-use) and value (which he erroneously calls exchange value). This distinction is a great advance in the study of the law of value and one of the most important contributions.

The theory of value in classical political economy is not simply a labor theory of value but is more complex. Classical political economy opened the way for the development of a labor theory of value, as well as for other theories of value. Neoclassical utility theories of value are also the offspring of classical political economy. If the relationship between Marx and classical economists is not one characterized by a simple rupture, the same applies to the relationship between Smith/Ricardo and Jevons/Menger/Walras. In the science of value, all authors are trying to break with Smith, and yet they all inherit some

---

(1946). For a summary of the methodological strategy to relate Marx to the world of non-Marxian economists, see Oskar Lange's (1945) paper *The Scope and Method of Economics*. This work is the blueprint for Lange's *Political Economy* (Lange ([1959] 1963) and Lange (1971)), the 'book of his life, as he used to call it' (Felicje Lange to Piero Sraffa, 20 October 1965. See Sraffa 1965).

characteristics from him. It is like a parental relationship, a mixture of rupture and continuation between the old and the new.

In chapter 3, I explained that there was no adequate solution to the transformation problem of values into prices until the problem was explicitly announced and worked out by Marx in the 1860s. Engels also made a decisive contribution to this in the prefaces to *Capital* books 2 and 3, as well as in complementary commentaries on *Capital* book 3. The main argument I present here is that the end of classical political economy leads to two opposing paths: the labor theory of value of utopian socialists and the utility theory of value of mainstream economists, (whom I have referred to as the neoclassicals). My reason for this division is based on the idea that we need to criticize both theories of value in the same way. Marx's theory of value is not simply the choice of the labor theory of value over the utility theory of value. Marx's perspective is to unveil the class character of all types of theory of value that naturalize capitalist social relations of production.

The novelty of my argument is the claim that Marx's denuciation is not only directed at the apologists for capitalism in the emerging utilitarianism approach to political economy. His critique is not restricted to reactionary vulgar economics, but applies also to progressive vulgar economics. The division of vulgar economics into a reactionary and a progressive current may be useful, and I believe we should explore this insight further. My intuition is that this might contribute to a better understanding of the relationship between utopian and scientific socialism, in other words, between all non-Marxist anti-capitalist schools of thought and Marxism. This distinction is very poorly understood among progressive economists today. Of course, the purpose of the distinction is not to increase the distance between these two groups but rather to create a healthier environment for the exchange of ideas between orthodox Marxist economists and economists with the potential to contribute to the cause of the working class but who do not regard themselves as Marxists.

For this reason, I argued (especially in chapter 3) that vulgar economics is not just a feature of reactionary political economy. Progressive political economy in the 19th century was also vulgar in the sense that it did not investigate the socio-historical determinants for its own labor theory of value. Non-Marxian socialist economists thought that labor could generate value based on the direct relationship between human and nature. Marx's defense of the labor theory of value does not rest on any neutral or pure reasoning that could be empirically verified through standard protocols for studying human action on nature because value is not just a result of the interaction between humans and nature, as is the case in the paradigm of Robinson Crusoe. Value is the outcome of a triangular interaction (involving human-human as well as human-nature) where natural economic resources are appropriated through a specific institutional scheme of relations among many humans.

Humans modify the external, natural world by working within historical social rules. Social relations of production are fundamental for the phenomenon of value. In other words, value cannot be entirely understood when we consider only the physiological dimension of production. It is true that a concept of abstract wealth, and therefore both exchange value and value, can be derived directly from the dimension of use value, as the exercise of Robinson Crusoe shows. But any theory of value (whether it be labor or utility) can be derived from this exercise. On the other hand, value is not just a product of pure social conventions either. All elements of the superstructure are rooted in the material basis of the economy. The dialectical unity of the natural and the social worlds is crucial.

Marx's contribution that deals simultaneously with the physiological and sociological dimensions is unique. His approach to value is fundamental for avoiding the transformation of political economy and economic science into methodological individualism. In this sense, I argue that any theory of value that naturalizes the phenomenon of value also naturalizes the law of value, and consequently naturalizes capitalism. Theories of value constructed on this basis are vulgar economics, regardless whether they are politically reactionary or progressive.

Inspired by Isaak Rubin's history of economic thought, I also explored in chapter 3 the bifurcation after the end of classical political economy. Two strands of economic thought emerge from classical political economy. Both strands are dealt with in Marx's *Critique of Political Economy* and I developed this critique symmetrically. The scheme I proposed (figure 1) suggests that this bifurcation should not interrupt the interaction between Marx's followers and those of non-Marxian political economy. There must always be some sort of communication. Marx did not construct his system based on 'previous Marxists' because economic thought is produced by real persons who are not equally conscious of class struggle and there is no such thing as a 'Marxists economics' completely separate from other currents, such as mainstream neoclassical economics, institutional or heterodox economics, Keynesian economics, Austrian economics and so on. Economics is a science, and every school of economic thought must be mastered by the class-conscious economist. To ignore the world of non-Marxian political economy is a mistake because this leads to defeat in the battle for commanding the mainstream. It is necessary to engage seriously with all sorts of vulgarization in political economy because, despite their obvious propagandist purpose, they also reveal minor truths that should be appropriated. Furthermore, education in economics in capitalist countries is dominated by a non-Marxist mixture of various disciplines that do not constitute a coherent unity. Communicating with non-Marxian economics and economists is essential if we want to influence teaching in economics.

Chapters 4 and 5 revise the two main strands of value theory that are offered to the undergraduate student of economics. I want to break with the idea that these two strands directly reflect the opposition between labor and capital. It is not true that a student must choose one side or another. Before making a choice, a student should further investigate this clash. There must be time for him/her to comprehend his/her own position in a class society. Moreover, by this parallel presentation, I argued that we need to give an equal treatment to progressive and reactionary vulgar economics. This equal treatment is necessary to emphasize Marx's contribution to economic science since Marx's perspective on value means that he is against both kinds of naturalizing value theories. Methodologically, both the labor theory of value of the utopian socialists and the utility theory of value of the marginalist economists should be rejected. This does not mean that these two opposing sides are the same regarding their political content. While the naturalizing labor theory of value is progressive, the utility theory of value is reactionary. In this sense, the critique of both theories must be done with strategic caution.

My presentation of Marx's political economy and his investigation of value argues that Marx developed this cautious and strategic critique to achieve two things. First, he wanted to show that the traditional approach to value was dominated by the fetishism of the commodity. Accordingly, all economists and utopian socialists can be seen to construct their theories of value based on the Robinson Crusoe model. The essence of this experiment is to analyze how an abstract human interacts with the natural surroundings in order to survive. There emerges an idealized economy where the society is made up of only one person. Logical reasoning in the context of utilitarianism and capitalism leads to the hypothesis that Robinson Crusoe organizes his available time and energy so as to increase his material wealth and/or utility. Because of this, the traditional approach to value is limited to the relations of the kind human-nature. All expansions of this model arrive at the same place: simple commodity production.

Second, Marx wanted to present a theory of value that would utilize the political status of the labor theory of value, but would also show that labor does not naturally create value. This explains why he divided labor into two concepts: concrete labor and abstract labor. This was necessary to expel the naturalizing component in the labor theory of value of his predecessors (from Adam Smith and Ricardo to pre-Marxian socialists). So, Marx's theory of value is a 'special' labor theory of value in the sense that labor is both a physical/

chemical/biological metamorphosis and a social endeavor. It is labor in the duality concrete and abstract, according to his dialectical definition of the commodity.

In chapters 6 and 7, I presented how we should comprehend Marx's approach to the law of value. In brief, we should separate the law of value from the concept of the theory of value because they are not the same thing. The law of value is the real phenomenon, while the theory of value is the analysis and mental synthesis about that real phenomenon. Accordingly, every value theoretician (from utopian socialists to the most ardent capitalist apologetic author) develops some sort of theory of value that derives from the concreteness of the law of value. Theories of value are tools to both understand and manipulate the real phenomenon of the law of value.

Marx's critique stands out as the unique perspective that relates the theory of value to class struggle. Because of this, the issue for economists is not to look for 'correct' theories of value and to discard 'incorrect' theories of value through the traditional methods of empirical research. All theories of value partially describe the functioning of the law of value and make normative suggestions as to how to behave towards it. Letting it act freely (laissez-faire, laissez-passer), regulating it, surpassing it, or even destroying it, are all economic policies that could be drawn from theories of value. All theories of value are politically orientated, whether the value theoretician is aware of it or not.

The perspective I have presented means that there must be another kind of relation between Marxian and non-Marxian economics regarding the theoretical core of political economy. Marx's system should absorb non-Marxian systems, just as Marx did when processing the literature of political economy of the 17th, 18th, and 19th centuries. Purism does not lead to a stronger school of economic thought. Of course, horizontal syncretism is also not the approach. What we need is a rigorous development of the working-class political economy, where the abstract dimension of the discipline is free to absorb alien elements while also expelling the pro-capital discourse in them. I have indicated that Oskar Lange was one of the proponents of this method of battling in the arena of economic science and that his legacy may contain valuable insights for new generations of communist value theoreticians.

Finally, in chapter 8, I developed the concept of capitalist economic planning. This notion is not new. It resembles the description of high stage capitalism where the state and the totality of private capitalists become one single entity to dominate the world. I focused on the theoretical dimension of this historical phenomenon by showing that the law of value achieves full development in a planned environment. Accordingly, economic planning under the rule of capital leads to the reinforcement of the law of value. Therefore, the only way to overcome such a dystopic outcome, is to increase consciousness about the political struggle around planning.

We must further explore the law of value because there is still much to learn. This concept was a unifying element of political economy until the last decades of the 19th century. It allowed a perspective of totality in the discussions of the theory of value. Science must lead all competing theories to the same battle arena. This is the only way to put economics back on the track of serious investigation of real relations of production. Activating Marx's work in a way that it can interact with, learn from, and teach non-Marxian economic theories is the way to fight the enemy. In this sense, I invite the reader to make his/her own readings of Karl Marx's *Capital* and to creatively work out its relations with non-Marxist economics as a solid way of studying the core of political economy: value theory.

References

Amin, S. ([1977] 1981). *La Ley del Valor y el Materialismo Histórico*. México: Fondo de Cultura Económica.

Amin, S. ([1978] 2010). *The Law of Worldwide Value*. New York: Monthly Review Press.

Anderson, K. (1995). *Lenin, Hegel, and Western Marxism: a critical study*. Urbana and Chicago: University of Illinois Press.

Angeli, E. (2014). A agenda de pesquisa heterodoxa da mainline economics. *Economia & Sociedade*, vol. 23, no. 3, pp. 731–756. https://www.scielo.br/j/ecos/a/JTp97QRY rk53QBnwp5wHrfR/?lang=pt [08/11/2021]

Ashraf, N., Camerer, C. F. and Loewenstein, G. (2005). Adam Smith, Behavioral Economist. *Journal of Economic Perspectives*, vol. 19, no. 3, pp. 131–145.

Backhouse, R. (2016). *A Short Note on the Place of Mainstream Economics in Samuelson's Family Tree of Economics*. Available at SSRN: https://ssrn.com/abstract=2783 085 or http://dx.doi.org/10.2139/ssrn.2783085 [29/10/2020].

Babeuf. G. ([1796] 2016). *Manifesto of the Equals*. Source: Ph. Buonarroti. La conspiration pour l'égalité, Editions Sociales, Paris, 1957. https://www.marxists.org/history/france/revolution/conspiracy-equals/1796/manifesto.htm [20/07/2020].

Barone, E. (1908). Il ministro della produzione nello stato collectivista. *Giornale delli Economisti*, 37(9), pp. 267–293.

Beggs, M. (2012). Zombie Marx and modern economics or how I learned to stop worrying and forget the transformation problem. *Journal of Australian Political Economy*, no. 70, pp. 11–24.

Bellofiore, R. (2008). Sraffa after Marx: An Open Issue. In: Chiodi, G. and Ditta, L. (Eds.). *Sraffa or an Alternative Economics*. New York: Palgrave Macmillan, 2008, pp. 68–92.

Bharadwaj, K. (1990). Vulgar Economy. In: Eatwell J., Milgate M., Newman P. (eds) *Marxian Economics*. London: The New Palgrave. Palgrave Macmillan. pp. 373–376.

Bianchi, A. M. (1988). *Pré-História da Economia—De Maquiavel a Adam Smith*. São Paulo: Hucitec.

Binns, P. (1986). State capitalism. *Education for Socialists*, no. 1, March 1986. http://www.marxists.de/statecap/binns/statecap.htm [17/09/2020].

Bockman, J. (2011). *Markets in the Name of Socialism: The Left-Wing Origins of Neoliberalism*. Stanford, CA: Stanford University Press.

Boettke, P. J. (2000). Introduction: Towards a History of the Theory of Socialist Planning. In: Boettke, P. J. (Ed.). *Socialism and the Market: the socialist calculation debate revisited*. London and New York: Routledge. pp. 1–39.

Boff, E. O. (2018). What's the problem, Mr. Smith? Shedding more light (than Heat) on Adam Smith's view of man. *Economia & Sociedade*, vol.27, n.1, pp.1–28. http://www.scielo.br/scielo.php?script=sci_arttext&pid=S0104-06182018000100001&lng=en&nrm=iso [29/08/2020].

Böhm-Bawerk, E. v. ([1889] 1985). *Teoria Positiva do Capital.* Volumes I e II. São Paulo: Nova Cultural.

Böhm-Bawerk, E. v. ([1889] 1930). *The Positive Theory of Capital.* New York: G. E. Stechert & Co. https://cdn.mises.org/The%20Positive%20Theory%20of%20Capital.pdf [20/07/2020].

Böhm-Bawerk, E. v. ([1896] 2007). *Karl Marx and the Close of his System.* Auburn, Alabama: Ludwig von Mises Institute.

Böhm-Bawerk, E. v. ([1921] 2010). *A teoria da exploração do socialismo-comunismo.* São Paulo: Instituto Ludwig von Mises Brasil.

Borges Neto, J. M. (2004). As várias dimensões da lei do valor. *Nova Economia*, vol. 14, no. 3, pp. 143–158. https://revistas.face.ufmg.br/index.php/novaeconomia/article/view/439/437 [30/10/2020].

Bortkiewicz, L. v. (1907). Zur Berechtigung der grundlegenden theoretischen Konstruktion von Marx im dritten Band des "Kapital". *Jahrbücher für Nationalökonomie und Statistik*, volBd. 34, S. pp. 319–335, Stuttgart.

Bryceson, D. F. (1983). Use values, the law of value and the analysis of non-capitalist production. *Capital & Class*, vol. 7, no. 2, pp. 29–63.

Bukharin, N. ([1917] 2001). *Imperialism and World Economy.* https://www.marxists.org/archive/bukharin/works/1917/imperial/ [25/06/2021].

Camarinha Lopes, T. (2013a). Reviving the Cambridge Controversy by Combining Marx with Sraffa. *World Review of Political Economy*, vol. 4, no. 3, 2013, pp. 300–322. doi:10.13169/worlrevipoliecon.4.3.0300 [29/06/2021].

Camarinha Lopes, T. (2013b). The shift from contradiction to redundancy in the critique of the labour theory of value. *International Journal of Pluralism and Economics Education*, vol. 4, no. 3, pp. 263–273.

Camarinha Lopes, T. (2014). Continuidade e Ruptura em Economia Política ou quantidade e qualidade na teoria do valor. *Economia & Sociedade*, vol. 23, no. 3, pp. 697–730. https://www.scielo.br/scielo.php?script=sci_arttext&pid=S0104-061820140003006 97&lng=en&nrm=iso&tlng=pt [06/08/2015].

Camarinha Lopes, T. (2019). The Transformation Problem of values into prices: from the law of value to economic planning. *New Proposals: Journal of Marxism and Interdisciplinary Inquiry.* Vol. 10, no. 1, pp. 29–42. https://ojs.library.ubc.ca/index.php/newproposals/article/view/188058 [29/08/2020].

Camarinha Lopes, T. (2021a). Comrades do Not Always Agree: How to promote cooperation between the followers of Marx and Sraffa? *Review of Radical Political Economics*, vol. 53, no. 3, pp. 535-541. March 2021. doi:10.1177/0486613421992555.

Camarinha Lopes, T. (2021b). Technical or Political: the socialist economic calculation debate. *Cambridge Journal of Economics*, vol. 45, issue 4, pp. 787-810, https://doi.org/10.1093/cje/beab008 [28/06/2021].

Camarinha Lopes. T. and Neder, H. D. (2017). Sraffa, Leontief, Lange: The political economy of input-output economics. *EconomiA*, vol. 18, issue 2, pp. 192–211. https://www.sciencedirect.com/science/article/pii/S1517758016301035 [07/08/2020].

Carson, K. A. (2004). *Studies in Mutualist Political Economy*. Fayeteville: Ark. https://www.researchgate.net/profile/Kevin_Carson3/publication/228910244_Studies_in_Mutualist_Political_Economy/links/5a9b176baca2721e3f301b5c/Studies-in-Mutualist-Political-Economy.pdf [03/09/2020].

Chattopadhyay, P. (2018). *Socialism and Commodity Production: Essay in Marx Revival*. Leiden and Boston, MA: Brill.

Clark, J. B. ([1907] 2013). *Essentials of Economic Theory as applied to modern problems of industry and public policy*. New York: Macmillan.

Clarke, S. (1991) The Marginalist Revolution in Economics. In: Clarke, S. (1991). *Marx, Marginalism and Modern Sociology*. London: Palgrave Macmillan. Pp. 182–206.

Cleaver, H. ([1979] 2000). *Reading Capital Politically*. Leeds, UK: Anti/Theses.

Cockshott, P. and Cottrell, A. (1993b). *Towards a New Socialism*. Nottingham, England: Spokesman.

Cockshott, P. and Cottrell, A. (1997). Labour time versus alternative value bases: a research note. *Cambridge Journal of Economics*, 21, pp. 545–549.

Cockshott, P. (2018). *Did Marx have a labour theory of value?* https://paulcockshott.wordpress.com/2018/04/05/did-marx-have-a-labour-theory-of-value/ [29/10/2020].

Cockshott, P. (2019). *How the world works: the story of human labor from prehistory to the modern day*. New York: Monthly Review Press.

Collison Black, R. D., Coats, A. W. and Goodwin, C. D. W. (1973). *The Marginal Revolution in Economics: interpretation and evaluation*. Durham, N. C.: Duke University Press.

Cottrell, A. and Cockshott, P. (1993a). Calculation, Complexity and Planning: the socialist economic calculation debate once again. *Review of Political Economy*, vol. 5, no. 1, pp. 73–112.

Defoe, D. ([1719] 2004). *The Life and Adventures of Robinson Crusoe*. Project Gutenberg. http://www.dominiopublico.gov.br/download/texto/gu012623.pdf [28/06/2021].

Dickinson, H. D. (1933). Price Formation in a Socialist Community. *The Economic Journal*, vol. 43, no. 170, pp. 237–250. https://www.jstor.org/stable/2224464?seq=1#page_scan_tab_contents [15/01/2018].

Dobb, M. (1946). *Studies in the Development of Capitalism*. London: Routledge & Kegan Paul.

Dobb, M. (1969). *Welfare Economics and the Economics of Socialism: towards a common-sense critique*. London: Cambridge University Press.

Dooley, P. C. (2005). *The Labour Theory of Value*. New York: Routledge.

Economics Institute of the Academy of Sciences of the U.S.S.R ([1954] 1957). *Political Economy*. London: Lawrence & Wishart. https://www.marxists.org/subject/economy/authors/pe/index.htm [25/09/2020].

Engels, F. ([1844] 1976). *Umrisse zu einer Kritik der Nationalökonomie*. In: Marx-Engels Werke. Berlin/DDR: Dietz Verlag, pp. 499–524. http://www.mlwerke.de/me/me01/me01_499.htm [07/08/2015]. English version: Outlines of a Critique of Political Economy. https://www.marxists.org/archive/marx/works/1844/df-jahrbucher/outlines.htm [23/07/2020]. Versão em português: Engels, F. ([1844] 1979). Esboço de uma Crítica da Economia Política. Revista Temas de Ciências Humanas, no. 5, pp. 1–29. São Paulo: Editora Ciências Humanas.

Engels, F. ([1876] 1934). *The Part Played by Labour in the Transition from Ape to Man*. Progress Publishers: Moscow. https://www.marxists.org/archive/marx/works/1876/part-played-labour/index.htm [01/09/2020].

Engels, F. ([1883]). *Speech at the Grave of Karl Marx*. Highgate Cemeitery, London, March 17, 1883. https://www.marxists.org/archive/marx/works/1883/death/burial.htm [23/07/2020].

Engels, F. ([1885a] 1985). Prefácio. In: Marx, K. ([1885] 1985). *O Capital. Livro Segundo: O Processo de Circulação do Capital*. São Paulo: Nova Cultural.

Engels, F. ([1885b] 1955). Preface to the First German Edition. In: Marx, K. ([1847] 1955). *The Poverty of Philosophy*. Moscow: Progress Publishers. https://www.marxists.org/archive/marx/works/1847/poverty-philosophy/pre-1885.htm [25/06/2021].

Engels, F. ([1886] 1975). Ludwig Feuerbach und der Ausgang der klassischen deutschen Philosophie. In: Marx-Engels-Werke (MEW 21), pp. 265–273. Berlim: Dietz Verlag. First published in Die Neue Zeit, Vierter Jahrgang, Nr. 4 und 5, 1886. http://www.mlwerke.de/me/me21/me21_259.htm [04/08/2015]. English version: Engels, F. ([1886] 1946). Ludwig Feuerbach and the End of Classical German Philosophy. Moscow: Progress Publishers. https://www.marxists.org/archive/marx/works/1886/ludwig-feuerbach/index.htm [24/07/2020].

Engels, F. (1895-1896 [2003]). *Wertgesetz und Profitrate*. Erster Nachtrag zu Buch 3 des Kapitals in: Marx, K.; Engels, F. (1871–1895) Manuskripte und Redaktionelle Texte zum dritten Buch des "Kapitals", [MEGA, II, 14, Text, 2003], Akademie Verlag 2003. http://www.mlwerke.de/me/me25/me25_897.htm [20/07/2020].

Ekelund, R. B. and Hébert, R. F. (2002). Retrospectives: The Origins of Neoclassical Microeconomics. *The Journal of Economic Perspectives* 16, no. 3, pp. 197–215. http://www.jstor.org/stable/3216957 [16/09/2020].

Farjoun, E. and Machover, M. (1983). *Laws of Chaos. A probabilistic approach to Political Economy*. London: Verso Editions and NLB.

Feuerbach, L. ([1839] 1972). *Towards a Critique of Hegel's Philosophy*. https://www.marxists.org/reference/archive/feuerbach/works/critique/index.htm [23/07/2020].

Fisher, I. (1930). *The Theory of Interest as determined by Impatience to Spend Income and Opportunity to Invest it*. New York: Macmillan.

Freire, P. ([1968] 2015). *Pedagogia do oprimido*. São Paulo: Paz e Terra.

Furtado. C. (1956). Resenha do Manual de Economia Política. *Econômica Brasileira*, Rio de Janeiro, vol. 2, no. 1, pp. 52–54.

Ganssmann, H. (1983). Marx Without the Labor Theory of Value? *Social Research*, vol. 50, no. 2, pp. 278–304.

Geogerscu-Roegen, N. (1971). *The entropy law and the economic process.* Cambridge, Mass: Harvard University Press.

Gintis, H. and Bowles, S. (1981). Structure and Practice in the Labor Theory of Value. *Review of Radical Political Economics*, vol. 12 no.:4, pp. 1–26.

Gontijo, C. (2009). O valor-trabalho como fundamento dos preços. *Economia & Sociedade*, vol. 18, no. 3, pp. 493–511.

Gorender, J. (1985). Apresentação. In: Marx, K. ([1867] 1985). *O Capital: Crítica da Economia Política. Livro Primeiro: O Processo de Produção do Capital.* São Paulo: Nova Cultural. Pp. 5–66.

Gossen, H. H. (1854). *Die Entwickelung der Gesetze des menschlichen Verkehrs, und der daraus fließenden Regeln für menschliches Handeln.* Braunschweig: Friedrich Vieweg und Sohn.

Graeber, D. (2011). *Debt. The first 5000 years.* New York: Melville House.: New York.

Guevara, Che. (1982). *Textos Econômicos para a transformação do socialismo.* São Paulo: Edições Populares.

Hagendorf, K. (2014). The Labor Theory of Value: A Marginal Analysis. *World Review of Political Economy,* vol. 5 no. (2), pp. 231–257. doi:10.13169/worlrevipoliecon.5.2.0231 [09/09/2020].

Hahnel, R. (2015). Environmental sustainability in a Sraffian framework. *Review of Radical Political Economics*, vol. 49, no. 3, pp. 477–488.

Hahnel, R. (2017). *Radical Political Economy: Sraffa versus Marx.* New York: Routledge.

Hahnel, R. (2021). Response to Moseley. *Review of Radical Political Economics*, vol. 53, no. 3, pp. 525-534. May 2021. doi:10.1177/04866134211003340.

Harvey, D. (2018). *Marx's Refusal of the Labour Theory of Value.* Reading Marx's Capital with David Harvey blog. http://davidharvey.org/2018/03/marxs-refusal-of-the-labour-theory-of-value-by-david-harvey/ [17/09/2020].

Hayek, F. ([1941] 2009). *The Pure Theory of Capital.* Auburn, Alabama: The Ludwig von Mises Institute.

Hegel, G. W. F. ([1833] 1979). *Vorlesungen über die Geschichte der Philosophie.* In: Hegel, G. W. F. Werke in zwanzig Bänden. Band 18, Frankfurt am Main: Suhrkamp. http://www.zeno.org/Philosophie/M/Hegel,+Georg+Wilhelm+Friedrich/Vorlesungen+%C3%9 [25/06/2021].

Heinrich, M. ([1990] 2014). *Die Wissenschaft vom Wert.* Münster: Dampfboot.

Hobbes, T. ([1646] 1918). *Grundzüge der Philosophie.* Zweiter und dritter Teil: Lehre vom Menschen und Bürger. Leipzig: Hofenberg.

Hobbes, T. ([1651] 2003). *Leviatã.* São Paulo: Martin Claret.

Hobsbawm, E. ([1977] 2014). *A era das revoluções: 1789–1848*. Rio de Janeiro: Paz e Terra.

Hodgskin, T. ([1825] 1986). *A defesa do trabalho contra as pretensões do capital*. São Paulo: Nova Cultural.

Horvat, B. (1970). *Teoría de la planificación económica*. Barcelona: oikos-tau s.a. ediciones.

Horvat, B. ([1982] 2020). *The Political Economy of Socialism: A Marxist Social Theory*. New York: Routledge.

Howard, M. C. and King, J. E. (2001). 'State Capitalism' in the Soviet Union. *History of Economics Review*, vol. 34, issue 1, pp. 110–126.

Hunt, E. K. (1981). *História do Pensamento Econômico*. Rio de Janeiro: Campus Elsevier.

Hutnyk, J. (2020) Robinsonades: pertaining to allegories from the East India Company in Ceylon and other islands, from Marxism to Post-structuralism, and in which, dear reader, a 300-year-old adventure book may still have something to say. *Inter-Asia Cultural Studies*, vol.21, no.:2, pp. 279–286, DOI: 10.1080/14649373.2020.1766236 [30/10/2020].

Huxley, A. ([1932] 1998). *Brave New World*. New York: HarperCollins Publishers.

Jaffé, W. (1976). Menger, Jevons and Walras de-homogenized. *Economic Inquiry*, vol 14, no. 4, pp. 511–524. https://doi.org/10.1111/j.1465-7295.1976.tb00439.x [03/09/2020].

Jevons, W. S. ([1871] 1888). *The Theory of Political Economy*. London: Macmillan. https://oll.libertyfund.org/titles/jevons-the-theory-of-political-economy [23/07/2020].

Jevons, W. S. ([1871] 1983). *A Teoria da Economia Política*. São Paulo: Nova Cultural.

Judson, D. H. (1989). The convergence of neo-Ricardian and embodied energy theories of value and price. *Ecological Economics*, vol. 1, no. 3, pp. 261–281.

Kaldor, Y. (2020). The cultural foundations of economic categories: finance and class in the marginalist revolution. *Socio-Economic Review*, vol. 18, no. 4, pp. 1133–1151. https://doi.org/10.1093/soceco/mwy043 [03/09/2020].

Karacuka, M. and Zaman, A. (2012). The empirical evidence against neoclassical utility theory: a review of the literature. *International Journal of Pluralism and Economics Education*, vol. 3, no. 4, pp. 366–414.

Karagöz, U. (2014). The Neoclassical Robinson: Antecedents and Implications. *History of Economic Ideas*, vol. 22, no. 2, pp. 75–100.

Kauder, E. (1965). *A History of Marginal Utility Theory*. Princeton, N. J.: Princeton University Press.

Kautsky. K. (1914). *Ultra-imperialism*. First published in Die Neue Zeit, September 1914. https://www.marxists.org/archive/kautsky/1914/09/ultra-imp.htm [25/06/2021].

Keen, S. (1993). Use-Value, Exchange Value, and the demise of Marx's labor theory of value. *Journal of the History of Economic Thought*, vol. 15, no. 1, pp. 107–121.

Keynes, J. M. (1936). *The General Theory of Employment, Interest and Money*. Cambridge, U. K.: Macmillan Cambridge University Press.

King, J. E. (1983). Utopian or scientific? A reconsideration of the Ricardian Socialists. *History of Political Economy*, vol.15, no.3, pp. 345–373.

Knight, F. H. (1936). The Place of Marginal Economics in a Collective System. *The American Economic Review*, vol. 26, no. 1, pp. 255–266. https://www.jstor.org/stable/1807786?seq=1#page_scan_tab_contents [15/01/2018].

Knight, F. H. (1937). Note on Dr. Lange's Interest Theory. *The Review of Economic Studies*, vol. 4, no. 3, pp. 223–230.

Kowalik, T. (1964). Biography of Oskar Lange. In: Organizing Committee of the 60° Anniversary of Oskar Lange (Ed.) *On Political Economy and Econometrics: Essays in Honour of Oskar Lange*. Warszawa: Polish Scientific Publishers Pergamon Press. PWN, p. 1–13.

Kowalik, T. (2018). Lange, Oskar Ryszard (1904–1965). In: Durlauf, S. e Blume, L. (Eds.) *The New Palgrave. A Dictionary of Economics*. The Macmillan Press.

Kurz, H. (2018). Marx and the Law of Value. A critical appraisal on the occasion of his 200th birthday. *Investigación Económica*, vol. 77, no. 304, pp. 40–71. Facultad de Economía, Universidade Autónoma de México (UNAM). http://www.scielo.org.mx/scielo.php?script=sci_arttext&pid=S0185-16672018000200040#fn1 [29/10/2020].

Laibman, D. (1992). *Value, Technical Change and Crisis: explorations in Marxist economic theory*. New York: M.E. Sharpe.

Lampa, R. (2011). Scientific Rigor and Social Relevance: the two dimensions of Oskar R. Lange's early economic analysis. (1931–1943). These Abstract. *Journal of the History of Economic Thought*, vol. 33, no. 4, pp. 557–559.

Lampa, R. (2014). When Science Meets Revolution: the influence of Rosa Luxemburg on Oskar Lange's early project (1931–1945). In: Bellofiore, R. Karwowski, W. and Toporowski, J. (2014). *The Legacy of Rosa Luxemburg, Oskar Lange and Michal Kalecki. Volume 1 of Essays in Honour of Tadeusz Kowalik*. London: Palgrave Macmillan. Pp. 122–140.

Lange, O. (1935). Marxian Economics and Modern Economic Theory. *The Review of Economic Studies*, vol. 2, no. 3, pp. 189–201.

Lange, O. (1936). On the Economic Theory of Socialism: Part One. *The Review of Economic Studies*, vol. 4, no. 1, pp. 53–71.

Lange, O. (1936b). The Place of Interest in the Theory of Production. *The Review of Economic Studies*, vol. 3, no. 3, pp. 159–192.

Lange, O. (1937). On the Economic Theory of Socialism: Part Two. *The Review of Economic Studies*, vol. 4, no. 2, pp. 123–142.

Lange, O. (1945). The Scope and Method of Economics. *The Review of Economic Studies*, vol. 13, no. 1, pp. 19–32.

Lange, O. ([1959] 1963). *Moderna Economia Política. Princípios Gerais*. Rio de Janeiro: Fundo de Cultural. Edition in Spanish: Lange, O. ([1959] 1966). *Economía Política I: Problemas Generales*. México: Fondo de Cultura Económica. Edition in English: Lange, O. ([1959] 1963). *Political Economy*, vol. 1. General Problems. Oxford: Pergamon Press.

Lange, O. ([1961] 1967). *Introdução à Econometria*. São Paulo e Rio de Janeiro: Editora Fundo de Cultura. Edition in English: Lange, O. ([1961] 1962). *Introduction to Econometrics*. Oxford, London, New York, Paris: Pergamon Press. Warszawa: PWN Polnish Scientific Publishers.

Lange, O. (1970). *Introduction to Economic Cybernetics*. Warszawa: Pergamon Press.

Lange, O. (1971). *Political Economy*. Vol 2. Oxford: Pergamon Press.

Lazzarini, A. and Brondino, G. (2019). Sraffa's visit to China in 1954. In: Carter, S. *Digital Sraffa Website*. May 17h 2019. https://sraffaarchive.org/f/sraffa%E2%80%99s-visit-to-china-in-1954 [29/06/2021].

Lee, C. (1993). Marx's Labour Theory of Value Revisited. *Cambridge Journal of Economics*, vol. 17, pp. 463–478.

Lee, C. (1998). The Distinction between Social Value, Individual Value, Market Value and Market Price in Volume III of Capital. In: Bellofiore, R. (Ed.) *Marxian Economics: A Reappraisal. Volume 2: Profits, Prices and Dynamics*. London: Macmillan. Pp. 86–100.

Lerner, A. (1934). Economic Theory and Socialist Economy. *The Review of Economic Studies*, vol. 2, no. 1, pp. 51–61 https://academic.oup.com/restud/article-abstract/2/1/51/1540829?redirectedFrom=fulltext [15/01/2018].

List, F. ([1841] 1909). *The National System of Political Economy*. London: Longmans, Green & Co. https://oll.libertyfund.org/titles/list-the-national-system-of-political-economy [24/07/2020].

Locke, J. ([1690] 1999). *The Second Treatise of Civil Government*. https://www.marxists. org/reference/subject/politics/locke/index.htm [22/06/2021].

Louzek, M. (2011). The Battle of Methods in Economics: The Classical Methodenstreit— Menger vs. Schmoller. *American Journal of Economics and Sociology*, vol. 70, no. 2, pp. 439–463.

Machiavelli, N. ([1513] 2016). *The Prince*. The Project Gutenberg EBook of The Prince. http://www.gutenberg.org/files/1232/1232-h/1232-h.htm [19/07/2020].

Mandel, E. (1951) The Theory of "State Capitalism". *Fourth International,* vol.12 no.5, September-October 1951, pp.145–156. https://web.archive.org/web/20060526002538/http://www.ernestmandel.org/en/works/txt/FI/theory_of_statecapitalism.htm [17/09/2020].

Mandel, E. (1968). *A formação do pensamento econômico de Karl Marx*. Rio de Janeiro: Zahar.

Mandeville, B. ([1705] 2017). *A fábula das abelhas ou Vícios privados, benefícios públicos*. São Paulo: Editora Unesp. Mandeville, B. (1988). The Fable of the Bees or Private Vices, Publick Benefits. https://oll.libertyfund.org/titles/mandeville-the-fable-of-the-bees-or-private-vices-publick-benefits-vol-1 [27/10/2020].

Marshall, A. ([1890] 1985). *Princípios de Economia*. São Paulo: Nova Cultural.

Marx, K. ([1843] 2009). *On The Jewish Question*. First published in February 1844 in Deutsch-Französische Jahrbücher. https://www.marxists.org/archive/marx/works/1844/jewish-question/ [23/07/2020].

Marx, K. ([1844a] 2009). *A Contribution to the Critique of Hegel's Philosophy of Right.* First Published *Deutsch-Französische Jahrbücher*, 7 & 10 February 1844 in Paris. https://www.marxists.org/archive/marx/works/1843/critique-hpr/intro.htm [23/07/2020]. Edition in German: Marx, K. ([1843] 1976). Zur Kritik der Hegelschen Rechtsphilosophie. Kritik des Hegelschen Staatsrechts. In: Karl Marx/ Friedrich Engels—Werke. (Karl) Dietz Verlag, Berlin. Band 1. Berlin/DDR. 1976. S. 203–333. http://www.mlwerke.de/me/meo1/meo1_203.htm [07/08/2015].

Marx, K. ([1844b] 2009). *Economic & Philosophical Manuscripts of 1844.* Moscow: Progress Publishers: Moscow. https://www.marxists.org/archive/marx/works/1844/manu scripts/preface.htm [23/07/2020]. Edition in German: Marx, K. ([1844] 1968). Ökonomisch-philosophische Manuskripte. MEW 40. Berlin (DDR): Dietz Verlag, 1968: http://www.mlwerke.de/me/me40/me40_465.htm. [07/08/2015].

Marx, K. ([1845] 1978). *Thesen über Feuerbach* („1. ad Feuerbach"). Written in 1845 and published for the first time with alterations by Engels in 1888. Republished in Marx-Engels-Werke (MEW), vol. 3, Berlin. Marx's version of 1845 is available here http://www.mlwerke.de/me/meo3/meo3_005.htm [04/08/2015]. Engels' edited version for publication in 1888 as appendices to the text Ludwig Feuerbach und der Ausgang der klassischen deutschen Philosophie is here: http://www.mlwerke.de/me/meo3/meo3_533.htm [04/08/2015].

Marx, K. ([1847] 1955). *The Poverty of Philosophy.* Moscow: Progress Publishers. https://www.marxists.org/archive/marx/works/1847/poverty-philosophy/ [20/07/2020].

Marx, K. ([1857–1858] 2011). *Grundrisse.* São Paulo: Boitempo.

Marx, K. ([1859a] 1971). *Zur Kritik der Politischen Ökonomie.* In: Karl Marx/Friedrich Engels Werke (MEW), Band 13, 7. Auflage, 1971. Berlin: Dietz Verlag. http://www.mlwerke.de/me/me13/me13_003.htm [08/08/2015].

Marx, K. ([1859b] 1977). *Preface. A Contribution to the Critique of Political Economy.* Moscow: Progress Publishers: Moscow. https://www.marxists.org/archive/marx/works/1859/critique-pol-economy/preface.htm [23/07/2020].

Marx, K. ([1862–1863] 1968). *Theories of Surplus Value.* Moscow: Progress Publishers. https://www.marxists.org/archive/marx/works/1863/theories-surplus-value/ [11/02/2014].

Marx, K. ([1865] 1969). *On Proudhon. Letter to J B Schweitzer.* First Published in: *Der Social-Demokrat*, Nos. 16, 17 and 18, February 1, 3 and 5, 1865. Marx Engels Selected Works, volume 2. https://www.marxists.org/archive/marx/works/1865/letters/65_01_24.htm [20/07/2020].

Marx, K. ([1867] 2015). *Capital. A Critique of Political Economy. Book One: The Process of Production of Capital.* Moscow: Progress Publishers, Moscow, USSR. https://www.marxists.org/archive/marx/works/download/pdf/Capital-Volume-I.pdf [22/06/2021].

Marx, K. ([1868] 1928). Marx an Ludwig Kugelmann in Hannover. Letter written on 11th July 1898 to Ludwig Kugelmann. First published in: *Pisma Marksa h Kugelmanu*, Moscow-Leningrad, 1928. Reprinted in: Marx/Engels Werke, MEW v. 43, Berlin: Dietz Verlag, 1990.

Marx, K. ([1873] 1985). Posfácio da Segunda Edição. In: Marx, K. ([1867] 1985). *O Capital: Crítica da Economia Política. Livro I: o processo de produção do capital.* São Paulo: Nova Cultural. Edition in English: Marx, K. ([1873] 1887). Afterword to the Second German Edition of Capital Volume One. https://www.marxists.org/archive/marx/works/1867-c1/p3.htm [23/07/2020].

Marx, K. ([1875] 1970). *Critique of the Gotha Programme.* Moscow: Progress Publishers: Moscow. https://www.marxists.org/archive/marx/works/1875/gotha/index.htm [01/09/2020].

Marx, K. ([1885] 1956). *Capital. A Critique of Political Economy. Volume II. The Process of Circulation of Capital.* Moscow: Progress Publishers. https://www.marxists.org/archive/marx/works/1885-c2/index.htm [30/10/2020].

Marx, K. ([1894] 2010). *Capital. A Critique of Political Economy. Volume III. The Process of Capitalist Production as a Whole.* New York: International Publishers. https://www.marxists.org/archive/marx/works/download/pdf/Capital-Volume-III.pdf [30/10/2020].

Marx, K. and Engels, F. ([1845] 1956). *The Holy Family or Critique of Critical Criticism. Against Bruno Bauer and Company.* Moscow: Foreign Languages Publishing House. Moscow. https://www.marxists.org/archive/marx/works/1845/holy-family/index.htm [23/07/2020]. Edition in German: Marx, K. und Engels, F. ([1844] 1972). *Die heilige Familie oder Kritik der kritischen Kritik gegen Bruno Bauer und Kursorten.* Berlin: Dietz Verlag: Berlin/DDR. http://www.mlwerke.de/me/me02/me02_003.htm [07/08/2015].

Marx, K. and Engels, F. ([1846] 1932). *The German Ideology.* Marx-Engels Collected Works, volume 5. https://www.marxists.org/archive/marx/works/1845/german-ideology/index.htm [23/07/2020]. Edition in German: Marx, K. and Engels, F. ([1845–1846] 1969). Die Deutsche Ideologie. MEW 3. Berlin (DDR): Dietz Verlag 1969. http://www.mlwerke.de/me/me03/me03_009.htm [07/08/2015].

Mata, M. E. (2007). Cardinal versus Ordinal Utility: Atónio Horta Osório's contribution. *Journal of the History of Economic Thought*, vol. 29, no. 4, pp. 465–479.

Mauss, M. ([1925] 1966). *The Gift: forms and functions of exchange in archaic societies.* London: Cohen & West.

Meek, R. ([1956] 1973). *Studies in the Labour Theory of Value.* London: Lawrence; Wishart.

Meek, R. (1973). The law of value in Ricardo and Marx: A reply to Mr. Pilling. *Economy & Society*, vol. 2, no. 4(4), correspondence session, pp. 499–506.

Menger, C. ([1871] 2007). *Principles of Economics*. Auburn: Ludwig von Mises Institute: Auburn. http://www.hacer.org/pdf/Menger04.pdf [23/07/2020].

Mill, J. S. ([1885] 2009). *Principles of Political Economy*. New York: D. Appleton and Company. https://www.gutenberg.org/files/30107/30107-pdf.pdf [31/08/2020].

Milonakis, D. (1995). Commodity production and price formation before capitalism: A value theoretical approach. *The Journal of Peasant Studies*, vol. 22, no. 2, pp. 327–355.

Milonakis, D. and Fine, B. (2008). *From Political Economy to Economics: Method, the Social and the Historical in the Evolution of Economic Theory*. London/New York: Routledge.

Mises, L. v. (1920). Die Wirtschaftsrechnung im sozialistischen Gemeinwesen. *Archiv für Sozialwissenschaften*, vol. 47, pp. 86–121. Edition in English: Mises, L. von ([1920] 1935) Economic Calculation in the Socialist Commonwealth. In: Hayek, F.A. (Ed.) (1935). *Collectivist Economic Planning*, London: Rouledge & Kegan Paul Ltd. pp. 87–130.

Mises, L. v. ([1949] 1998). *Human Action*. Alburn, Alabama: Ludwig von Mises Institute.

Montes, L. (2010). Is Friedrich Hayek rowing Adam Smith's boat? In: Farrant, A. (Ed.). *Hayek, Mill and the Liberal Tradition*. London: Routledge. Pp. 7–38.

Moscati, I. (2018). *Measuring Utility: from the Marginal Revolution to Behavioral Economics*. Oxford: Oxford University Press.

Moseley, F. (2021). A Marxian Reply to Hahnel: The Relative Explanatory Power of Marx's Theory and Sraffa's Theory. *Review of Radical Political Economics*, vol. 53, no. 3, pp. 511-524. March 2021. doi:10.1177/0486613420957148.

Moseley, F. and Smith, T. (Eds.) (2014). *Marx's Capital and Hegel's Logic, a reexamination*. Leiden and Boston: Brill.

Napoleoni, C. (1970). *Smith, Ricardo, Marx. Considerazioni sulla storia del pensiero economico*, Torino: Boringhieri.

Oishi, T. (2001). *The unknown Marx: Reconstructing a unified perspective*. London: Pluto Press.

Orwell, G. ([1945] 2009). *Animal Farm*. Boston and New York: Mariner Books Houghton Mifflin Harcourt.

Pannekoek, A. (1936). State Capitalism and Dictatorship. *International Council Correspondence*, vVol. 3 III, nNo.1, January 1937. https://www.marxists.org/archive/pannekoe/1936/dictatorship.htm [17/09/2020].

Pareto, V. ([1906] 2014). *Manual of Political Economy*. Oxford: Oxford University Press.

Pasinetti, L. (2009). *Keynes and the Cambridge Keynesians*. Cambridge, UK: Cambridge University Press.

Petty, W. ([1690] 1996). *Aritmética Política*. São Paulo: Nova Cultural.

Petrovic, P. (1987). The deviation of production prices from labor values: some methodology and empirical evidence. *Cambridge Journal of Economics*, vol. 11, no. 3, pp. 197–210.

Phillips, L. and Rozworski, M. (2019). *The People's Republic of Walmart: How the world's biggest corporations are laying the foundation for socialism.* London and New York: Verso.

Pigou, A. C. ([1920] 1932). *The Economics of Welfare.* London: Macmillan.

Pilling, G. (1972). The Law of Value in Ricardo and Marx. *Economy & Society*, vol. 1, no. 3, pp. 281–307.

Pilling, G. (1973). A reply to Professor Meek. *Economy & Society*, vol. 2, no. (4), correspondence session, pp. 499–506.

Praag, B. M. S. van (1991). Ordinal and cardinal utility: An integration of the two dimensions of the welfare concept. *Journal of Econometrics*, vol. 50, issues nos. 1–2, pp. 69–89.

Prado, E. (2014). Do socialismo centralista ao socialismo democrático. *Revista da Sociedade Brasileira de Economia Política*, vol. 39, pp. 60–77. https://www.revistasep.org.br/index.php/SEP/article/view/61 [08/11/2021]

Preobrazhensky, E. ([1926] 1965). *The New Economics.* Oxford: Oxford University Press.

Proudhon, P. J. ([1846] 2007). *Sistema das Contradições Econômicas ou Filosofia da Miséria.* Tomos I e II. São Paulo: Escala.

Proudhon, P. J. ([1847] 1888). *System of Economic Contradictions or: The Philosophy of Poverty.* Rod Hay's Archive for the History of Economic Thought, McMaster University, Canada. Translated from the French by Benjamin R. Tucker. 1888. https://www.marxists.org/reference/subject/economics/proudhon/philosophy/index.htm [20/07/2020] and https://theanarchistlibrary.org/library/pierre-joseph-proudhon-system-of-economical-contradictions-or-the-philosophy-of-poverty#toc39 [20/07/2020].

Quesnay, F. ([1758] 1996). *Análise do Quadro Econômico.* São Paulo: Nova Cultural.

Rakowitz, N. (2003). *Einfache Warenproduktion: Ideal und Ideologie.* Freiburg: ça ira Verlag.

Ricardo, D. ([1817] 2010). *On the Principles of Political Economy and Taxation.* Project Gutenberg. https://www.gutenberg.org/files/33310/33310-h/33310-h.htm [19/07/2020].

Roemer, J. E. (1982). *A General Theory of Exploitation and Class.* Cambridge, Mass.: Harvard University Press.

Ricardo, D. (1951). The Works and Correspondence of David Ricardo, Vol. 10: Biographical Miscellany. In: Sraffa, P. (Ed.). *The Works and Correspondence of David Ricardo.* Cambridge, UK: Cambridge University Press.

Roberts, M. (2020). Marx's law of value: a critique of David Harvey. *Human Geography*, vol. 13, no. 1, pp. 95–98.

Rojas, R. (1989). *Das unvollendete Projekt: zur Entstehungsgeschichte von Marx' "Kapital".* Berlin, Hamburg: Argument Verlag.

Rosdolsky, R. ([1968] 2020). *Zur Entstehungsgeschichte des Marxschen "Kapital". Der Rohentwurf des "Kapital" 1857–1858*. Freiburg: ça ira Verlag.

Ross, L. (2020). On Disentangling Alienation, Estrangement, and Reification in Marx. *Rethinking Marxism*, vol. 32, no. 4, pp. 521–548.

Rubin, I. ([1928] 1987). *A History of Economic Thought*. London: Pluto Press.

Rubin, I. ([1928] 1973). *Essays on Marx's Theory of Value*. Montreal: Black Rose Books.

Saint-Simon, H. ([1803] 1980). *Um sonho*. In: Duarte, M., Vilarinho, J. and Pestana, M. (ed.) O socialismo pré-marxista. São Paulo: Global. pp. 29–33.

Saint-Simon, H. ([1819] 1980). *Parábola de Saint-Simon*. In: Duarte, M., Vilarinho, J. and Pestana, M. (ed.) O socialismo pré-marxista. São Paulo: Global. pp. 35–38.

Samuelson, P. A. (1971). Understanding the Marxian Notion of Exploitation: A Summary of the So-Called Transformation Problem Between Marxian Values and Competitive Prices. *Journal of Economic Literature*, vol. 9, no. 2, pp. 399–431.

Samuelson, P. A. (1982). The normative and positive inferiority of Marx's values paradigm. *Southern Economic Journal*, vol. 49, no. l, pp. 11–18.

Schefold, B. (2017). *Great Economic Thinkers from the Classicals to the Moderns*. London and New York: Routledge.

Schonhorn, M. (1991). *Defoe's Politics: Parliament, Power, Kingship and Robinson Crusoe*. Cambridge, UK: Cambridge University Press.

Sekine, T. T. (1980). The Necessity of the Law of Value. *Science & Society*, vol. 44, no. 3, pp. 289–304.

Sen, A. (1999). *Sobre Ética e Economia*. São Paulo: Companhia das Letras.

Shaikh, A. M. (1998). The empirical strength of the labour theory of value. In: Bellofiore, R. (Ed.). *Marxian Economics: A Reappraisal*, vol. 2. London: Macmillan. Pp. 225–251.

Simmons, A. J. (1993). *On the Edge of Anarchy: Locke, Consent, and the Limits of Society*. Princeton: Princeton University Press.

Smith, A. ([1759] 1869). *The Theory of Moral Sentiments*. London: Alex. Murray & Son. https://oll.libertyfund.org/titles/theory-of-moral-sentiments-and-essays-on-philosophical-subjects [19/07/2020]. Project Guthenberg: http://www.gutenberg.org/files/3300/3300-h/3300-h.htm [19/07/2020].

Smith, A. ([1776] 1981). *An Inquiry into the Nature and Causes of the Wealth of Nations*. Liberty Classics: Indianapolis. http://www.gutenberg.org/files/3300/3300-h/3300-h.htm [28/06/2021].

Smith, M. E. G. ([1994] 2018). *Invisible Leviathan. Marx's Law of Value in Twilight of Capitalism*. Leiden: Brill.

Sraffa, P. (1928–1931). *Notes on Advanced Theory of Value*. In: Sraffa D2/4, Trinity College, Cambridge, https://mss-cat.trin.cam.ac.uk/manuscripts/uv/view.php?n=Sraffa. D2.4#?c=0&m=0&s=0&cv=1&xywh=-260%2C629%2C3120%2C1741 [27/10/2020].

Sraffa, P. (1960). *Production of Commodities by Means of Commodities*. Cambridge, UK: Cambridge University Press.

Sraffa, P. (1965). *Felicje Lange to Piero Sraffa, 20 Oct 1965.* Correspondence (C162). In: Papers of Piero Sraffa (1898–1983), economist. Wren Digital Library. https://archives.trin.cam.ac.uk/index.php/papers-of-piero-sraffa-1898-1983-economist [08/11/2021].

Steedman, I. (1977). *Marx After Sraffa.* London: New Left Books.

Steedman, I. (Ed.) (1995). *Socialism and Marginalism in Economics: 1870–1930.* Routledge: New York.

Stewart, D. ([1811] 2002). *Biografia crítica.* In: Smith, A. ([1759] 2002). Teoria dos Sentimentos Morais. São Paulo: Martins Fontes. pp. XI-LXXXII.

Stalin, J. ([1952] 1972). *Economic Problems of Socialism in the U.S.S.R.* Peking: Foreign Language Press.

Taylor, F. M. (1929) The Guidance of Production in a Socialist State. *The American Economic Review*, vol. 19, no. 1, pp. 1–8. https://www.jstor.org/stable/1809581?seq=1#page_scan_tab_contents [15/01/2018].

Toporowski, J. (2014). Lange and Keynes. In: Bellofiore, R. Karwowski, W. and Toporowski, J. (2014). *The Legacy of Rosa Luxemburg, Oskar Lange and Michal Kalecki. Volume 1 of Essays in Honour of Tadeusz Kowalik.* London: Palgrave Macmillan. Pp. 141–153.

Traverso, E. (2019). *The Jewish Question: History of a Marxist Debate.* Leiden and Boston: Brill.

Tribe, K. (2008). "Das Adam Smith Problem" and the origins of modern Smith scholarship. *History of European Ideas*, vol. 34, issue no. 4, pp. 514–525. https://www.tandfonline.com/doi/full/10.1016/j.histeuroideas.2008.02.001 [29/08/2020].

Truzi, M. (1966). Adam Smith and contemporary issues in social psychology. *Journal of the History of Behavioral Sciences*, vol. 2, no. (3), pp. 221–224.

Walras, L. ([1874] 1954). *Elements of Pure Economics* . Homewood, Illinois: Richard D. Irwin: Homewood, Ilinois.

Wicksell, K. ([1893] 1954). *Value, Capital and Rent.* London: George Allen & Unwin Ltd.

Wieser, F. von ([1889] 1893). *Natural Value.* London: Macmillan. https://oll.libertyfund.org/titles/wieser-natural-value [29/10/2020].

Wright, I. (2008). The Emergence of the Law of Value in a Dynamic Simple Commodity Economy. *Review of Political Economy*, vol. 20, no. 3, pp. 367–391.

Wright, I. (2019). Marx's transformation problem and Pasinetti's vertically integrated subsystems. *Cambridge Journal of Economics*, vol. 43, issue 1, no. 17, pp. 169–186.

Index

www.ingramcontent.com/pod-product-compliance
Lightning Source LLC
Chambersburg PA
CBHW070922030426
42336CB00014BA/2502